"SO ACHINGLY HONEST
IT TAKES YOUR BREATH AWAY...
At its heart, *The Boy and the Dog Are Sleeping* is a love story, one
that radically and defiantly redefines what a family is. . . . This is
not a story you have heard before."
—*The Miami Herald*

"Every parent knows how the love of a child is life-changing, but
in his gripping memoir *The Boy and the Dog Are Sleeping*, Nasdijj
takes us deeper into the bond between father and son than we
ever thought possible. That the circumstances are tragic does
not make the experience unbearable; quite the contrary, this tale
of an unexpected, unlooked-for love shows us how a great grief
can be borne. The son's gift to his father—an appreciation of
life, not just death—becomes the author's gift to us."
—JESSE GREEN
Author of *The Velveteen Father*

"Remarkable . . . striking in the poetic quality of its language,
touching in the outpouring of love, heartbreaking as an emotional passage of the characters, and eye-opening for its reflec-
tions on reservation medical care, pain management, and moral
values. Don't miss it!"
—*Library Journal* (starred review)

"[A] passionate, emotionally wrenching narrative . . . an exceptionally moving redemption tale of two souls who discover the joy of living by loving each other."
—*Kirkus Reviews*

"Among the most powerful merging of visceral poetry and hard-truth narrative imaginable, helping make *The Boy and the Dog Are Sleeping* a restless, moving, and spiritual trek, where unnatural suffering is eased by nature's terminal beauty."
—*BookStreet USA*

"A window into the larger question of what's really important in life . . . Nasdijj writes about love and the way love shows people how to live. This is a powerful and rare display of visceral, emotional writing."
—*Publishers Weekly* (starred review)

"The poetry of Nasdijj's writing is raw and emotive. A beautiful tribute to an extraordinary boy."
—*Booklist* (boxed and starred review)

"Nasdijj's moving meditation about the devastation AIDS has on his adopted eleven-year-old son is an essential and eloquent reminder of an ongoing global catastrophe."
—*Washington Blade*

THE

BOY

AND

THE

DOG

ARE

SLEEPING

ALSO BY NASDIJJ

The Blood Runs Like a River Through My Dreams

Nasdijj

THE

BOY

AND

THE

DOG

ARE

SLEEPING

BALLANTINE BOOKS
NEW YORK

This book is for Tina Giovanni. My wife. My love. My dog trainer. You made this book possible. By salvaging my heart, my mind, my soul. By taking me into your life. With my rants. My lostness. And my sons. I owe you everything.

Nasdijj

Chapel Hill, North Carolina

August, 2002

Contents

1. The Songs of Gods to Me

Sometimes I think I am insane.

Why would anyone sane adopt a child with AIDS?

It terrifies me to write this book. I am afraid. I am afraid of dragons.

I am afraid of losing my mind. I want something no one is allowed to have.

I want the mad ones. The children mad enough to struggle and survive. I want the children who have seen war. The children mad enough to question everything. The children who have had everything taken away from them. The children who are broken and mad enough to attempt to repair themselves. The children mad enough to spit and fight. Mad enough to laugh outrageously. Mad enough to make a music of their own. Mad enough to see themselves as individuals. I want children who will dance in rain. I want the mad, crazy ones. I want the ones insane enough to love hard, and brave enough to be vulnerable.

I do not know where this book begins.

I am haunted by deep, electric flashes of music, memory, dragons, and madness.

I was out of my mind to do it. The child was *sick*. I did say no.

I was fishing with my dog up at Navajo Lake on the Navajo Nation.

It started to rain. I don't fish in the rain. I want things dry and safe. I pulled my anchor up. I have a small Johnson outboard motor mounted to an aluminum rowboat. I beached it. The dog jumped out. A Navajo man about my age helped me pull the boat in.

A young Navajo boy stood behind the man, sort of like a shadow. The boy appeared to be about ten. He kept staring at me with sharp, darting, black desert eyes.

I had never talked with these people before in my life. We were the only people at the lake. The shadows in this place danced a choreography of darkness and light.

There was thunder in the distance. There was lightning.

Thunder, rain, and lightning are not insignificant events in this place on the Navajo Reservation. This high-desert sacred landscape of coyotes, rock, and jackrabbit. Thunder, rain, and lightning are gifts from Begochiddy, the sun god.

Begochiddy has given thunder and lightning to his son, Monster Slayer, so he might use these gifts to defeat the dragons who have been devouring the Navajo people. I believe in dragons. I believe in the power of the mythology I grew up with. Even if I am not entirely an Indian. My father was an Anglo. With skin as pink as peaches. Mythology is oblivious to the blindness of race. When you grow up surrounded by language and stories, you become the stories and the languages you know. The desert does not care who your parents were. Only people care about their genetic pedigree. I am a desert mongrel who howls at midnight moons.

The mountains around us are the sleeping bodies of the dragons. Evidence that the skeletons of mythology are real.

The Navajo know these stories. The Pueblo people and the Apache people know this mythology, too. They understand how old the mythology is. They understand the power of the enigmatic, and of things that breathe fire and fly about the midnight sky.

I did not know who the man and the boy were. And yet I knew exactly who the man and the boy were. Magic speaks to me.

I had to sit down. I was a little breathless, and more than a little bewildered.

My heart was racing. This could not be happening.

Yet it was. It was unfolding exactly the way it had unfolded at least a thousand times in dreams. Dreams of this rain. Dreams of this thunder. Dreams of this lightning. Dreams of this man and his son.

This was madness. I was losing my mind.

It was beginning to pour. The man suggested we could go sit in his truck. He had whiskey in his pickup if I wanted some. I did, but I declined.

The man wanted to talk to me. The boy said nothing. He was painfully shy. I suggested we sit in my jeep. I knew exactly what was coming. I had seen it all a thousand times, and I would wake up, drenched in sweat.

We sat in my jeep. I had a thermos of hot coffee, and some Styrofoam cups.

The man and I sat up front. The boy and my dog, Navajo, sat in the back.

I cannot relate the exact conversation. For one thing, I do not remember it. It is a blur. For another thing, I agreed not to do that. The issue of privacy is something I take very, very seriously. In the religious ceremonies of the Navajo, masks are worn by dancing participants. The masks must not be removed. To do so would be to strip away the faces of the gods, and you might not like what you see. The only thing I remember vividly is the sound of the rain on the top of the jeep. It had a soft top then. A top you could put down. Since then I have had a hard top put on the jeep since I am not someone who drives with the top down anymore. In my old age I am conservative and cautious. I avoid the wind.

It poured like hell.

It pounded on the top of the jeep like a drum at a Yeibeichai. When it rains in Navajoland, you remember it.

Parents often seek me out. My work with disabled children in school districts all over the Southwest is not a secret. What I know comes from having worked with children in real, hands-on ways. It comes from experience. Not a book. The people in this part of rural New Mexico know about my memoir, *The Blood Runs Like a River Through My Dreams*. They've read it. Usually the parents are looking for advice. Simple. Sometimes they want you to actually work with their kid. Not so simple. Sometimes you can. Sometimes you can't.

The man was sick. I could see that. His eyes were in that beyond exhausted place where everything goes numb.

He moved his long, Navajo hair away from his neck.

He wanted me to see. I did see, and then I looked away. Outside the window of the jeep, rain. I could not even see the lake. I looked over at the man again. *I am not a doctor.*

Purple lesions ran up and down his neck like a road map. Something had exploded inside a plethora of dark veins that spread themselves out not unlike a spider. Now I knew what this was about.

Something inside of me grew very quiet. Very sober. The man had AIDS. I would learn his wife had AIDS. The boy in the backseat with the dog had it, too.

Thunder. Lightning. Pouring rain. The sky had gone black again.

I do not know if the gods of white people actually speak to them. I think not. My gods speak directly to me. Unlike the traditional Navajo who live here, my gods look at you right in the eye, and they are not always good or benevolent.

Begochiddy is no god I ever want to know. Begochiddy is the mythical Navajo sun god who cast his sons out, sending them to earth with enormous, almost impossible tasks to complete. Armed with lightning, intelligence, and the ability to adapt to an always changing world, the war twins defeat the ravaging monsters. Their father was always testing them.

My little jeep shook.

I could not do this. I was sorry. But I could not take some boy I did not know into my home. Into my life. The responsibility.

Even if my house is empty not unlike the way some men are vacant shells.

I am not a candidate to care for some child with pediatric AIDS.

I had no advice. Sometimes you can be real slick, coolly professional, give parents referrals, and sit back smugly, like you've really helped them out.

It is professional bullshit. You fool no one.

The kid had AIDS. The parents could no longer care for him. They had probably done a rotten job of it from day one. But they had tried. They were putting their affairs in order. They were not terrific parents, but they wanted this child to have a chance at life.

Or these two people would not be here.

I'm sitting there thinking: just fuck me.

Why me?

I have gone by that house a hundred thousand times.

It is on the way to town.

You take the paved road through what we call the Checkerboard. The Checkerboard exists at the edges of the Navajo

Nation, and it is mainly lost sheep, scrub, rock, snake, coyote, cactus, goats, and drifting sand. It is where my people come from. Migrating sheep camps. Cow range. Anasazi ruins everywhere.

Uranium mines.

The Checkerboard and the surrounding terrain is populated with a vast moving mixture of Hispanic people, Navajo people, Pueblo people such as the Acoma, and the Zuni. To the east, there is the enormous Jicarilla Apache Reservation. It is a place of canyons, horses, reservations, cultures that cling precariously to existence, voices from the past, and, above all, languages.

Tongues.

Songs.

Drums and flutes.

Old men who still play their classical Spanish guitars with the seductive, dark arrogance of the conquistador.

The Checkerboard is the enigma of the living desert, above which sits a sky as blue as my first lover's eyes. In New Mexico you can reach up, pull the sky down, and taste it.

We are only creatures who walk the surface of the earth (which is how the Navajo refer to themselves in their mythology).

There it is on the right. That tarpaper place with the beer cans everywhere. Whenever I went by I bit down on my teeth and tried my best not to look at it. The poverty was the poverty of the people who had brought me into the world. The people who live at the edges of existence. It is a defeated place. It was like slowing down when you come upon an accident. Some horrible thing has occurred here, and people are hurt forever.

When I didn't want to see it, I would take the long way into town. It was painful to look at.

All the dog shit in the mud. We call this kind of mud the Big Mud. It was a sea of mud. The mud and bright orange, plastic tricycles stuck in thickness. The remnants of disposable diapers torn and littered here and there. Can't you just please pick up the fucking diapers? The windows broken. The clothesline heavy with clothes left in the rain. The rusted hulks of cars. That chicken-scratch shack.

I hated it.

The coyote eyes looking out like prisoners.

I looked into the rearview mirror.

Yaaaaa. His eyes. They would haunt me in my dreams. I said *no*. They left.

I hoped forever. But the sun gods were not done with me.

I had moved back to the reservation one more time. I had left a woman I loved. I loved her more than anything, but I could not live with Tina. Not now. For the moment. We are so different. She was an *urban* person and functioned well in cities. Tina was happy there. She did good work there, and taught children no one wanted. The disposable ones. Children almost everyone had washed their hands of. I had *been* a kid like that. Children always balanced on the razor's edge that divides this world from the world of the institution. Tina is often their only hope. She was mine, too; I was just too self-involved to see it. I am in awe of her. I do not have half the brains this woman has. I am not urban, and I don't function well in cities.

They leave me confused and anxious. They overwhelm me especially with noise. I had every learning-disabled diagnosis in the book.

I was alone again, and sliding into some vacuum of suicidal blackness. There was a vacuum in my guts and it was eating me alive. I was without Tina and she is my rock.

I had asked her so many times to move with me back to the reservation.

But the reservation scares her. I do understand. It is so remote.

From my front porch I can see three hundred miles north and not a single solitary house or soul. All of it mountains, desert, and jackrabbit. The nearest store is hours and hours away. Going to town is an expedition.

There are no jobs on the reservation. Not one. What woman is going to live here with me?

I drove my dog home and went to bed.

Those eyes. That boy. The thunder and the rain.

I was in a bookstore in White People Town. I was there to read my book.

I am told that when writers do this reading and speaking it sells books, but I am not sure I believe it.

When you're finished reading, bookstore owners expect you to play questions-and-answers with white people who want to know things like what do you really think of Tony Hillerman?

I can only shrug. Tony Hillerman writes Navajo mysteries.

The Navajo are the real mystery.

I do not claim to know them. Does anyone know the Navajo? Is it possible? I exist outside the context of any group or clan. I was a *migrant worker*. Just another brat born into a sheep camp. I do not belong to any tribe. I can only speak for myself.

It is only within the context of recent history that the Navajo defined themselves within tribal perimeters. They had always been a loosely knit band of roving clans. For centuries, the warriors were beholden to no one specific leader, no chief, and warriors could join the ranks of any guiding star they wanted their family to follow. When the grazing was good at the upper levels, they moved their sheep there. When the mountain weather turned ugly, they moved their sheep down into the valleys.

The fundamental notion of the sheep camp is one of movement. People are always moving to and from the sheep camp.

This included my mother, who met a white man (we call them Anglos) who (no accident) was a migrant worker but saw himself as a cowboy. My parents could work just about any job on any ranch. But they also picked cash crops, because at the end of the day, they could and did count their money. And then they moved on.

I look just like my Anglo dad.

I have lived on many reservations. I have lived among the Navajo, the Tewa, the Chippewa, and the Mescalero Apache. I have worked with the children of these tribes. The reservation with its poverty and its rich sunsets and its coyotes who laugh, howl, and disappear.

I am never asked in bookstores about poverty on the reservation. I am never asked by Anglos about the death that comes from the uranium mines imposed upon us. I am never asked why the Navajo do not have water. Yet the coal mines and the gold mines and the silver mines and the uranium mines and the copper mines have all the water they need. All over the West. All over the West the water goes to them. I am never asked by Anglos about health care on the reservation. I am never asked about the schools on the reservation where if you dared to speak in Navajo you got your mouth washed out with soap. I am never asked about tuberculosis on the reservation. I am never asked about starvation on the reservation. Those people who have the reservation in their blood just know. *We know* about these things. These events in bookstores seem to be about as relevant as a tea and crumpets party given by the Methodist Ladies Society. I am asked about Tony Hillerman. I do not understand these events.

I do not know Tony Hillerman. Why would I read him? To study the Navajo? It's like you've made some jewelry, and you've taken it to the flea market. You sit there at some card table, and white people come along, and want to know if you know Tony Hillerman.

I try not to look at white people.

I saw him then.

I saw him walk into the bookstore.

The bell above the door rang.

The boy at the lake. It's late at night. It's dark, and I am wondering how he got here. We are miles from the reservation, and he's dressed in a thin T-shirt.

I saw him steal a book.

He stood in line.

I signed it.

"Who am I signing this for?" I asked. I knew his name. His dad had told me. Up at the lake. In the rain. In the jeep. Purple veins up and down his neck like a road map into hell. With the gods above us and the dragons screaming blood.

"Awee," he said. "A W E E."

For Awee. What are you doing here, and how did you get here, and why do I smell cigarettes on you, and where is your coat?

He does not like what I have written in the book he stole. He frowns.

"I'm here to ask you one more time—*pleeeeeeze*—and I don't gotta coat. I know boys you worked with."

Yaaaaa. So what?

This is not unusual. There is a pipeline among these kids. The mad ones. Kids who live at the edges of the system. Foster kids. Kids in jail. At the edges of the desert blacktop with their thumb out. Hitchhiking into that yellow twilight at the edge of town. The ones who will not graduate from high school this year.

Adults get rated. You are someone they can tolerate. Or you are someone to be avoided at all costs. Once you have made it to the *to be avoided at all costs list*, there is no way in hell or shit that you will ever make it back to the *tolerated* list again. Children are intransigent. These are children fighting for their lives.

"How did you find me?"

"It was in the paper. Do you gots a cigarette?"

The chances of my having a cigarette were not good. He was shivering. "You're freezing, Awee."

"Yes."

I buy him something hot to drink.

I give him my coat.

"They're gonna put me in a foster home if you won't take me," he said. "I will run away. I will. I know how to hitchhike. I hitchhiked here. I don't need nobody. I can take care of myself. I am not no fucking baby."

"It's really dangerous for a boy your age to be out there hitchhiking," I lectured. I have worked with boys who hitchhike in the dark in New Mexico. It's like asking to be raped.

We find bodies of nude boys in ditches. No one knows who they are or where they came from. Strangled and dumped in the desert.

"Please. I know you had a son once. Everyone knows that. You wrote about it. He died. It was in the paper. I read about it. We could do this. You and me. I'm alive. I won't be any trouble. I'll just stay out of your way, okay? But the foster homes are bad. Really bad. They won't let you be on no baseball team in the foster homes, and I just wanna play some baseball is all I want. Do you gots a cigarette?"

Why would anyone sane adopt a child with AIDS?

Because one comes to you. Because you can. Because he needs you. Because he is asking you to adopt him. Because you know about the bureaucratic strings and how to pull them. Because he is going to be one more dead Indian child and not even shit as a statistic. Because he has no coat and he's shivering. Because the two of us are all by ourselves. Because he likes baseball.

Even here, sitting in a bookstore coffee shop drinking hot chocolate with a raggedy kid, I am out of place, out of context, and so alone.

The reservation in the darkness sings the songs of gods to me. The reservation is my home.

2. Blue Jays

I have these dreams where he is playing baseball.

Awee is at a baseball game. The sun is going down. The municipal park is green and filled with kids, dogs running around, families at picnic tables, baseball bleachers filled with moms and dads. I sit slightly removed from most of this at the top of the bleachers where he can see me. Every few minutes, he turns to look.

Yaaaaa. I'm here for you.

My memories of him are images of victory, dirt, and sweat. Baseball T-shirts and dirty socks.

Awee, oblivious. Now his focus is the ball.

The prince of shyness up to bat.

Hit it.

Awee, a blur of light between the bases.

Now all the other moms, and all the other dads, get up off their butts and stand in a mix of amazement, surprise, and electric fascination.

Yaaaaa. The blur of light is mine.

I want to tell you about my son. That is why I am writing

all of this down in some mad, frenetic attempt to share him with you.

If I do *nothing* else with what is left of my life, let me do this. Let me show you something extraordinarily unique, something more beautiful than *anything* you have ever seen. Something mad. Mad to live.

Inside a dream.

The story of Awee is very much like the story of Awee running bases.

You know he's going to make it home, but you hold your breath as he slides through the human obstacles that stand directly in his way.

I could take his picture. He's standing there with his teammates. Their arms draped around him because they love him. But it really wouldn't tell you much about who Awee is.

Awee is that boy who trips the light in dreams fantastic. Every moment with him forces me to see something new. Something I have never seen before. So I write in journals (when there is time). I have notebook journals. I have loose-leaf journals. I have computer website journals. Everything is such a blur, and not unlike the way in which Awee runs base to base. Stealing moments when he can.

Awee was eleven years old when he came to me. Adopted.

This *entire* book (and then some) could be about his eyes.

I have tried and tried and tried and tried to put his story into some kind of linear order. I have banged my head against the wall to do it. I simply do not understand how to do that kind of cultural storytelling. It isn't how I think. It isn't the kind of storytelling I know. Memories are like fragments from the past. They are the junk from exploded hand grenades.

I try to stand events up like a line of dominoes, but all I ever end up with is a room with thousands of pieces of paper because that was Awee, too. Thousands and thousands of pieces of him flying everywhere. I do not know how to assemble him so that the thing is orderly and intact. Like something rendered from sanity. I do not know that it can be done.

What I know and understand and write about is chaos.

I have worked with boys who lived in foster homes. I am told there are good foster homes, and I believe it. I am an optimist and in denial about a lot of things. I just haven't seen any *good* foster homes. The foster homes I have seen have been places I wouldn't leave a dog.

I have many social worker friends who call me up when they are facing a crisis with some kid they want to go to the wall for in order to save. Even in our burned cynicism we believe there are kids who are still worth it.

Kids on their way to prison.

When we were young our idealism was breathtaking. We would save the world. We were the mad ones who joined such soldierships as the American Indian Movement. We demonstrated. We got our names put on FBI lists. We took over Alcatraz. Now we are quiet about the work we do. We change things. Quietly.

We are no longer interested in saving the world. We know in our bones that the world does not deserve or desire to be saved. We also know that there is a difference between the *world* and an *individual child* who might, indeed, deserve to be saved.

I pulled strings to get Awee. I called in favors that were owed to me. Here was a kid who deserved more than he had received. *Change is one child at a time. Change is one family at a time. Change is changing the madness of culture into the spirituality of the individual one social structure at a time.*

Begochiddy gave his son, Monster Slayer, the weapons of lightning and the ability to adapt so he might defeat the dragons and turn their bodies into the mountains that we know.

I sit back here in the shadows of the bleachers alone, apart from the families, and the children laughing, screaming, the sounds of the baseball game, the cheers of neighborhood teams. My son running like the wind to some home plate slide. The dust of conquest. *Safe.*

I call him my son now. He calls me Dad.

Or Daddy.

After Awee moved into my house on the Checkerboard, I stopped dreaming about him. I was usually too exhausted to dream.

I can reach into the moments, and I can show you something of the light in that time we spent together.

We eventually left the Rez for a while. We were living in White People Town. Not too far from the hospital.

I could get there fast.

You could even see the lights from the hospital as it loomed over the city from the top of the baseball bleachers.

Awee was a sight in his white baseball pants, his Nikes, his official Municipal Park Baseball Program T-shirt with the words *Blue Jays* emblazoned in big blue letters on the front and back.

There wasn't a mom in our lives. There was only us. We bought the groceries. We made the meals. We did the laundry. We would have to be enough.

Awee strictly instructed me to wash his Blue Jays baseball shirt properly. I was not to just throw his baseball shirt in with the other laundry. It was a *special* shirt. It required *special* consideration.

After all, he was the captain of the Blue Jays. He was apt to beat (he claimed) the pants off every team in the T-shirt league, and if he had his way about it, he would challenge the great and mighty Wal-Mart Lions.

Any team that defeated the Wal-Mart Lions was a sure bet to get their picture in the paper.

No one had ever defeated the Wal-Mart Lions. They reigned supreme.

His baseball stuff was special.

In fact, it was so special, his highness could help me with the laundry, a chore Awee loved about as much as eating liver.

I had gone off on a serious nutrition/health binge. Nutrition is not my specialty. Guilt is my specialty. I fried up onions and liver once a week, and I made him eat it. "Onions," he claimed, "do not help."

Yuck.

All real baseball people eat liver three, four times a week. The Wal-Mart Lions eat liver three times a day, every day.

He would smile and say that sarcasm did not suit me.

We made a deal. We made a lot of them. Liver for laundry. Awee would eat liver once a week if I washed his Blue Jays base-ball T-shirt with special consideration.

I was amused that even at eleven, the boys out on the baseball field wanted very much to look the part.

Awee was a sight in his baseball cap, which could never quite contain his unraveled, dark Navajo hair that spilled like a black waterfall from some ebony river glinting in the sun.

Awee sliding into third.

Awee stealing second.

Awee on the run.

Awee popping flies that no Dairy Queen Red Socks boy could catch. Awee popping flies to heights no Wal-Mart Lions boy could match.

We were having a good period. For however long it lasted.

Like any parent, I wanted to be there for the good times. Like any parent, I would endure the bad times for the privilege.

The Blue Jays and the Dairy Queen Red Socks were not feared by the other teams. But everyone was afraid of the Wal-Mart

Lions. The Wal-Mart Lions were fearsome, and they had real uniforms.

They could hit the ball so hard, legend had it, that they had broken bats.

This did not deter my son.

Awee could hit 'em hard.

It is a mistake to think that his Indianness had nothing to do with his success at baseball. His Indianness set him apart. We had left the reservation, and now we were somewhat surrounded by a culture Awee did not really know intimately. He knew that people did not merely glance at him. No. They drank him in slowly. An Indian boy. He never saw himself as an Indian boy. Awee was a Navajo. I don't care what anyone says about White People Town anywhere in the Southwest. I know for a fact that White People Town looks down its nose at the Navajo. You can either succumb to this stupidity or you can stand up to it and challenge it with as much pride as you can muster.

It was the way he carried himself that made people look at him. Awee was a quiet soul, and dignified. You had to know him like I did before he let his guard down. I could tease him, and tickle him, and put my lips up to his belly and make fart sounds so he would laugh and scream until he threatened to throw up on me, which he would do.

"You are teasing me!" he'd say. Then he would get all silly, and act like he was eleven. He claimed he wanted to be fifteen, but I did not believe it. Most of the time, when he first came to me, Awee acted like he was twenty-seven. Awee did not want to be twenty-seven. If push came to shove—and eventually it did— Awee liked being five, maybe six. Twenty-seven was too mature. Too removed. Too willing to shoulder responsibilities bigger than he was. Yaaaaa. I teased him. I liked him somewhere right around four.

What the baseball boys saw was the twenty-seven Awee. Cool. Very quiet. Self-contained. His dignity drew people to him. You wondered if it was really as beautiful as it looked. It was. You wondered if you could touch it.

I did not want anyone to touch him.

My job was to care for him. My job was to protect him.

When most kids hit a baseball, most people watch the ball—you want to know where it's going to land. I knew that mainly it would land just to the left at the rear of the outfield over by the railroad tracks in the weeds. This is where the two of us had practiced hitting it when no one was here. We had come here long before baseball season, and we had lost more than a few baseballs in the river behind the railroad tracks. I did not know at that time that Awee would want to return to this place and play real baseball with boys his age. I did not know at that time if Awee would even make it to baseball season. If you are going to pop some baseballs, you better pop them now. Life with Awee had an immediacy to it that was inescapable.

You did things now. You hugged him now. You did the dishes with him now. You took him places now. You talked late into the night with him now.

There was no *later-safe* to store your valuables in.

My beautiful, newly adopted eleven-year-old had AIDS.

He had had it all his life. He had fought it valiantly, courageously, with tenacity and vigor. Many children who were born with this virus have done so, and many of them have lived far longer than was originally assumed. Many, too, have died. Many have reached adolescence. We are learning many things from them.

Over time, Awee's parents were so sick themselves that it was becoming increasingly impossible for them to care for the child at all. Awee described them as mostly passed out on the bed in their coats. Awee took on AIDS alone.

AIDS had knocked him down. It had knocked him around. It had knocked him out. But Awee was a fighter. He always got back up again. Now he was with me.

Now he was the captain of a baseball team. I held my breath a lot. I wanted us to make it through the season.

I wanted us to make it through the season without a hospitalization. I wanted us to make it through the season without a medical crisis to have to stare down, like tumors, or cancer, or blindness, or infections, or pneumonia, or neuropathy, or any of the things that haunted him. I wanted us to hit a couple of home runs. That was all. Awee was on a lot of medication. It was very complicated. It was a full-time job. At first I was ambivalent, and I was not sure I could do this. Care for a child with AIDS. Then I wanted him. I wanted us to be together.

Baseball was more than I had asked for. Baseball was pure dessert. I never thought we would have anything as good as baseball. We were not in a place I particularly liked. White People Town is not my cup of tea. I am more comfortable on the reservation, but the kind of medical care we required was not on any reservation. We had moved here to have as many medical options as we could get.

I was back among the white people again. Quick, my sword.

The medications were working, and I would take baseball gratefully, and be happy as a pig in shit about it.

For however long it lasted. Often, the AIDS medications work for a time, and then they stop working. When they stop working, you find yourself back on the medical merry-go-round, and you try to find something that works. What works for one person does not always work for other people. Many people can take an AIDS drug like Zerit, and they're fine, and the drug is effective. Other people take Zerit, and the resultant nerve damage cripples them.

You have good periods. You have periods that are nightmares.

If Awee got any better at baseball they were going to have to sign him up with the Wal-Mart Lions, and I thought they played too serious a game of baseball. One where the parents (who did not know how to behave) screamed for blood.

We were doing this for fun.

We were doing this because it reminded us that there was more to life than fighting a disease.

When Awee hit a baseball, you had to consciously pry your eyes off him to find the baseball falling from the sky, devouring gravity, a scorched pyrotechnic rock that burned holes in mitts and hands.

Parents in the stands screaming *don't drop the ball* long before the ball falls into the mitt of some eleven-year-old who not only drops the ball but falls to the ground screaming Jesus.

Every now and then Awee's black eyes connect to me.

Go play.

You don't need me.

You can do this yourself.

The dust from the game was hot as it rose, an apricot cloud of sand and grit so penetrating you could taste it, like mustard in your mouth, and everyone in the bleachers was slugging carbonated pop kept cold on ice from coolers brought there by moms now jumping up and down and screaming for the head of some umpire they did not agree with.

It was getting dark. The Blue Jays had won again. They were walking off the field as the cold, white lights blinked on, flooding everyone in the radiance of conquest, and the shadows of defeat.

The losers seemed to melt away. The Dairy Queen Red Socks were a sad and sorry lot. You never saw a single dad with a single boy. These were boys alone, or boys with moms.

They never won.

Every other team that participated in the Municipal Park Baseball Program loved to play them. They had their own sand lot somewhere in the suburbs. But they never won. Often, they never even got a hit. They made a mess of everything, and people laughed at them. When they lost, which was every time they played, they cried.

Eleven does cry. Eleven is still a baby, and it will cry given the right circumstances.

You would pass some kid riding his bike home after the game. He is pedaling fast. He is pissed off. Why did *he* have to get stuck with the Dairy Queen Red Socks. His dad never came anyway. If his mom so much as dared to ask him who won, he was going to slam his bedroom door in her face. He's alone, weaving in and out of traffic, his mitt dangling from his handlebars, and the kid is crying. It is far too dark for this child to be out here on his bike.

Even in those few brief moments when they could throw the ball, it seemed heavier than anything they had ever held, and when they went away, off to parking lots, they left like individuals, one kid here or there, kicking imaginary stones, never having sweat, never having been touched by anyone.

The winners took their shirts off.

No one told them to do this.

No one knew why, and no one questioned it. The winners bathed themselves in dust and light. The winners threw their mitts into the air. Mitts so big they threatened to swallow the boy to the elbow, twirling up, meeting Helios, the limelight of the sun dogs, flush with the crimson blood of rout, coming down, to yet be caught by princes, conquerors of doubt, and the Blue Jays seemed to converge, their arms around their buddies' necks, owning the dirt they walked on, stars ascendant, the prizes of the night.

Even your brother has to admire you now.

Somewhere in the middle of this baseball field, in the middle of this mass of huddled flesh and hair and mud and uniforms was my son. The Blue Jays had congregated around my son. I could feel his heart beating wildly. I could taste the shipwrecked adrenaline in his preadolescent veins implode. I could see the wildfire flash electric in the pony blackness of his eyes.

I knew how he felt.

I knew how he thought.

I knew how he loved.

I knew how he did everything.

The Blue Jays had never had a real Indian on their team before. Not like Awee. There had never been a warrior dragon who could lead them into the caustic eyes of victory. They loved him. He seemed to dissolve into the gnarled bones and elbows of a dozen eleven-year-olds. It was a really big deal to the boys to touch him. To pour ice and water on his head.

He looks around for me.

Yaaaaa. I'm up here. Sitting in the sober shadows, boy. Our eyes locked for an instant of discovery. It was time to take him home.

I knew the price he would pay for this.

I knew his guts and secrets.

I knew that smile. "We won," he said.

Yaaaaa.

Now, individual boys approach. Give him five—*slap*—and then they run away to moms and dads and brothers and showers and dreams of the boy who was a cool mystery to them. I saw the eyes of the moms and the dads dart to Awee. So, this was the Indian boy their son has talked so much about. Yaaaaa. He's softer than he had seemed at a distance. And painfully shy. "Are you okay?" I asked.

"I think we better get home," he said.

I nodded.

He had given everything he had. Everything he could find down inside his guts to pull up as blood and spunk. No other boy had given it that—it was simply municipal baseball to them, not something you sacrifice your life over.

But Awee had done exactly that. His shot at immortality.

Awee was not like them.

Awee hád to do his living now.

We arrived here from a *reservation*. Where the support systems necessary to deal with the stresses a disease such as AIDS imposes on you do not exist. The American government will scream that they exist. But our experience proved otherwise, and we do not have the luxury of time to argue about it. We were either going to get our butts to a place where there were some medical options, or we were going to limp along that shining reservation path of numbness and defeat.

We were on a quest. To find doctors. To find treatment. To rest a bit. To be somewhere for a while where no one knows us.

When I get him in the door, he's going to collapse. I know the drill by now. He's either going to pass out on the bed, or he's going to make it to the bathroom where he's either going to throw his guts up or shit blood or both. None of the boys who adore him know he's sick. We trusted no one.

At first I was ambivalent about baseball, too. I was not prepared for the emotional and physical intensity.

I never scream at some poor eleven-year-old who has dropped a burning baseball or missed one with his bat.

Sitting up here in the shadows is a sedative. This is much, much better than TV.

"You don't have to come to every practice, you know," Awee says. I know. But the Blue Jays knock me out, especially with their desperation to connect.

I don't want him to feel smothered by me.

But I don't want anything bad to happen either.

Every game is life or death. You will only remember the ones you win. Those of us up here in the darkness of the bleachers know that. The boys will tell you it's about the pitch. Or it's about that base they stole. Or it's about that home run they hit. It is about these things. But it also goes to the heart of something more profound.

It is about my love for him, and his love for me. Fathers and sons. Yaaaaa. I see you out there. I'm here. Watching. Baseball is about an insurgent thunder. It is about an ear-splitting detonation when the ball connects not to the bat but to the boy. It is about that abrupt upheaval where a human being in his skin and bones and iron determination meets the unmoved thing that is the earth.

Each boy has a uniform supplied to him by Sparkle Dry Cleaners, Gino's Bar and Grill, and Freddie's Plumbing Fixtures. Parents are required to supply their sons with appropriate Nikes, socks, and an athletic supporter.

My son did not understand what this was.

"It's a jockstrap," I explained.

"Oh."

I say nothing.

"Why?"

"To protect your balls."

"Oh."

"You have to go to Wal-Mart to buy one. And then you have to go into the little room to try it on. And then you have to come out and let me see if it fits. And you have to stand in front of the mirror and turn around. Sorry."

I do not know why I do these horrible things to him. The look of sheer panic on his face. Me cracking up. Rolling on the floor laughing. Him sitting on me. Holding me down with his skinny arms. Sitting on me with his skinny butt. Like anyone would care to see him in a jockstrap. He has never worn one, and for all of his pretend sophistication, he has no idea what it is.

We go to Wal-Mart. The jockstraps are in boxes. Small. Medium. Or large. We go with small. He will *not* go through the checkout with the jockstrap. He makes me do it. I can feel him behind me in his silence turning red. We take the jockstrap home. He takes his jockstrap box into the bathroom and closes the door.

He's in there for twenty minutes. I timed him with my watch. First, you have to try it on backwards. Then, you have to put it on your head. Every male who has ever worn a jockstrap has stood in his bedroom and put the jockstrap on his head. Everyone.

"*Daaaaad.*"

"What?"

"Come in here."

"No, you come out here."

I sigh.

"Something is wrong."

"Looks fine to me."

"There's no *butt* on this thing. My *butt* is hanging out. I don't like it."

"Your butt is supposed to hang out."

"I'm not wearing this *thing* with no butt."

"Then, don't wear it."

The first game the Blue Jays played in their jockstraps they lost to the Kmart Giants, who had worn their jockstraps for about a week longer than the Blue Jays, and their Kmart jockstraps were free. The Blue Jays emerged from their cars with their moms and the whole team walked funny, like a bunch of ballerinas, into the outfield. Every moment of their lives was an initiation into something. There was a lot of whispering among them.

Their sisters laughed during that game louder than the sisters usually laugh when the Blue Jays lose.

Becoming a man is never comfortable.

"We're not wearing them *things* no more," Awee announced to me at dinner one night.

"Then don't."

It was a quiet liberation. The Blue Jays arrived in their underwear, lost in their underwear, went home in their underwear, and the earth just kept spinning.

Every now and then, they won one.

The Dairy Queen Red Socks just kept losing. You take your victories when life offers them to you. Most of the time you get trounced, and life is just a place where your butt hangs out.

The Dairy Queen Red Socks received free banana splits at the end of the season. They got their picture in the paper, too. The other boys were outraged. "I think *we* should have gotten free banana splits and *our* picture in the paper," the captain of the Blue Jays maintained. It was liver night. Lots and lots of onions. Onions are good for you.

The Blue Jays had whipped the Dairy Queen Red Socks eighteen to nothing. Really, your heart had to go out to these boys who had played the best game they could. But they had lost, and in America, it's about winning. Period.

My son was with the winners.

There was cold pop and a lot of very masculine patting on the back and dads all puffed up like big blowfish. Your son has won hooray.

I went up to my son and hugged him *hard*.

Daaaaad.

I know. I know.

Someone might see.

I loved him *so much* in that winning moment on that hot sum-

mer night when the Blue Jays were giddy with screams of glee
and look at us—eighteen runs to zero—and three of those runs
had been hit into the stratosphere by my kid. My kid. One home
run whack had hit the ball so hard no one could find it way out
there in the weeds where it gets dark fast. The Dairy Queen Red
Socks were back there in the weeds kicking up crickets to lo-
cate the baseball, but it had probably gone all the way to China
by then.

Awee like a pony. Base to base. The light fantastic. All the
cheering done. He looks back at the empty field one last time.

The pony is my son.

3. Something of the Light Will Last

When I was Awee's age and younger, whenever we moved to a new migrant camp, the first thing we did was scrub it down. My worn brown mother on her hands and knees.

Even my white dad scrubbed. We could not afford soap, but a bucket and a brush and hot water would do.

The week before I adopted Awee, I scrubbed everything.

Waiting for that day to arrive was like watching some slow shadow of a cloud drag its length along. It seemed forever. I really wanted him.

The day Awee moved in is hard for me to remember because I had been waiting and waiting and waiting and then *finally* he was there.

The light that day was slow, too, and not unlike the way my woodstove heats the coldness of the house. You get up and the floor nips at your toes with teeth. You put wood into the fire.

I don't remember being sane until the moment he arrived.

Then I saw that I had set the table. I had probably set the table days ago.

There were two plates at my table. It had been awhile since there were two plates. For a long time, there had only been one.

One plate in such a house saddens me. I want my house to bulge at the seams with the pandemonium of children. I needed to add at the very least one more plate to this table of loneliness.

Two would do.

For now.

I want the mad ones. I want the children who grind their teeth. I want the ones who have been kicked out of every school. The ones who cannot read. I want the ones who are at risk for every goddamn thing.

I never saw Awee as a boy with AIDS.

Awee was mad with hope. I do not know why. I do not know if it was a hope that he could or would get better. It was a hope for connection. Now that he had finally found his way into something of a family, he wanted us to *do* things together. Awee's lists of the things we would do were endless. We would see every movie ever made, hike every trail ever blazed, go to every spring baseball game in Arizona where the Colorado Rockies, his favorite team, would reign undefeated.

We did not see every movie ever made. We saw a few. We did go to a Colorado Rockies' baseball game in Tucson, and they got whipped, and Awee just shrugged and knew in that brief moment you weren't going to have . . . everything.

Over time Awee became hopeful in the smaller things.

Now there was someone who would hold him.

You don't hear the word *orphan* much anymore, but if you had seen Awee on the day he moved into my house, you would have said *orphan*, and you would not have been wrong. Awee looked abandoned. I saw that I was going to have my work cut out for me. I was okay with that. I hung his toothbrush next to mine. He watched me. He followed me around.

"Our toothbrushes are together now, huh?" he asked. "I

guess maybe you needed a boy here." He looked around. He saw a very quiet loneliness. I seemed to have passed some kind of test. There would be others. "Can I ask you something?" he said.

"Sure."

"What do you want me to call you?"

It was a good question. Obviously I was going to call him Awee. That was his name. There would be other terms of endearment, but those would come later. He could call me Nasdijj if he wanted. But I don't think he wanted to call me Nasdijj. The boy was really asking about what I expected from him.

I was not his friend. Awee would have a lot of friends. He was bright and lovable. But I was his dad now, and that was what I wanted him to call me.

Dad.

I liked the ring of it. I wanted to be someone's dad.

"Call me *Dad*," I said.

I was serving dinner.

Awee was tired. I could see that. He looked like he was hot, perhaps running a small fever. I was putting a steak on his plate.

"Dad?"

He put his head down in his hands. He was beyond exhausted.

I thought: *new dad, new house*. It would be a lot for any kid. Awee was not any kid.

"Daddy, I think I might fall."

Might fall?

"Awee, are you okay?"

Awee could only look at me with his pony-black eyes and his long warrior hair.

He fell off his chair. His silverware crashed to the floor. He was mortified. He tried to pull himself up.

I went to him. Dinner could wait. He did not feel like sixty-five pounds.

He felt more like fifty.

I carried him into his room and set him on his bed. Care for coyotes (a term we had adopted) means you carry them, yaaaaa.

Awee was frantic. "But it's only seven, it's not even eight yet. Only babies have to go to bed at seven." He was terrified that it might become a rule.

Bedtime was a battle that never really ever went away.

"Awee, what do you sleep in?"

"My underpants."

Tonight he would have a brand new pair of blue pajamas. But it would be awhile before we were going to get to them.

I knew I had to be considerate here. I also knew that the next thirty minutes were going to be real important. There were certain things I had to know.

Awee *was* fragile. I undressed him. Awee sighed and let me do it.

He put his hands up so I might take his T-shirt off. I undid his shoes and pulled them off. The old socks smelled really bad. They were definitely going to go. The pants came off and so did the underpants. Awee was not circumcised. These small things were not going to be polite little secrets. You are asking yourself: Why does he need to know this? Why does he need to tell us this? Why doesn't he just leave well enough alone?

A child with AIDS can develop fevers even from small infections. The foreskin of his penis was infected. If you are uncircumcised, you simply have to know how to take care of it. Dads teach boys these things. How to peel it back and keep it clean, and most of all how to dry it without hurting yourself. Sometimes a boy's foreskin won't retract all the way until he is actually old enough to masturbate. Awee's foreskin was a mess of crust, blood, and infected puss. His hair was crawling with lice.

A nice long hot bath with special shampoo (I keep it around as I have worked with a lot of Head Start kids like Awee) would do the trick. Awee was neither self-conscious nor embarrassed. I put him into the tub and got a washcloth.

There were purple strap marks on Awee's butt.

There was no point in even pursuing it. Awee was finally *safe*.

If you were going to function in this world where the children who inhabited it essentially did not have parents, and the system of social services that hangs over everybody and everything like fog was one that was essentially retributive, and more about punishment than anything, you learn early on that in order to be effective here, in order to survive longer than a day, you *picked* your battles. Going after people who were confronting death was just something I did not have the stomach for. They were punished enough. Enough. I wanted to symbolically put their relative importance, now, into the brown paper sack Awee had arrived with—with his pathetic *junk*—and be done with it. It was important to *move on*!

I had to look carefully at the purple strap marks to make sure they were not Karposi's sarcoma. Karposi's sarcoma is a rare form of cancer that is often seen in AIDS patients. The cancer causes purple lesions on the skin. Awee's dad had it. These were strap marks.

I didn't know if this would work (I never really know if the things I do are going to work), but I went into his room, and got a few of the toys I had purchased for his arrival. I was of the distinct impression that now that he was actually feeling a little safe, Awee would go back maybe a bit to this space where he could feel free enough to play. I was hoping anyway, because if he could do this it was going to help me enormously. But if he was going to hang on tight to being a big tough guy (and he could do that), it was going to be difficult.

"What are these, please?"

"They're called Hot Wheels."

Hot Wheels are cool. They're small cars and trucks. Awee did not know them.

He played with them while I washed his hair.

This meant that Awee was going to give me the benefit of the doubt, and he would go back into childhood a little bit.

I handed him a soft soapy washcloth.

"Okay, I want you to wash your penis very carefully."

"You mean my dick?"

"Yaaaaa. Awee, is it hurting you?"

"Sometimes when I pee it hurts me."

"Well, it could be any number of things. But we'll start with keeping it clean, and then we'll just go from there."

Awee washed himself. "The skin gets stuck," he said.

"Being in the warm bath will help."

"I gotta tell you something. Will you promise not to be mad, okay."

"I won't be mad, Awee."

"Yeah, well, but you gotta promise cross your heart and hope to die, and stick a needle in your eye."

"Okay. Cross my heart, and hope to die, and stick a needle in my eye. What is it?"

"Will you get mad?"

I lifted his foot out of the water. "Did you know I eat toes?"

"No, you don't."

"I promise I won't get mad."

"I might wet the bed."

"Oh. Is that all?"

"They used to spank me if I wet the bed. With a belt. Do you gotta belt?"

"I will never spank you. I will never hit you. I will never punish you like that, Awee. Those days are over. I'm your dad now, remember?"

"Yeah, but you might got a belt and you might wanna whip me."

"I will never whip you. I promise. This is serious. I will never hurt you. I want you to hear that."

I want the ones brave enough to cry on me.

Awee drove his hot wheels car up the wall. He was suspicious.

The thought of anyone whipping him just made me sick. Awee was the most gentle kid I had ever met. He didn't have a mean bone in his body.

I got him out of the tub. The infected penis and the lice in the hair were little problems we could deal with immediately. The feeling safe and trusting stuff would happen, but it was going to take some time. Awee was trusting me to allow him to be about four years old that night.

He was so tired (he said he had not slept because he knew the adoption was happening) that he simply gave himself to me in one fell soapy swoop.

"It's the lice shampoo kind, huh?"

"Yaaaaa."

He knew.

The best part about going to bed just as it is getting dark is that you get to eat peach pie. "Can I feed Navajo some pie, please?"

Navajo was hiding under the bed in the not too subtle hope a crumb might fall. She is a herding animal. Now she had something new to herd. A boy. She adores boys. She is essentially a shameless flirt.

Navajo does not need peach pie in bed even if she does beg for it.

"Well, only a little bit."

"Can Navajo sleep in my room?"

"I don't see why not. If you feed her any more peach pie, you'll never get rid of her."

Before the end of the peach pie, Awee was fast asleep.

His ponyblack eyes drag his soul to me.

Keep this whipping in the past. I am carving something solid here. Something of the light will last.

4. Care for Coyotes

The first few nights with Awee were not nights of sleep.

I would get up and check on him. He was fine. I would get up and check on him again. He was fine. I was getting up again (to check on him) when I realized Awee was in my room.

He was standing in the dark. I want the mad ones.

"What's wrong?" I asked.

"I just wanted to know . . ." he said, "if you were still here."

Yaaaaa. I was there. "I'm here," I said.

Awee started crying. There was that quick intake of breath. That swallow he did when he was choking it down.

"What's *wrong*?!?"

"I'm gonna be sick. Don't yell at me."

I didn't know I was yelling.

I was.

Awee bent over in the darkness of my bedroom and threw up. All over my bed. All over me. All over the floor. All over his new blue pajamas.

For a moment I did not know what to do.

He was crying and throwing up.

Awee never threw up a little. When Awee threw up, it was buckets.

Vomit everywhere.

At first I thought it was nerves. But after I smelled the vomit, I knew. This kid was sick.

You learn real fast about a lot of things with pediatric AIDS. I got him into the bathroom. Awee pleading with me not to whip him. Suddenly, without warning, shit starts pouring out of his butt. Black liquid shit. Everywhere. Awee screaming.

I pick him up, and put him on the toilet. It was coming out of both ends of this kid.

Vomit all over his chest. Shit all over his feet and legs. Vomit and shit are all over the house. On the floor. In my bed.

"It just does that to me!" Awee's voice is three pitches higher than normal. "I *hate* it! I *hate* myself."

"Calm down. I'm just going to hold you here on the toilet. Just let it all come out of you Awee, and then we'll wash you, and make you clean again."

"But you won't *want* me, and I will have to go away! Oh, please don't make me go, please."

I was not about to make him go anywhere. I would fight like hell to keep him. The idea of him going away was ridiculous.

To me.

But not to him. We never see things from their perspective. They do have one.

This time I put him in the shower. I dried him, and gave him one of my T-shirts to wear. It looked like an oversized dress.

I cleaned the house in rubber gloves. Stripped the beds (his was soaked). Put a huge load of laundry to do later into big, black, plastic bags. It looked like fall, and we had been raking leaves. I put Awee into my sleeping bag, flipped his mattress over, and put him to bed.

I got a blanket and went to go sleep on the couch.

Awee was in his room crying.

This time openly.

"Will you sleep with me? Will you hold me, please. I neeeeeeeeeeeeeeeeeeed someooooooooooooooone!"

The kid had lost it. *Is this when we go to the hospital? Is this when I panic? Is this when . . .*

No. No. No. Just hold on.

I hadn't slept in a little boy's bed in years. There wasn't much room. His brand-new bed smelled like pee. I did not care. Awee, dressed in my T-shirt, inside the sleeping bag, slept in my arms that night.

Dreams. Tina would have approved, and smiled, and turned out the light.

Why would anyone sane adopt a child with AIDS?

It isn't like that. Sane or insane.

Parents who have gone through the process of adoption know. You are adopting them—*yes*—but they are adopting you, too. It is a two-way street.

The connection you are making with the kid is fragile, and rather private. He would embrace me and I could smell his breath. It was an intimacy like the intimacy of light as it lingers when the sun goes down at the edges of the desert. I got a cold. That was all it was. Just a cold. It was no big deal. I went to bed, and I did not want Awee to catch this cold (and he didn't), but he came into my room with hot tea and crackers. I thanked him.

"Care for coyotes," he said. Our song. Our dance.

I had to laugh.

If Awee cared about you, he let you know it.

A new AIDS drug had hit the market. I drove about three hundred miles with Awee to a university medical school infectious disease specialist to discuss the idea of putting Awee on Sustiva.

People living with AIDS were extending their lives with Sustiva. The specialist explained about the side effects. One was a possibility that Awee would have very intense nightmares. The term *LSD-like* is often used in connection with Sustiva, which does, indeed, reach HIV in the central nervous system and the spinal cord. That there would be neurological involvement with this very powerful drug was not a surprise.

Later that night I woke up. He was in my bed. Clinging to my leg.

I woke him up. He did not know who he was. Or where he was. Or who I was.

A small voice begged me not to whip him. It was not a voice I knew. He promised that if I would not whip him, he would stop turning himself inside out if only he could figure out how to make it stop.

"Are you inside out now?" I asked.

"Yeah."

He didn't like it much when he turned himself inside out because his guts were hanging out.

I said: *Awee, honey, are you awake with Daddy?*

Nooooo.

There's a green vinyl chair in a hospital room that has green-tiled floors, and ugly green-painted walls, and white ceilings made from tiles with 372 holes per tile, and long, flickering fluorescent lights. The green vinyl chair sits between the hospital bathroom and the machine with red numbers that flash. The machine beeps when the numbers go below 88, and I sit day after day in the green vinyl chair staring at the numbers on the machine, willing them to go from 88 to 89. Can't they give me that, one small jump. And this is where I learned to watch him breathe.

Down the hall there are other children. Sick ones. There is a certain contained chaos here. There are little yellow ducks painted on the wall in the hallway.

He's lived eleven years with HIV. It even sounds evil. *Hiiivvv.* Like something a cat might spit with its back arched up and its hair sticking out. *Hisssssssssssssing.*

This is where I learned to watch. Silent witness to the precipice.

That green vinyl chair and the green vinyl room and the beeping machine I wanted to smash with a baseball bat.

Pneumonia again.

The flu can be fatal.

I do not keep leftovers in the fridge. Do *not* feed him peach pie, please.

When Awee had diarrhea he would usually pass out on the toilet.

Underneath all the plastic tubing, there was a boy.

My new son.

I do not care about the past.

I care about today. Right now.

There were needles in his veins. Tubes in his nose. Tubes down his throat. They had to strap his arms down with restraints to the sides of the bed because, even in his deep morphine un-consciousness, Awee would pull the tube in his penis out. He knew how.

How many times did we fight the battle of the tube. I want the mad ones. The ones who insist they are human and not a compliant number.

NO! I'm NOT going to NO hospital cuz they're gonna put a TUBE in my penis! I won't DO IT AGAIN. I won't, and you can't MAKE me!

The truth is that Awee never said penis. He did not know what a penis was.

Awee said dick. Dick is the word he came to me with.

I did get him to use the word *penis*. We talked a lot about words. About the kind of power they had.

He would look down at it. "It's not a very big dick, is it?"

Digiz is the Navajo word for crooked. "It only grows when you say penis," I said. "Nice people say penis. Only not very nice people say dick."

I had a lot of really stupid moral idiocies I believed in. Like only bad people did drugs. I was worse than some frumpy, old grandmother from Bible State University. Awee would challenge everything.

"I don't like that fucking tuuuuuuuuuuuuuuuube in my peeeeeeeenis," he wrote in his journal.

I mention this violation repeatedly because it happened to him so repeatedly. If we even drove by a hospital on the way to the grocery store, Awee would turn away, bitterly, and refuse to look at it. It was hard when he shut me out.

There were lots of battles. But the one battle Awee and I fought over, the tube in his penis, was the one that never went away. Like bedtime, it never got resolved, and Awee would kick and spit and bite and hit and scratch and scream and refuse to coop-erate in any way with a thing he saw as essentially a violence per-petrated against him. If they even came into the room with that tubing, Awee would climb the walls. I got so sick of it. Hospital staff would look at me like *please, help us with your kid. Tell him it's going to be okay.*

But it was not okay. It was not going to be okay. I would leave the room. I would not help them by telling some lie he was going to see through. Finally, his urethra had been poked so many times it developed infections and allergies to latex and formed so many internal scars, that they had to leave well enough alone, which is something they find difficult to do in pediatrics.

So he wet the fucking bed.

He did not know I was there when I washed his tummy. He didn't know I was there when I washed his hair with the washcloth. He didn't know when I washed his feet. He had no idea I had cut his toenails (the red toenail polish he loved wore off). "You can't eat my Nibbles if I paint them red," he would say, and he would scream when I tried. He didn't know when I washed his butt. He didn't know when I washed his fingers. And he did not know when I kissed them.

He didn't know when I talked to him or what I said or when I begged him to live.

Awee. You came to me and you promised. You promised that time you begged me to adopt you. You promised and I did. You promised, Awee, you would fight to live. If you can't do it for yourself anymore, please, honey, I need you to do it for me.

Someone came to me once with a form that needed signing.

I was sitting in the green vinyl chair.

My empire's throne. I was holding his hand.

They say talk to them. I don't believe it. I say: *Touch them.*

It's absolutely ridiculous to think you have the slightest idea what you are signing in a hospital room with the door half-closed, the curtain half-closed, the light coming halfway into the room, and they're handing you a clipboard with some form on it, and you can smell the coffee outside the room being delivered on carts, and you've been up all night, and sign here, please.

Where?

Here.

What is this?

A form that says no extraordinary measures will be taken if he codes blue.

My heart jumps. Codes blue? I turn to look at him. He is not blue. He is brown and soft and naked and beautiful and tubes are coming out of every hole of his small, perfect body and what do they mean—*codes blue*.

Hell, no, I say.

I am what they refer to as a *difficult* parent.

Which means I do not always go along with the dog and pony show.

I want every fucking machine known to God and science pushed into this room. You stick him with every needle you've got. You put the paddles to his chest and you plug it in and crank it up. Stand back. Hit it. You crash cart this kid until the cows come home. You wake up every sleeping son-of-a-bitch doctor in this place and you *make* him live. You take extraordinary measures, and you do everything you can do.

I know. I want them to leave him alone and I want them to save him. It is a contradiction. Deal with it.

Where do I sign?

I sign most forms they push into my face. I have no fucking idea what I am signing when I sign things in hospitals. The idea that I am cognizant of what I am signing is ludicrous. *I can't even see the print.*

Excuse me, nurse. My son is naked. Do you think we could put a blanket over him, please?

They will not do it.

I move the green vinyl chair over by the door so I might guard the room. Sometimes I feel I'm in Grand Central Station with every ward clerk and every secretary coming in here with forms for me to sign. *Sign here.* Everyone glances at the beautiful naked boy in the bed with all the tubes in him, and all the machines, and all the beeping.

Morphine is a goddamned miracle.

Finally I get sick of asking for things. I find a blanket and I cover him and fuck them and fuck what they think about it.

Awee never really knew that he was naked. Awee never really knew that he had been connected to all those machines. Awee doesn't remember that hospitalization at all. There have been too many. We don't like to talk about hospitals too much, and we cannot stand to watch hospital dramas on TV.

I think he knows I read his journal. But Awee has no idea I get up ten, sometimes twenty times a night to go into his room and stand quietly in the shadows where I watch him breathe. I am the man who counts the holes in the ceiling tile. I am the man who sleeps not too soundly in a green vinyl chair. I am the man who signs the forms. I am the man who pays the bills. I am the man who cleans up shit and vomit. I am the man who washes every toe. Every finger. Every inch of him.

I am the man with two plates at the table. I am the man the nurses call: *Awee's father.* I am the watchman lighting lamps.

All is well.

We're living in the city now. I have to laugh. It seems like it was just the other day when he said: *I don't need you. I'll go to the baseball game by myself. I will. You watch me.*

Here we go again.

His medication has changed. It confuses him when they do that, and they do not discuss it with him. He hates the big pills. He gags on them. It had been very difficult to keep up with all the changes. Our lives revolved around the medication schedule.

Awee understood what each pill was about, and what each pill was for. Awee could tell you the side effects, and he could even tell you about the molecular structure of the medicine because he studied these things on the Internet.

I want the mad ones. When the literature says that medical professionals appreciate the well-informed patient, the kind of patient who takes the time to read things, to understand the disease in question, they do not mean eleven-year-old boys with AIDS. Eleven-year-old boys with AIDS are treated with disdain. They are too big to be treated like little baby boys, but they are too young to be allowed to take responsibility for their own medication.

Awee is not just a case of pediatric AIDS.

Awee with his ponyblack eyes is more than the sum of his diseases. Awee is sweet and shy. Always asking why? Why? Why? Awee is light from the stars and sun. Awee is pieces of the sky.

5. Grits His Teeth

I did not take Awee to Indian hospitals because I believe their approach to medicine kills Indian people. Doctors and nurses who work in these places will bristle indignantly. Native people will bristle indignantly. But it's what I believe.

I dare you to go to any Indian community and find a majority of Indian people who will say: *Our community hospital is a modern, clean, technically proficient health care delivery system run by a government that cares for and about the Indian people it serves, and is connected to all the latest research and advances in medical and computer science.*

How many community hospitals built and designed for Indians participate in AIDS-drug research?

Go to any Indian community. This is what you will find: *You better be careful because they kill people in there.*

How many health care delivery systems are designed to bring health care to Indian people and actually go so far as to find difficult-to-reach populations of Native People to test them for HIV?

How many programs actually reach beyond the realm of superstition and fear and silence and bring in men, women, and children, not to just be tested for HIV but to participate in AIDS-drug research trials? I am not asking how many programs *exist*. I am asking how many of these programs reach the people they are supposed to reach. How many Indian women are tested for HIV during pregnancy? Virtually none.

How many Indian women even receive any medical care whatsoever during pregnancy? Very few.

This despite the fact that many Indian hospitals are fundamentally designed to assist Indian women having babies.

The idea that we can base AIDS funding on the number of people with HIV is wrong when we have no real idea how many people are infected. The statistics the government keeps are skewed. These programs go to white people and white hospitals. The AIDS-drug trial medicines are not available to Indians. There is little public dialogue in Indian communities concerning AIDS as AIDS is perceived within a sexual context.

People are not comfortable with sexual issues. People are afraid to be tested (and who can blame them) and have their names on lists. I no longer believe in statistics. The statistics the government puts out are bogus because no one really knows who has HIV.

I did not take Awee to Indian hospitals. Ask any Indian hospital how long it takes them to get viral genetic testing results returned to the *patient* so the *patient* can decide what form of treatment he or she will or will not participate in.

Duh . . .

Chances are good that they don't provide that kind of medical care at your corner community Indian hospital, where mainly they are equipped to (1) treat diabetes, (2) deliver babies, (3) refer you to an alcohol program.

How many Native Americans are informed enough to decide what drugs to take? How many Indian people are getting the ap-

propriate medications? You cannot just hand an Indian medication that requires refrigeration because too many Native Americans do not even have electricity. Nor do they have running
water. How are people who do not have electricity or running
water supposed to get health care delivery systems that reflect
who they really are?

When it comes to health care, Indians do not just live in the
dark ages, they live in an ice age.

White people often take their access to such things as medical insurance for granted. If they don't like the care they're receiving, they can take their business somewhere else.

Anglos would never tolerate the kinds of limited options
Indians have to live with every day.

The reality is that most Indian hospitals would have been an
immediate death sentence for Awee, so I did not take him there.
When I did take him to a hospital or to an infectious disease
clinic, I never once checked the little box that indicates race. It is
not legal to ask me that although they all still do. I am not compelled to answer.

You cannot deny me treatment on the basis of racial identity.
Yet if you identify yourself as Indian, many of these white places
will show you the door. Why? Because Indians are treated at Indian hospitals.

Oh, no. We don't do that here.

Translation: *The welfare hospital down the street serves you welfare people.*

In Gallup, New Mexico. The *Indian* hospital is literally across
the street from the White People Hospital, and health care is
delivered by a system based on race.

Racism is not limited to the birthplace of Jesse Helms, who
has advocated for the elimination of AIDS funding altogether.

In America, the term *AIDS* is synonymous with the words *gay* or *homosexual*. This is a sexual minority American conservatives feel get what they deserve: death as the natural consequence of anal sex. That this notion is a fantasy based on antediluvian fears of sex and sin will never be recognized by ideologues who resist, too, the notion that *family* might be something more than mom (who stays home and bakes pies), and dad (mom and dad never have anal sex because it is against the law), and the prerequisite children whose purpose is to reproduce social structures designed to keep the powerful powerful. The powerful have access to health care as that is their right.

I wanted Awee to have the same kind of access to health care that white boys have. I wanted Awee to get the same kind of treatment white boys get. I wanted Awee to get the same kind of treatment Senator Helms would get. In the United States, cutting-edge AIDS-treatment is connected to research and Indian hospitals are not connected to AIDS research. AIDS research is inherently connected to the development of drugs. Go to any Indian community hospital and ask how long it takes them to get results from blood tests for viral loads and CD4 counts (ratios of T-cells).

I want these test results by the next day at the latest.

Time is of the essence here.

There are some medical centers in the United States (North Carolina for one) that are taking as long as *six weeks* to get this information to the patient. Often, even the large, state-run public health hospitals that have full-time labs do not have enough lab testing kits on hand because they do not order them. AIDS is not a laboratory priority, and it is not a cultural priority either. Six weeks is intolerable.

That's six weeks you could be using the right medication. Six weeks on the wrong medication for a person with AIDS is not acceptable. That would be like saying to a person with tuberculosis: *Look, we're going to give you aspirin for your TB, and we're going to charge you a hundred bucks a pill, and the aspirin might not treat the tuberculosis, we don't know, we won't know for six weeks until we get your blood tests back, have a nice day.*

The idea that I would have Awee on the wrong medication for six weeks is ludicrous. I won't do it. I will find an alternative. Six weeks on a drug like Zerit can be dangerous for some people as it has been known to damage nerve cells, and six weeks of ongoing, active, overt nerve damage is like asking someone to take a sledgehammer to your feet and legs and pound away at you for forty-two days.

I fought with doctors. I fought with nurses. I fought with the federal government. I fought with insurance companies. I fought with AIDS programs. I fought with so many things, I was like some cosmic dragon breathing fire. I fought with Awee.

I go into his room early in the morning. He groans. *Oh, fuck . . .*

Go away, Daddy.

Okay, buddy, I know yesterday was hard, but today we're getting up at four in the morning, and we will drive five hundred miles to a hospital in a big city (hopefully there will be a place to park) where I am going to fight with everyone, and you are going to take your clothes off and allow them to inspect you on the inside and the outside—climb right up here so they can stick their fingers in your butt—and I want them to roll that lump you have in your testicles around, and then we are going to take X rays, and add five huge pills to the regimen of pills you already have to take, and won't that be fun?

Awee was depressed.

It was more fun than he could handle. He thought that he could eventually stash enough OxyContin to kill himself. The eleven-year-old was right.

That's the scary thing about eleven-year-olds. They are often right about the wrong things.

Open your mouth.

Why?

I want to see if there are any pills under your tongue.

Swallow it, Awee . . .

It's life I do not trust.

I'm the man who grits his teeth and winces when you walk out of the house with that skateboard. I'm the man who rocks you when you don't know where you are, who you are, or what happened. I'm the man who wishes I was the one who had this terrible disease, not you. I'm the man who sneaks into your room to watch you sleep. I am the man who is at *war*.

With everyone.

I stand alone in shadows of the dragon. I stand alone among all the wild creatures of mythology. Athabaskan mythology is deeply imbued with eroticism. Coyote is always having sex with someone.

I should be ashamed.

To see that the sleeping eleven-year-old body has an erection.

I am not ashamed.

I am his dad. I take it as a great and extraordinary victory. The male body lost in REM. A sexuality struggling to survive.

I want Awee to have everything he can get, every hard-on, every hold on happiness he can have for the time he is going to have among us.

Only his dreams belong to him.

I didn't see his unconscious erection any differently than I saw his lungs as they attempted to rid themselves of pneumonia. Fight, Awee, fight.

Welcome to the world of men.

I know every inch of him, and every smell, every movement of his chest, every gurgle in his throat, every wet eyelash, every drop of moisture that lingers on him, every sour taste of every breath.

I stand in the shadows of a gnawing grief.

Daddy!

What, honey?

Why are you standing in my room watching me sleep?

I don't know. It's just what I do sometimes.

Daddy, will you rub my back?

Sometimes it puts him to sleep. Sometimes not.

Knock knock.

Who's there?

Morning light is just about to spill into the room. Ssshhh, little boy, do not get up just yet. No knock-knock jokes. Time lingers in the transition from night to light. Just outside the window of his room a small flock of sparrows flies away into the distant trees.

I am haunted by the indifference of the world.

I am haunted by the beauty of a child.

I have answered all his questions.

The ones about death are very hard to deal with. He asks them less and less because he knows they hurt me.

He wants to show me where it hurts. *It hurts right here. And then when I walk it hurts me in the ice picks.*

In the ice picks?

When the ice picks come, and then they're stabbing you so hard. And I don't want them to. It's hurting.

I wish I knew a joke, Awee. I don't know any jokes today.

Daddy, knock knock.

Who's there?

Awee.
Awee who?
Awee gonna go to the movies, pleeeeeeze!

I would make him do his chores.

Awee was part of a family. He contributed.

"No, Daddy, I'm too tired to do my chores."

He would sigh.

"Awee, chores."

He would do his chores.

"Daddy, you said we could go to the movies."

"No. Today I will tell you about my grandma Sa."

He settles. We sit together. He likes to sit by me. "Tell me the one where you didn't talk no more, and you lived with Grandma Sa, please."

Awee was the Story Monster.

"Truly, the place where Grandma Sa lived was magical, Awee. Especially for a kid like me who did not talk. We were living in a sheep camp. She told me all the stories. I owe her everything, including my ability to write."

"But did she know monsters?"

"All her stories had at least one monster. Sometimes several."

"But Daddy, tell me the one where you loved a beautiful lady and then you adopted this boy who was sick, you know, like AIDS, and then you did not ask her to come live with you cuz it was too much to what is it?"

"It is too much to ask of someone, honey, to come inside our house. It is more than I could ask of someone else. Even if she wanted to. Still, I cannot ask her."

"But you love her, huh?"

"Yes, I do."

"But tell me the one where you're gonna stay with me, okay, cuz I want that one."

His face is on my lap. He is taking my hand and running it up and down his cheek.

"The one where you're gonna stay with me, please."

He nags.

"Once upon a time there was a beautiful woman I loved very much. I still do. She lives far away in a city. I could not live there. The city was smothering me. I could not breathe. So I came back to the reservation and adopted a boy who was the best boy ever ever, and although I still love the beautiful woman very much, I am not going anywhere without the boy. Is that the one?"

"Yeah, tell me that one, please."

He is talking to my knee.

He is biting my knee. My knee is wet.

"Once upon a time there was a beautiful woman I loved very much . . ."

We talked about it on the telephone late at night.

"I want to try," she said. "I want to help you with him, Nasdijj."

I believed her. But it was too much to ask.

"You always take the hard ones home."

I am tired of defending it.

For many people I know, life is a love affair with the reservation. On again. Off again.

My diminutive home on the reservation waits for me in hopelessness to come (live there), and yet I never move in too permanently amid the songs, cousins, and empty, clear cold skies. There *are* no women who will live here with me, really. We are too far away from town.

We are too surrounded here by HUD reservation houses with disposable diapers in the mud, and heavy clothes wet with rain that have been hanging on the same clothesline for twenty thousand years, and mops, and rusted tricycles, and broken cement block steps that lead into a double-wide universe where everyone has been horsewhipped. The kind of home Awee is from.

What woman would come here—just to be with me, to sleep nude with her breasts and hips against me—out here with the coyotes, the jackrabbits, the horses, and the sun.

On the outside, I looked okay. I seemed sane enough.

I had just published a book—much of it set on this very reservation—and yet I was deeply contemplating suicide (I had it all planned down to the gun I would blow my head off with, pills are for sissies) because I could not go on. I spoke to no one of this. Why would I?

I would numbly stare at that one fucking single plate.

I did not see it as depression, but the reality is that I was acutely depressed. I had grown despondent over the publication of my book *The Blood Runs Like a River Through My Dreams*. Not because the book was published badly, no.

But white people *do* have a very difficult time understanding the extent to which (or why) native men, or even a mongrel such as myself, might feel deeply conflicted with the invasiveness of the never-ending questions, the interviews where you were expected to respond cheerfully, the analysis of not just your work but your life.

You have enough trouble analyzing yourself. You do not need another take on it.

If it could be kept focused on your work, fine. That would be one thing. But what they really want is a piece of you. The radio shows. The question-and-answer sessions where you have to sit at some long table of educated white people who know what they are doing (writing in English), and you *know*, in your dissolving bones, you don't. The photographers who show up at your home. The magazines. The Why did you do this? And the Why did you do that?

And can you send us a better photograph of your deceased son, and what year was it he had that final seizure?

I wanted my life back. Writing about it had been enough. More, really, than I thought I could do.

How does my writing a memoir make it the business of anyone to know the names of the women I have slept with?

Well, you wrote about your life, so now you are compelled by God to tell us every little private thing.

The birth dates of my children are *my* business.

They are for me to celebrate. Not you.

Why I name my dogs Navajo is *my* business. I felt beyond invaded. I felt like the dead corpse of my first kid had been dug up and ripped apart by hyenas. I felt like I had been raped, and had spilled the secrets of the tribe.

I wanted the woman I loved to love me and she did. But I could no longer live with anyone in a city, any city, it doesn't matter which one, all of them (to me) are quite the same. They are all much too loud.

The ones in North Carolina where she lives are growing and expanding like mold organisms in a petri dish. A shallow covered glass dish used to culture bacteria. The construction of highways leading to the construction of bedroom communities whose only purpose is to spread the urban sprawl. All the little perfect houses lined up perfectly in rows. Mommy in her dress and heels reading the *Ladies Home Journal* and baking peach pies. The reality, of course, is that Mommy works in a busy office in a bank, and Baby comes home from school to an empty house. The gap between the reality of these places and the unreachable fantasy these places were designed around and for cannot be bridged by a sameness where the hampsters in their plastic cages all run the same frantic wheel whose destination gets them to the place where they first got on. *All aboard!*

Everybody run.

I could never tell where I was in the North Carolina suburbs because they all seemed to be the same. Raleigh was Charlotte and Charlotte was Greensboro and Greensboro was Durham and Durham was Cary and Cary was another suburb where the malls and the pagers and the perfect parking lots were indistinguishable one from the other. All the malls had the same shoes for sale, and all the pagers had the same message, and all the perfect parking lots were filled with perfect facsimiles of the same car. I was done with being lost. I found Awee. He came to me like this enormous gift.

I am difficult to know. I have one friend. Crow Dog is seventeen. Ever since the sixth grade, Crow Dog has always been around. We are distantly related. His cousin's cousin's mother's uncle married my aunt's third stepsister who divorced my grandfather's second child by his third wife in another clan.

Crow Dog wears hearing aids. He is able to hear but not well. He stutters. He knows a lot of American Sign Language. He knows a lot of Indian sign as well. Crow considers himself to be stupid and semiilliterate, yet he knows English, Navajo, Spanish, American Sign Language, and Indian Sign Language.

Crow Dog also knows all of Grandma Sa's old stories. He should. I told them to him.

Crow started losing his hearing when he was beaten up and knocked around by the men his mother frequently brought home. Beating Crow Dog up was considered to be something of a reservation sport, like shooting squirrels with a .22 from the trailer steps.

Hey, kid, go get me a beer.

Every other week, the man changed, but Crow was expected to call all of them *Daddy*. For someone with so many daddies, Crow had no idea who his real daddy was.

Crow remembers the night the cops came and took his dad away in handcuffs.

Crow's dad had been in prison far away in Santa Fe.

I found Crow Dog in the backyard of his mother's house one night hanging from a tree with a rope around his neck. Crow was the same age Awee is now. I cut him down in time and took him home. One long silent ride through mountains. Crow Dog whimpering. Finally, he just put his head on my lap and wept. I want the mad children. Too many Indian men just don't fucking make it. I never saw myself as Crow Dog's dad. But Crow did.

"I don't understand you," he said.

"I know."

"But if this is what you want—Awee."

"It is."

Crow threw his ax much too forcefully into the piece of fire-wood we'd been chopping. He grunted to pull the ax out. He sent the ax into the wood again. Wood chips were flying everywhere. Sweat was pouring from him. "Then I have to love you for it, don't I? This boy is going to be *tough*, and you know it. Tougher than this fucking wood."

We had been chopping aspen like a father and his older son might. Because in time, the cold would come. We do many things to not be cold. Months from now.

Aspen is a hard, tough wood to chop. It takes me four or five cords to get through a winter on the reservation. Some people use as many as nine cords to make it through a winter. A tar-paper shack does not hold the heat in well.

"I think he's really unique," I said.

"He's sick," Crow reminded me with that ability he has to yank me back into a landscape of starkly sober reality, a place I often feel compelled to resist.

"I know."

"No. I don't think you do. I think you block it out. I don't know that you weigh how it might impact the rest of us who love you." Crow Dog's fist hit his chest by his heart. He meant that I could hurt his heart. "But it doesn't matter, now, okay, Nasdijj. All that matters is that he's here. It's done. There's no going back. How am I going to know you through this? Now that there's a new one who will sort of take my place as your new lost cause. You *do* do that. Don't say anything. Don't tell me you don't. For once, just *shut up*. It's done. And he's so . . . so vulnerable."

Crow unconsciously made the Indian sign for wounded.

I didn't know if he meant himself or Awee.

"You must have pulled a lot of strings."

Yaaaaa. I make kite string with the strings I pull. Big balls of kite string you take out into the high-desert mesa of Dinetah to fly kites with.

I did not know how he (or anyone) was going to know me through this. We went back to chopping wood.

I told Awee all the old Navajo stories. Awee loved the tales of the War twins. Tobajishinchinii, Child Born for Water, and Nayanee Nezghanii, Monster Slayer. How did two small brothers defeat the power of the monsters? Not with thunderbolts given to the twins by their father Begochiddy who was the sun. How did these boys turn the monsters into the mountains that we see? With love. And sacrifice. On the backs of birds. "Daddy, tell me the one where Monster Slayer dies." And then Awee would snuggle in his pillow and melt into the bed.

He had been sent to me.

Younger brother, I shall now leave you forever, you will never see me again, but when the summer comes, you will watch for the storms, and when you see the he-rain you will say: There is my brother. For I shall be like lightning and dragon-fire in the storm that you behold.

That is the burning of the candles in the stories we are told.

6. Scars

It was the pain that was the worst. First there was the pain from the peripheral neuropathy. This was a pain that just about crippled Awee.

Diabetics often get it in their hands and feet. It can be described as a *tingling* sensation.

It is my belief that medical science wishes it could be just a *tingling*. It is peripheral neuropathy that strips off the mask science wears to expose contemporary medicine for the ineffective thing it is. There is no such term as AIDS-neuropathy in medical literature where this is referred to as HIV-related neuropathy. Medical literature has a long way to go to catch up to the reality of disease. We do not really know what neuropathy is or what causes it.

We throw a plethora of neurological pharmaceuticals at it, but nothing in our bag of tricks works too well. Neurologists and pain specialists do not want you to know that. Neuropathy is nerve damage. And it can be far, far more debilitating than just a *tingling*.

It can cripple you.

It will knock you off your feet with a pain so intense, it will take your breath away, and you will hyperventilate because you are not getting the kind of oxygen to your brain that you need to maintain rhythmic breathing patterns. Between the pain and the breathlessness the pain facilitates, you will think you are having a heart attack.

Typically, you get referred to a neurologist who is going to prescribe Neurontin. If Neurontin doesn't work, then they will shrug and wash their hands of you.

Neurontin only made Awee vomit.

I would hold him around the waist so he didn't completely collapse on the bathroom floor.

His head in the toilet.

Vomiting Neurontin.

Awee needed something that could help him with the pain from the peripheral neuropathy and the nausea.

Crow Dog reluctantly suggested marijuana. Crow thought drugs were basically bad things.

"I can't do *that*," I said.

"It's not for you. It's for him."

And then Crow walked away, which is what he always does when he thinks I am being a jackass.

"You should take him for rides on the bike, too," Crow maintained. "Get his mind off himself."

I had a motorcycle. It had been at Crow's.

"I couldn't do *that*," I said. "Awee has AIDS."

"Bring him over to my trailer and we'll play cards when you get over yourself, okay," Crow said. Then he left.

Awee did not know about the motorcycle. Crow Dog had borrowed it. I borrow many things from Crow. And Crow borrows many things from me. We sometimes forget whose is what. I had been so busy with Awee (doctor visits, drives to town, drives to different university medical clinics, my failed attempts to find someone who would help us with this pain) that the Harley had sort of escaped me. I own a jeep. Awee loved to ride in it with the top down. His hair in the hot Las Cruces wind.

My bike was a tenuous connection to a youth that had sort of slipped away (I did not miss it). Crow Dog and his smiles came over on the Hog.

Wanna ride?

Awee was really pissed. Why hadn't anyone *told* him about the bike.

That he was going to go live with someone who actually owned a Harley-Davidson.

He would have gladly died to touch it. We shrugged. It was a toy to us. But to Awee, it was as awesome and as mysterious as the world he did not know. He stomped around (wincing), and demanded that we tell him everything. We laughed. Never in a million years. At eleven? Turning twelve. You will *not* know everything. You will know things as we tell them to you.

We were spending the night in Crow Dog's little trailer. Down the dirt road. Not far away, but far enough so that when we visited, we did not want to drive home. Sometimes we did that because Crow has a VCR, and Awee loves to watch movies that he rents at the Pinedale trading post.

Awee had knocked himself out with popcorn and that horrible red punch disgusting crap they sell at Safeway in plastic jugs (even our dog, Navajo, refused to lick it), and he was asleep in his Donald Duck underwear in Crow Dog's bed.

"He's not walking well," Crow observed. "He's falling a lot." Crow Dog bit his lower lip. I could not break him of the habit. He never listens.

"It's the pain from the neuropathy," I said. "They treat his HIV, but they won't treat his pain. The neuropathy has damaged a lot of him."

"Why not? Why won't they treat his pain? I don't understand."

Ever since he was in the sixth grade, I have been trying to make Crow Dog understand things. Indian Sign Language is a thing that grows on you. I am not always aware of it or that Crow and I are talking in it. I shrugged. "He's a kid. They think if they treat his pain, he'll become an addict. A junkie." Here, I make the sign for trouble, which is the same sign for heart. You hold the five fingers over your heart, palm almost touching, and by wrist action you vibrate the hands as in making the sign for perhaps. I also make sure Crow can see my lips. I watch his eyes carefully (a cultural taboo).

"They think the kind of pain he's in is better than being addicted? I told you—marijuana. It might help."

I sighed. "Whenever it's a choice between medicine or morality, guess what, morality always wins, Crow. Always."

Crow makes the sign for this is a joke: Hold the right hand with the back down, in front of the mouth, fingers separated, partly curved, and pointing forward, move hand to front and upwards. "It's getting worse. He's so unsteady on his feet, the wind could knock him over."

"The dog knocks him down and he pretends it's funny."

"It's not funny. I'm not laughing."

"I know," I said.

"What are you going to do?"

"Show him as much of the world and living as I can."

It was Crow Dog's turn to sigh. He makes the sign for land (meaning we might or we might not land on our feet): Push both flat hands toward the ground, then spread them sideways. "Does that mean I'm going to have to worry about the two of you?"

He's watching my lips. "That's up to you."

Crow Dog, always the responsible one, looked over at the clock. It was time for pills. "Show me how you do the pills," he said.

Easy.

You wake Awee up. He will be groggy. He might or might not cry.

Pill time.

At this time of night, it would be Sustiva. Such stuff as eyelids pull in heaviness, bewilderment, moonstruck, swift, swift, you dragons of the night. Awee will cry. No, not Sustiva.

I hold the glass of red punch up for him.

Shit.

He has wet the bed. His underpants are soaked.

This started happening when the ice picks came (this was how he described the sensation of the peripheral neuropathy), and overwhelmed any other feeling he once had. It was one thing for him to wet my bed. But to wet Crow Dog's bed. That was another thing.

You know who your friends are.

The bed is at the rear of the little trailer (it had been a gift from one of Crow Dog's aunts who had given it to him when Crow had earned his GED). It was the kind of camping trailer you could haul with a pickup truck (like Crow's). It represented his independence. There is only a bed, a tiny bathroom with a toilet, a tiny stove, a table (where we often played cards) that folded down, too, into a bed, and there was another bunk above the bed Awee was in. All in all, it could sleep six, but it would be crowded. Crow only had one set of sheets. We picked Awee up and put him on the toilet (holding him there so he didn't fall), and he peed. We peeled the urine-soaked underpants off. Then we lifted him up, put him in the top bunk in a sleeping bag, and stripped the wet bottom one. AIDS is work.

We lifted Navajo up into the top bunk, too, where she peered out at us curiously.

A blue heeler bird.

This left us with one sleeping bag, and the table in the kitchen area that turned into a bed.

It was dark. "He cries now."

"Yes," I said.

"It's okay," Crow said. "He should cry when things hurt him. I hate it that things are hurting him."

"He wants to be a man. But he's still a little boy."

"I was his age when you were my teacher. You taught me how to read. Sort of anyway."

Yes.

Now this. Silence.

"What do you hear?" Crow asked.

You listen. To the night. To the sounds that come on wings.

"I hear waves," I said.

Awee had never seen the ocean.

We left on the bike. Crow would take the dog. He hauled his little trailer over to my place.

The reservation is like that. Adobe houses (close to being shacks). Woodpiles. Rusted cars and trucks. Skunks. Four raggedy marijuana plants in the back (or twelve). Someone's trailer.

We were just two guys on a bike with a backpack. Set off to see the ocean. Crow Dog waved and held Navajo as we pulled away. I knew Awee would miss them, but we would be back.

I was not sure when.

I was not sure where this path was going to go. Only that we had to follow it.

Like the road unfolding in front of us, some things were simply not going to wait. You were either going to fly or watch the birds do it.

Awee (like many boys his age) lied a lot about how old he was.

He *wished* he looked old enough to get away with saying he was fourteen.

He was not fourteen. He did not look fourteen.

Twelve was pushing it.

We had discussed his pain. Awee described it as "the ice picks are stabbing me."

Sometimes he said he felt like he was walking on razor blades.

It made him shudder. It made him sweat. It made him fall down. It sliced away at the tougher fragments of him, that gristle children have, which struggles and refuses to yield.

We had been to a thousand different doctors. All of them were quite willing to torture him with tests. The nausea. The vomiting. All of them were willing to humiliate him with their fingers in his rectum. As the nurses held him down. Awee screaming. But none of them were willing to help us with Awee's pain.

The antidepressants they prescribed for him were a joke. I finally threw them out. They did not touch his agony. We *tried* them. They did not help. We could perhaps attempt to outrun the pain.

He refused to wear a hospital gown ever again. I cannot say I blamed him. The ice picks and the razor blades were killing us.

Nucleoside analogue reverse transcriptase inhibitors. Non-nucleoside analogue reverse transcriptase inhibitors. Zerit. No one understands the long-term side effects. At what point do you consider changing a child's medication? When he complains that he is having trouble walking? The virus that causes shingles and chicken pox (Awee had both one right after the other) destroys your nerves. The razor blades have come. You will be denied pain management because it is not designed for children. Our fear of addiction is far more visceral than our fear of death.

My boots against the stones. Our flesh and tits against the night, and the air is thick with frogs.

You, shirtless on a bike again. Aboriginal. Blue exhaust behind every curfew. The bike is but the thief of what was the night before. Teaching me to see the stars. Old grandfather burns my legs. How many sunbeams now have passed to dance attendance on the spokes of spurs. To vanish once again into the bedlam.

Lean.

With me, boy. We were so alike.

Into the turns. Pleasure at the helm. To eleven-turning-twelve, everything is sex.

The bike goes on, ripping up the countryside. I had out-distanced cop cars on such a thing. To be weak is to be miserable. Just touching the chrome handlebars brought it all back. Like touching the vertebrae of a naked woman sitting upright on the motel bed. Ten thousand times up and down her spine, and gently press. Here and here. The old days when your blood was red and only liquid. The inside of your thighs soft against the leather seat. Motorcycles are for young men.

I was not really sure we could do this.

This ride through New Mexico and Texas. Even looking at the map was daunting. He worshiped me. But Awee would have worshiped anyone. We camped by Elephant Butte Reservoir just north of Las Cruces, and you could have touched the moon as if it were a cookie, and eaten sugar fragments of it in the blackness, or licked it clean with tongues.

The campgrounds had a shower. We found it crowded with dads and screaming meaming hordes of naked little boys. Awee bravely wades into this by himself. With his toothbrush and soap. It was everything he could do to stand up, to not fall down, but he grit his teeth, and would not let them see him do it. He was *that kid who arrived on a Harley*, and they were in awe of him as if he were a prince. He was mine. Bikerboy.

There were times when I did not like to share him.

What I remember are the nights. The single headlight, the spur of the occasion, the road hot, and waiting like a patriarch.

The mighty bike unborn to sky. The inevitability that all of us will die. Cutting through the night like lead. Soon enough, we are all the dead. The taste of desert cactus in the dust. I stop and point out the migrant workers stooping in the distance. He nods as he thinks he must.

We cannot know what it is like to be him.

There is not a woman on the face of the earth who would have approved. Not one. Certainly not my T. . . .

You have taken a child with AIDS, and put him on a motorcycle. You have taken him to the desert. It is heresy.

You're supposed to die softly in a nice cocoon. The stone sarcophagus precluding sound. Do not inconvenience the living. Between commercials. Sex and death are like the stars—we do not look up to see them. Beyond depth, we look away. The clouds are swarms of insects. We are supposed to die in quiet sparseness. Polite. In hospitals. Our tongues thin. Our eyes reduced. And not at home or anywhere we might be inconsolable. Our death like sex, any number of times, restrained, rings the changes in, and counts immensity in minutes. How small we are. How small the things we do, the events we ride through, the seconds we accumulate in increments.

The road starts here in the land of rogues. Stay dry. Road Warrior behind me knows. Legendary thunder, and alligator saddlebags. Raw-boned cruelty in a narrow frame. Twin cam bore and stroke, long, low, stable rides, shines like a switchblade, addicted to the fantasy of morphine, and John Lee Hooker, dark against the blacktop of a parking lot, get on, hold tight, and shut the fuck up.

Swerving to avoid an oil slick. A scoop guides the airflow directly to the oil cooler just below the headlights. Footpeg mounts are beefier (than any bike built previously) as they mate like bores welded to the chassis. Watch the tach needle drop down into the rumble of a perfect purr. Splitting lanes on the way to towns no one ever heard of, and then out of them. Peeling triumph. Get us out of here. Pagan boy grinds up the Interstate, hair spilling like excuses (I have none) in the Jesus wind, perhaps I should have left him alone, and safe, and washed in socks, archived inside the temple quiet. To give him birth in nutrients of speed. The same stinking motel beds of sadness flare with our eyes and bleed. To lean our weight against the curb. The father and the son are drenched and heard.

Or worse. The morning dogs await. The touch, the end, the kiss of fate. Sending us reeling over mountains to the sea. Stars back home break in ecstasy.

We turned off and down a side road in the middle of the desert, and followed an arroyo trail. It is said that Coyote and Badger are children of the sky.

Rain is just coyote piss.

We laughed and laughed and I could see Coyote's shadow in what light was left.

The desert is never absolutely dry. I will lose Awee to evaporation. And before darkness fell, the mud dried. The desert is an ocean. Our destinations were our dreams. Padre Island National Seashore. Brazos Island. Port Arnasas. Matagorda Island. This was going to cost more than I had, but how was I going to not do this? For Awee. You can see a lot of landscape from a bike. You are not enclosed in plastic or some traveling tin can. With any luck, we would take a boat out into the Gulf and go fishing. Because I wanted us to have this. Secret. Stealth on a Night Train. Not much backseat for a passenger. He would be mine now forever.

I was trying to save him. I admit it. From the ice picks. My backpack, a change of clothes, his medications in the saddlebag, and we were off the map. I am insane. I had no one's blessing, but I did not need it. There are some things I fear. I do not fear the six-hundred-pound bike. I do not fear time. I do not fear the vulnerability of tasting the blackness of the night. I do not fear jail. I do not fear the blacktop. I do not fear the boy behind me hanging on.

With his teeth.

I fear his house. The falling apart. I fear his death.

I do.

I listen to his words. I feel lost in them. They make me squirm.

I visualize my own shotgun in the corner of an empty room.

I have something to live for now.

I want to buy him ice cream. Texas ice cream in places where the teenagers come to sit in trucks in parking lots (at Dairy Queen), and they stare at him, he is so motherfucking cool with his leg propped up like that, just lick it. Coyote kid. They cannot touch his independence. They all have moms and dads and meatloaf on Friday night and spelling tests. He is a creature of the piss and wind.

I regret all of the medical tortures I have made him endure. The poking. The prodding. The pricking of his thumbs. The humiliations. The sticking of the needles. He winced when the nurses simply walked into the room.

It was not how he wanted to be. He is right. The doctors and the nurses are mean.

The serotonin reuptake inhibitors do not work. The anticonvulsants do not work (he doesn't have a seizure disorder anyway). These things are toxic and they could kill him. I cannot just remove him from some of these chemicals because if I did, he could have a grand mal seizure and die. I have allowed these poisons to be given to him as they were the only things he could get for pain. I was ignorant and trusting. None of these things were designed for AIDS-neuropathy, and none of the original testing of these drugs was done with children. The drugs they have required him to endure (I am reminded of when doctors bled people) like Neurontin were not designed to treat the pain from acute nerve damage, and these chemicals are simply given in lieu of narcotics. They are dangerous.

We sleep in cheap motels and eat pizza (he loves pizza), and smoke marijuana and watch TV and listen.

To salsa that we do not dance to but wish we could.

Do not think for a second I take the marijuana lightly. I don't. But I am the one who has to listen to him screaming in agony when the stabbing comes. I am the one who has to help him hold his head in the toilet. Marijuana is nothing in the face of that.

Another neon motel in Fort Stockton. The yellow light of town lingers like a coyote's eyes at the edges of the horizon.

Awee swims in the pool (the man said he could) out by where the trucks are parked at two in the morning in his Kmart Donald Duck underpants.

Swimming is the one thing he can do that does not claw at him with agony. Here, he has no weight.

There is only one ATM machine in Fort Stockton, by the railroad tracks, and the thing is empty. We find a cheap motel in Alice. Right next to the Grumpy Restaurant, Coffee Shop, Gift Shop, Truck Stop where truckers with their big rigs pull in to shower, and to eat eggs and pie.

Awee is frozen to the bike, and insists that he does not mind the seat, but then his butt and his balls are hard as marbles. The romance has worn off a bit. He will regain it in the morning. The kid is shit road tough, and more tenacious than a rattlesnake.

I unglue him from the spitting thing, the metal from the bike popping in the heat, and help him walk into the room. He almost falls. I catch him. Kick the door open. I hope they have

HBO. He is but a bag of twigs, gnarled, and soaked in sweat down his Levi jeans. I set him on the bed. His T-shirt now a wind-torn rag (his trademark).

I gotta find us food, and it's time for his medication, the Combivir, the acyclovir, the Allegra, the Bactrim, the Lamictal. I gotta get the bugs out of my teeth, and both of us ache everywhere.

Reverse transcriptase inhibitors are powerful retrovirals that attack HIV just after it enters a cell. Regimes fail.

I am too old for this tough-guy stuff.

My right leg is screaming like someone cut it with a chain saw. I limp.

The TV does not work. I give him the remote. Click. He gets it on. He laughs at me. I am technologically ignorant. The radio works, too. I am informed (he knows) that boy bands suck. What am I doing here. What have I done. I do not fathom it.

Ice picks.

"I'll find us some food," he says. So helpful. But the kid can barely stand.

I pull his tennis shoes off. His feet stink. His socks smell like ripe bear urine. I paw through our junk, find his HIV meds, and he swallows them dry.

Silent and come in from the desert of the great beyond.

Saying nothing. I touch his hair.

I go out to the parking lot in my black cowboy boots, crunching oyster shells and limestones, shirtless, my sweat melting down my belly in rivulets of salt and sacrilege. We need food. And then I remember it cannot be greasy food because you can't eat that kind of pig-road cuisine on AIDS medications. No high-fat content. No burgers, or fries, or a Coke. Fuck it. That is all there is at Grumpy's. The toilet stalls smell like diesel fuel, and the truck drivers have all left their cell numbers written on the door with permanent-ink markers. Daisy gives great head and so does

Fred. Wash your hands in here until they're red. Use soap. I put my shirt on.

Every time I look into a mirror, now, I see my dad. A white man. I am the spitting image of him in shit-hole toilets. But just behind my eyes, I hear the softer voices of my mother's songs.

"Two large fries, two large Cokes, four cheeseburgers, and a cherry pie."

Eyebrows raised.

"Yeah, the whole goddamn pie."

She writes it down. Pencil in the hairdo. This is Texas.

I am a failure as a father and a nurse.

There are migrants in this place. I recognize them. They recognize me. Always the hands. I know the fields are waiting for me out there.

Drawing me back to work.

The paper bag breaks halfway to the motel room, and the Cokes sweat harder than I do.

He is watching cartoons. Like the dead might. Leaned up against his pillow. Staring straight ahead. Ignoring ice picks. It's what he does.

Lesser men would call it courage. No energy to lift a French fry.

I feed them to him as if he were a baby. One French fry at a time. I stroke his hair. I like to smell it. Baby shampoo. Clouds. I want all my sons to go to Harvard.

He is smart enough.

"Ever see a migrant camp?" I ask him.

"I know you grew up in them," he says.

I did. Migrant camps. Reservations.

"Alice, Texas, ain't shit," he says. "You bought the whole pie."

We laugh a lot at the stupid things we do. I need someone in my life who can make me do that. I need him like I need my left leg.

I soak the fries in a sea of ketchup. He loves ketchup. Using those little plastic white things the ketchup comes in. We get ketchup on the bedspread.

"I'm having my period," he says.

Eleven is becoming twelve. What he knows about girls could dance on the head of a pin. Even if he thinks he knows everything. Has done everything. Has seen everything. Just not the ocean yet. He has never been in a bowling alley either. I will find him one.

Before you die, you should bowl just once.

I give him a full report (there is little we can't talk about or laugh at), and he makes stupid jokes about truck drivers, Fred, Daisy, cell phones, and permanent-ink markers. All shit holes are the same. He refuses to go into a Texas rest area alone (without me), and who can blame him.

"How well can you roll a joint?" I ask him. Usually, I roll them, but I am running out of spit.

"How well can you masturbate?"

Pretty damn well.

I throw him the backpack.

Close the motel curtains.

I think back to the witch's brew of drugs the people in the white coats have wanted him to take. And they pretend pot is bad for you. Many of the drugs they have wanted Awee to be on were designed to treat tissue damage after cancer chemotherapy. Modern Western medicine is a pig in a poke.

The kid could roll a hell of a joint, and we smoked it. Someday the white people cops are going to bust my ass. Until then, fuck their shit.

There are three categories of pain. All of them acute.

"You wanna dance?" he asked.

You bet.

Just last week, I was thinking: You know, I really wanna dance with an eleven-year-old kid whose feet smell like bear urine in a motel room in Alice, Texas. He fiddles with the radio.

I hold his shoulders. His arms around me again.

I put Awee in the bath and close the door. He always sings in there, and I realize he must sing, too, inside his head. Even when the hurt and the needles come. This boy needs his privacy more than most, not less.

Let him sing.

In his whole life, Awee has never hurt anyone or anything. Not once. What men can say the same.

I lean up against the wall.

I have a rule. You may speak your mind. Just say it. Anywhere. Anytime. No one is going to laugh or say that you are stupid. And if they do, it doesn't matter.

"What's it like to die?" he asks.

He plays flashlight shine-the-light like insects on the ceiling games. Quick here, then there. The insects flicker.

There are two beds in this room. I am in mine. He is in his. Our separateness, like the silence between us, surges softly backwards. His death his. My death mine. I am too tired. I look over at him propped up on a pillow in the dark.

He is afraid and wants to know.

"You're just not there anymore," I tell him. "It's being alive that is so hard. Dead is nothing to it."

"Does it hurt?"

I did not think so. But I did not know. I had only contemplated suicide.

"What do you want?"

I am unsure of what he means, although the voices in me know exactly what he means.

"What do you mean, What do I want?"

"What do you *want*."

"It changes. Sometimes I only want to be by you. With you. That is all I want. I want to protect you. Everything in me is about doing that. Even if it's complicated. I *want* to hang on to my children, please. I want everything that is essentially impossible."

"I will tell you what I want, okay?"

"Okay."

"I want to be with you. I never had nobody who wanted to be with me. And I miss my dog. I wish she was here."

We smoke another joint. I wish he would sleep. He is so dangerous. In his underpants.

He asks me to hold him. His dad had never held him. Had never had the strength. For just awhile. Okay.

I hold him. He sort of wilts. The ice picks will come soon enough.

"Is it sex?" he asks.

He means my holding him.

"Yeah, it's sex," I say.

A lie. But a nice one.

In the morning, he had wet the bed.

In the beginning, I was afraid of shit. The smell of it. With AIDS, you leave a lot of the things you were once afraid of well behind.

Shitty pants are put into the plastic bag and thrown away. Then, I do often clean his butt, as he can't feel what is or isn't there anymore. His strawberry rectum leaks blood. If he isn't clean, the fungal infections will eat him up. So he needs help and there it is. Another surrendering in the silence that we share. But I am not allowed to tell anyone I do this. He made me promise. Of all the things we share, we share silence here deeper than anything. The hole death lives in has no sound or smell.

There is no music there. Music comes from the rhythm and the chaos that is life. I will dance with him anywhere he wants.

I find us coffee in the morning. He likes his with sugar.

We find the islands not all that far from Alice. I set him on the sand. Waves.

I am exhausted. With him. With me. But I have given him something in this. This coming here.

We sleep on the ground behind a dune. It is still dark when I wake up sort of suddenly. He doesn't sleep for very long. The needles come. He is playing with the flashlight.

It shines into my eyes. For a moment, I am blind. I wince.

"I've never seen you naked," he says. "Not like totally naked. You always have a towel or something on."

There are things I hide from him. Like bikes. My penis.

Awee could be seductive. It scared me deep down into my bones where I hurt with him and me and all the things we could never be. Father and son would have to be enough. Even with AIDS, Awee stood poised on the cusp of adolescence, and in his anxiety, he wanted everything. His vulnerability was awesome.

I have seen him more than naked. I have seen the inside of his bleeding guts.

I stand in front of him completely naked.

Awee shines the flashlight on all my many scars. My scars from barns and hay and animals and tools and things that have cut me. I was shot once, too, and badly. I am harder here and there.

At first, he was almost speechless. "Wow. You never told me."

Everything.

Where would I begin.

In water, he is weightless. I show him how to float.

Finally, we sit upon the sand. In our nakedness, we hug our knees. Our hair like seaweed dripping down.

He holds my hand. His palm soft. His fingers very small.

We are the men.

The mingling of sunrise but a sound, and light itself advances up the beach like candles warm in a cathedral's cave. We are defeated in our familiar shapes, the void, and daytime dances over the horizon like a tongue, voluptuous and vast.

Night Train: Torque: 85 Oft. lbs. @ 3,000 rpm. Twin Cam 88B (balanced). Vivid black. Migrant trucks roar by.

Our separateness is no longer a thing defined by walls.

He is my son. I am his dad.

It is the sun that falls.

7. Head in Fridge

Finally, we found a town—a town big enough to rumble in the distance—where everything and everyone was hollow like the dead. The name of the town is irrelevant.

There were grocery stores here that took coupons and the place had jobs and high schools with football fields that were soaked in perfect dew every morning and car junkyards and cemeteries surrounded by black, wrought-iron fences where the steam came up dripping on the sweet grenadine flowers heavy with the dead and restaurants where cops drank coffee and inhaled cigarettes with a sucking sound and stucco houses where black mold had settled in the cracks and first-floor apartment buildings with bars on the windows and broken sidewalks pushed up by the roots from trees like snakes and perfect parks with paths worn down to dust and Dumpster dogs no one owned and downtown hookers who walked the streets and churches where on Sunday all the people went to pray and nice houses with perfect lawns where children lived and slept in rooms they would be safe enough to dream in and crows that danced high up on wires not put there for that purpose and bus stops where the air drifted in exhaust and hospitals where the windows were but yellow eyes and liquor stores with blinking arrows and dancing women in neon heels who kicked up their legs in light.

Anywhere. Anywhere.

I do not want to name it. Some things in this must be left to me.

I'm telling you, everything and everyone was hollow like the dead. The local Chamber of Commerce and the Junior League would deny it. Every city in America has one—some pom-pom, advertising cheerleading section that only wants to paint the pretty place mat picture—and Americans don't like hearing it. That it could be anywhere. Any town. Any city where the dead live at the margins and take the bus to work and do their laundry to the sounds of the madhouse down the block where Other People live. The early-morning garbage trucks arrive from nowhere.

We went there to look for drugs.

The Chamber of Commerce and the Junior League and the Police Department and the State Medical Board of Examiners and the County Health Department and the local School Board and the Ecumenical Council of Churches would not approve.

They would take my teaching license away, but I had already burned that motherfucker.

The name of the town was White People Town. This definitely does *not* mean there were only white people in it. Not by any stretch of the imagination. The people who washed the dishes and cleaned the toilets in the homes and dried the cars at the car wash and folded all the cotton hotel sheets were not white. The invisible are everywhere. White People Town only means that white people hold the power. They run the schools. They run city government. They are the police. They meet every month at the Chamber of Commerce on Mainstreet USA. They do not approve of people on motorcycles (one of whom has AIDS) from somewhere else trolling through their nice towns looking for drugs. White People Town does not have drugs.

White People Town was built on drugs.

They just don't know it, and when they do know it, they don't want to know it.

Crystalline. In dissolvable. Drugs.

We always have a strip mall. Dunkin' Donuts. The Family Doctor (walk-in care). Glenwood Cleaners. Resurrection United Church of Christ. Buy a mattress at our factory. WASP auto. Opticare. Rooms to Go. Security Storage. Pizza Hut. El Rodeo Mexican Restaurant. We Do Drains.

Every White People Town either has a park where men can meet at night or a toilet stall at Sears.

Everything has been decided.

White People Town has a lifetime warranty, and will go above and beyond the call of duty to make you a satisfied customer.

All we wanted were some drugs and to be left alone.

The blue coats came, and swept down like thunder from the mountains, all the warriors were gone, and the Indian village was destroyed. The corpses of the little boys were everywhere among the tepees with their genitals mutilated, cut off, scraps for dogs.

It cannot be.

Impermeable. Incompressible. You are your history.

It was never written. It was buried like the lesser writers at the local library in the State Historical Society section.

It was not a big big town, but a big enough town to have a few whores, made from baking brick, the town *and* the whores, concrete, tough, mute, and rough around the sneering edges, which is what we were, too. Any town big enough for a few whores to anesthetize themselves was big enough for us.

Awee's eyes had assumed an arrogance they had never had

before. Like wow. I'm a cowboy on a Harley-Davidson. Which he was even if he could barely walk and he wet the bed.

The malls and the shopping centers and the parking lots and the suburbs where the nice people with jobs at insurance companies lived had pushed themselves out to the edges, having gobbled up the countryside years ago, leaving the inner core to rot for us. It was hot and the city was embalmed. I find us a hotel.

How hard can it be? The hookers are right outside the door on the sidewalk.

Hello, ladies.

They like the bike. They sort of crowd around it. Admiring it. One touches it lightly with her fingers. Stroking. Licks her lips like you might lick a streetlamp in the freezing cold. Your spit will stick. They tease the boy, and they flirt with him. He has no idea what to do. How to react. They are not too sure about me, which is right where I want them.

All you need in this landscape is the cash upfront.

That is the standard upon which you will be judged. This part of the city was cavernous. Like urine passed through pores.

He has never seen a hooker in his life. Notwithstanding his mother.

We rarely ever spoke of her. It upset him to do so. I saw no point in speaking of things that now made him weep.

They don't even *take* credit cards at this hotel. The air in the lobby hangs heavy like the fat-soaked jowls of a bulldog. Every cigarette ever smoked in here continues to smolder. A memory of burning and tuberculosis. This is the kind of place that holds the money you pay with up to the fluorescent light. The desk clerk rubs the bills to see if the ink comes off.

The desk clerk lives here, too. Up on the third floor by the fire escape. He is a drag queen who has seen it all.

Nothing would be decided. Not today. The pay phone is down the hall, and the names and the numbers written on the wall there are but a passing and a pissing history scrawled by scribes and pimps and drunks and priests and the pool hall illiterates who live here.

Men stand in silent windows dying. World War Two was yesterday. The hair on their chest has grown white, and now they stand around Gold's Gym and watch the younger boys in silence. The night is slow, and the light is yellow, and the skid-row walls are thin as a geriatric hooker's lips, so thin you can smell the vodka sitting perfect in a juice glass in someone's room. Someone feeds table scraps and pasta to the starving cats in the alley below. We walk into our somber situation. The wallpaper is circa 1935. A bed. A table. A tiny stove. A bathroom (a luxury with a tub, I paid extra). A tiny refrigerator the size of a filing cabinet you could stick your head into.

I did.

It was another world. Clean. White. Plastic. And the lightbulb worked. There was beer in there, the kind you brought home in a paper sack, and the whores down the hall were nice. Most were only now getting up. Nothing surprised them.

Nothing.

Not mutilated corpses. Not history on a place mat. Not people looking for drugs. Not children with AIDS. Not men who had left their wives and families. Not housewives who arrived with faces black and blue. Not drag queen desk clerks. Not perverts. Not derelicts. Not girls looking for an abortion (or recovering from one). Not winos. Not three generations of migrants in the same room with the same name. Not the mafia. Not gentlemen with guns and suitcases filled with cash. They knew this: the Greyhound bus station was three blocks away, Wal-Mart was at the edge of town, and no one they were aware of took credit.

This included them.

We did not need the Chamber of Commerce. We had the advice of whores.

A doctor lived several floors above us. A real doctor. Everyone agreed. Someone had actually seen his diploma. Somewhere. A Harvard graduate from Kansas.

The whores liked him, but he might have to go to jail, nothing has been decided, everything was in limbo. They knew who his lawyer was. The doctor was a junkie, too, among the dead. "I can get you morphine," he told me.

We called him Doctor Doom because his skin was gray.

He made house calls.

We had been to some of the most medically advanced institutions in the modern world. No one there made house calls.

Doctor Doom had an old, black bag. There were treasures and secrets in it.

Awee and I liked him immediately.

He sat and smoked a joint with us. He listened. No doctor we had been to had ever listened. Not to the likes of us.

Doctor Doom was very kind, with his thin gray hands and veins as blue as the Aegean on a clear cold day at Jesus noon, and he was quiet as he touched Awee.

I could hear the blue coats coming down from the mountains now, their brown horses lost in smoke, to cut the penises of the boys whose saliva soaks the ground in hope.

Someone else is touching Awee, it makes me very nervous, and I have to look outside the window. It disturbs me. This sharing him. Awee on the bed looking at the wall.

Listens to his heart. Touches his brown tit, too.

Does not ask to see his penis. Does not stick his finger hard up inside Awee's hairless balls. Does not feel around inside his rectum. We are so glad for this. We are so glad for this.

Doctor Doom is a real doctor. Even if he is a junkie. We do

not inquire as to his addictions or his problems. "I can still write scripts," he says.

He tears one off.

Morphine is a miracle. So is OxyContin.

So is kindness.

"You stay here, and I'll go fill these," I tell Awee.

"No, I want to come, please."

Welcome to Wal-Mart. Doors swing wide. Swing low, sweet chariot. Coming for to carry me home.

I want a job where all day long I smile and say *Welcome to Wal-Mart* and look out for shoplifters and sing gospel music in my empty head. I do not want to be a writer.

The Wal-Mart pharmacist behind his bullet-proof glass gives us the evil eye.

Awee sits in the one dirty chair, waits, and stares at packages of condoms. Finally, we are released. We're leaving Wal-Mart with our morphine and our OxyContin. "How come some condoms say *ribbed*? What's a rib on a condom?"

He feels his own ribs. A point of reference.

I explain female anatomy.

Sort of like the neon woman at the top of the liquor store wears high heels that blink on and off, first blue, then red. Her skirt flies up. She has legs. Awee thinks I've gone mad again. We laugh all the way back to the hotel and almost get arrested. I have to watch the speed limit like a hawk and keep the big bike growling strictly at twenty-five in the school zone. Cop car on my ass.

Wal-Mart medication in the saddlebag.

They will arrest you for far less.

You do not look back. That's the thing with whores, and pain, and AIDS. Do not look back. Now when we walk into the lobby of the hotel, they know us.

Did we find Wal-Mart okay? Sleep tight. Don't overdose.

I made him take a bath before he had his morphine. He climbs into bed. Snug as a bug.

I love him. Shit. I am the devil.

"Okay, we're gonna do this, honey."

I called him honey. He liked it.

This was a first-class hotel, and there was even a water glass. Just one. One would do. First, the acyclovir, then the Allegra, then the Sustiva.

Then, the morphine.

Then, I tell him stories and he holds me tight. Tight until he begins to slip. He likes my stories about the migrant camps and how we used to travel like the wind. How I had a brother, and he was like my twin. How the earth was but a migrant camp where the sun had grown dim. How loneliness was but the rain. And sleep was safe with him.

His breathing goes regular and deep. I only cry when I know Awee is fast asleep.

I lie with him on the bed and feel the wind coming in past the curtains, through the window, and listen to the sirens.

The whore next door is making noise.

Getting fucked or praying.

It is not polite to listen to the weeping of your neighbors. To-morrow, we will all be different. It has been decided.

Finally, I untangle his heavy arms from me and stick my head into the fridge again.

The taste of cold beer like the Dog Star turns to liquid, the rush a sallow cold across my chest. I find a deck of cards (by the Bible in the drawer) yellow as the sun. I sit alone in neon light, the lady at the liquor store shivering, and flip my luck down by the river where the antelope run. It's a fantastic river, and one that only exists in dreams. In a couple of hours I will get him up to pee, set him on the toilet, hold him steady, and the urine will pour warm and effortless from him. I will pick him up and put him back in the bed and he will not remember. It is the first time in a long time that he has slept soundly and not twisted around like a snake, thrashing. He is not in pain, and I am glad for it. I will kiss his cheek and smell him. Soft like powder and urine. Sweeter than my beer.

I had grown used to waking up with him beside me or not too far away and having to help him dress. I had grown used to touching him. I had been needed. I wake up and it takes me a minute to realize that he isn't there. He has dressed himself. He is up and making breakfast. Coffee in a coffeepot about as old as the wallpaper. Awee is standing, walking on his own.

We have come to the right place.

To celebrate our release from this crippling prison Awee and I have lived in, we went to lunch. He thought it a superb idea. I have them now and then.

It was the waitress with the purple hair. I knew after she left our little booth that I would go back to writing.

He peers out, then pops his head back in the booth like it is a box, and he is a turtle.

I needed paper. I needed a pen. I had to write all of this down. I had decided. The town. The drugs. The hookers. The hotel. The sheets. The penis. The nakedness. The shit.

There is always Wal-Mart.

It was her purple hair. The piercings I can take or leave. The ring through the nose does nothing for me. But the hair.

Purple is as purple does.

We had our usual. Cheeseburgers. Fries. Coke. Apple pie. "When it comes to nutrition, you're really shit," Awee said.

I could not remove my eyes from her purple hair. She was chewing gum with the cook, and sneaking quick, furtive glances at the kid watching her.

Yaaaaa, honey. The kid is beautiful. And he's mine. It has been decided.

He blushed.

I could kick myself for being so fucking selfish. "I wish I knew about girls," he said.

Yaaaaa, me, too.

"I like her hair."

He would.

"Maybe I could get a nose ring, too."

Maybe not.

I was going to have to learn how to spell again. English drives me insane. I have no respect for it or the culture that it comes from. She had a pencil. The next time she passed our booth, I asked her for it.

I had embarrassed him.

"Do you always have to be so weird?"

Trust me.

I could write little notes on the paper place mat. Mostly, the place mat had little pictures of the town taken some time ago, and copy that seemed to be some kind of historical analysis.

Nothing had existed here until the white people came (on wagons) and discovered it.

His Coke was making rings on his place mat. I made him give it to me. I had two place mats. I flipped them over. Pure as milk.

He asked her for another place mat. She said, sure. He just rolled his eyes at me. Like I was not to embarrass him again, but considering my assigned status as an imbecile and a lunatic, it was to be expected.

"Are you writing again?"

"Yaaaaa. I think I will go back to it."

"Me."

"What me?"

"You're gonna write about me. I'm not stupid."

I never said he was.

"I saw naked women in a magazine." He smiled. Smugly.

I loved him for his really stupid moments.

"Yaaaaa. Where?"

"In the liquor store when you were buying beer." Like ha, ha. I am such a fuck.

I thought he had snuck around over to the magazines. The man in the liquor store had given me the evil eye (I was growing used to it by now), like can't you control your child.

Finally, Purplehead arrived with her arms filled with our order. All smiles. She smelled of grease and dish soap.

"You boys from around here?"

By now he knew this: Don't give too much of yourself away.

"I like your hair," he said.

She chewed her gum and touched it.

"I do it myself."

"My dad cuts mine."

He means me. I'm fucking cheap. And I am afraid of some barber cutting him. I see that straight-razor touching the soft skin of his neck.

"Well, he does a good job," she said. "You are *so* handsome."

He blushed again and she kissed the top of his unruly head.

He melts like a greasy French fry on the floor that someone might step on.

We're walking back to our hotel. I am wondering how long we will stay here. Nothing has been decided. I might write again.

He wants to stop in the liquor store. I ask him why.

"I want you to buy me one of those magazines."

Shit.

I don't want to do it. I am not Father of the Year material. I already feel bad about it. Living in some lymphatic place of cigarettes and whores. Our lives as liquid as vodka on a fire escape. But he was with us, and he was not in pain.

"I just want to look at girls, okay. Do you mind? Is it that bad to do that?"

I have answers for very little.

I have no answers for masturbation.

We get the evil eye again. The evil eye only makes me worse. I ignore the sign about minors, and let him pick the magazine.

The girls in the magazine have huge tits and huge smiles and huge red wet cunts with huge pink assholes with fingers in them. I plop the magazine down. Hey, you're the one selling it, dickhead. Awee stands behind me like the crows in this town perch on wires.

That'll be ten bucks.

For a magazine.

I *am* Father of the Year. I have the fucking halo and the balls to prove it.

He asked for privacy. I told him he could have all the privacy he wanted. Just don't lock the bathroom door.

"But what if you come in."

I might. That was how it was.

I reserved my right to intrude upon him. I do not do it maliciously. I do it for me. In case I have to scoop him up. He walks into the bathroom with his magazine like it's the most natural thing in the world because it might be.

How much time were we really going to have? Our history would be written on a place mat.

Monster that I am I will kiss upon the beauty of your bones. And sleep fitfully in sadness like a lover lost in moans.

8. Milkweed Pods

Mad glorious summer by this thief of shadows in the sun. He came charging in, and charging in, and charging on the run.

Buzzed whispers in my mouth forever. Echoes. Light rippling. The eddies of the wind. He was delight, alone, and unfolded.

Pockets heaped with stones.

When he was well, when everything was perfect, he was always charging everywhere. I was in awe of him, and all the charging places. My Romeo. Right through cobwebs. Wiping them from his face. He did not have time for spiders. Time was not a thing he had to waste, and he knew that, too. Suddenly, the door would slam.

Praise be to the goddess of morphine.

"You've *got* to see this!" He was out of breath. When he discovered something, anything, new, he wanted me to see it; it was important that I was a witness.

He pulled me by the hand.

This way. This way.

Dad.

He called me "dad" a lot. It was like some tender gift he

gave to me from his mouth and his lips and his summer eyes of swallows.

I was never fast enough. "What *is* it?" I asked.

He stops (briefly). "I don't know," he said.

There was a field littered with old tires out back behind the Whore Hotel parking lot.

It was an ordinary place where people discarded their trash. Beer cans. Bums. Old condoms. The more distance you put between yourself and this field of junk, the less urban the world became.

Behind the field was a ravine. If you went down into the ravine, there was a small stream. If you followed the small stream, you came to another small stream exactly like the one you had been following. Go left. Now you are getting away from things. Sounds. People. You could hear the street like a whisper.

He had been exploring.

If you go to the end of the field the stream runs through, there is a path. Through trees. If you take the path up the hill, you come to what was once an apple orchard. It was nothing now. There were apples there, some raggedy trees, but mostly it was the realm of boys, and bikes, and dogs, and forts. This electrified him.

Sunstruck. Half-spread wings. And now he seems to me to dance, haunted, light upon the uncut hair of Indian graves. Mounds. Memories that stand amused, complacent, look down, bend a side-curved head, curious, the dead can only wonder what comes next.

This was not a kid who ever thought he would walk again.

Now, the agony came and went.

A drug called nortriptyline had helped immensely when combined with Lamictal.

Lamictal is an anticonvulsant used to treat bipolar neurology. The problem with it at the doses he was taking was that he could never be off the drug. Were his blood levels of Lamictal to go down, he would have a seizure, and die.

It was a price to pay but his neuropathy was better.

At the end of the abandoned apple orchard was another field (this, too, was a great discovery, every weed, every tree, every bug, every wild creature in the woods). He was like Columbus.

The New World.

I was his slave.

Some pathetic creature pulled from the ship's hold.

In some ways, Awee was fearless. He was not ashamed of who he was because he did not know, really, who he was. He was only now exploring it. Finally, he stopped. He was breathing heavily. His chest heaved. The blood ran through him with great warmth and haste.

I could see the veins in his neck throb.

"We're there," he said.

I looked around. I saw nothing.

He raised both his arms as if to say: This is *it*. Everything. Look.

Obviously, whatever *it* was (or *there*), I was missing it.

Then, he waded out among them as if he were the pope. And these were his minions. We were in the milkweed pods. He had never seen anything quite like them.

The wind came up, and roused them from their silky sleep. Things now floated in the air. He screamed.

See! See!

Now he charged through the milkweed pods. A blindman's buff. Equilibrium unhinged. Hollering. Millions and millions of milkweed pods. Weedstalks. Long wet eyelashes. Exploding as he touched them. At his age, everything, everything is sex.

Everything. Even weeds.

Especially weeds.

He never did live safely in his socks. He rubbed the milkweed tassels on his skin, and in his hair, and he put some in his pockets, and he tasted them.

He ripped them open and he let them go.

I had lived so long among the blind. Things flew softly all around as though it were a miracle.

"Are you hungry?" he asked.

"Yaaaaa." I was hungry.

He had food in his pockets, too. Sometimes it was crumbs. Leftovers from something chocolate chip.

"I want to feed you," he said.

"Feed me?"

It was licorice. Black, thick, sticky.

He tore it in two.

Then he fed me. It was a giving up. Him feeding you. His candy fingers on the edges of your mouth. His eyes watching you to see if you would really eat it, curious as to whether or not you would actually allow him to do this. Feed you. Licorice. I did.

His fingers smelled of sweat, and dirt, and worms, and licorice, and pocket dust, and milkweed pods. They lingered on my lips.

He leaned back into the grass. Now he was exhausted.

"What happens when it rains?" he asked.

"What do you mean?"

"What are these?"

"They're called milkweed pods. They're beautiful."

"The milkweed pods get wet?"

"Sometimes."

"But can they still fly away?"

"Yes. They're seeds. They make other milkweed pods."

He nodded. "The milkweed pods have everything they want."

"I suppose they do," I said. "Do you?"

"Do I what?"

"Have everything you want."

He said nothing. He was with them on the wind.

"Do you have everything you want, Dad?"

"No, I don't have everything I want."

"Such as . . ." His fingers to my lips again.

Such as his life forever.

He did not care that someone might see us.

Mad glorious summer by this thief of shadows in the sun. Blowing milkweed seeds from our hands into the wind. He was not afraid to love, or be in love, or lay in it and wonder. I still live among the dull, the plodding, and the blind. I had to carry him home. He had grown weak again with time. I am a man who now pretends that everything is tamed. The truth is that in milkweed pods there are no trees of shame.

9. All His Good-bye-Buried Dreams

I would awake from dreams.

Sleeping with him. I am naked, chasing antelope on the high-desert mesa. The antelope herd comes to a river. It stops. At the edges of the herd, wolves.

This is the river that haunts me. This is the river I fish. This is the river I write poems to and let the river take them. This is the river I write books about.

I am awake. Reach out. Touch him. Feel him breathing. Hug him. Surround him with the deepness of my strength. Remind myself.

Who I was. Where I was. Who he was.

That we were here.

I had vowed that I would never live in an urban environment ever again. Home to me was a place where I could look out the window and see antelope. This was not that.

But I would do this for Awee. I would endure this urban place for him. For now.

Now I was living in the shit hole of a city so a boy with AIDS could have access to what medical care we could squeeze from what to us would always be white culture. White culture is a stone. I would squeeze and squeeze. If we could not get what I wanted—I wanted the best for him and I was willing to sacrifice and fight for him and with him to get it—we would get it somewhere else.

I learned this from AIDS treatment: It was not about sticking to one clinic or one doctor or one theory or any one approach to anything. Each place had something unique they could do that the other places did not do or do as well. Where one medical setting might treat the bone disease (avascular necrosis) that was creeping up on Awee, another might have a quicker response time to all the various blood tests. In some clinics you have reports back the next day. In others, results for the same tests take six weeks.

Some clinics had an awareness that stress from neuropathy pain was a piece of the total picture, where other clinics concentrated on the virus, the numbers, and that was it. The only consistency in AIDS treatment that I found was that all the clinics had the same bag of pharmaceuticals to pick from. But their knowledge of those pharmaceuticals could vary as could their access to them.

There is no consistency to AIDS treatment in America. That is a fact. The only concrete thing these medical delivery systems share is that you have to fight to get anything from them. The good ones and the bad ones. You fight to get in and get treated.

I had seen Indian men die from AIDS on the reservation. They folded up into a hardened cocoon of loneliness. Access to medical care on any reservation can be sporadic. Indian clinics are always closing. A few years ago, I drove a Navajo grandmother to a clinic in the Bisti Badlands, hours and hours away, only to arrive at a building that had been abandoned. The clinic had closed months ago. Grandma did not know. She was not aware of the fact that the government had withdrawn funding.

And white people wonder why Indians are often reluctant to expose themselves to Western medicine. Many Indians see Western medicine as something that hasn't been around for very long (certainly not as long as Navajo medicine), and when you need it, it often isn't there.

Doctors see their tenure on Indian reservations as temporary assignments. They have come here to practice medicine with a population of third-world people who are very unlike anything they have known before. They know they are going back to where they came from.

To where they came from.

White culture.

AIDS is not a disease you can treat sporadically. Awee's medical records indicated that his treatment at Indian clinics had been inconsistent. AIDS medications are typically given to Indians by the government in thirty-day supplies only. After thirty days you have to get back to the clinic, which isn't always possible. You can't just start the medications, stop, and then go back to them. You can build up a resistance doing that. What medications are available to you might not work.

Distance is a problem, too. Just getting to the doctor on a reservation can present insurmountable problems. On the Navajo Nation, a doctor can be hundreds of miles away. If you wake up in the morning with pneumocystis pneumonia— gasping for air, and you know what this fist in your lungs is all about—traveling three hundred miles to the nearest medical facility can be real difficult. You are too sick. You might not have a car.

There could be snow. Depend on it.

I was back living in an urban place so Awee could get treatment. Even if that treatment wasn't perfect—and it wasn't—it was better than no treatment.

We had one thing. One thing that held us together. We had that moment that existed briefly between the morbid and mystical, when it was late, and we had finally gone to bed, and we were ready for sleep, for what forgiveness it might bring to us, and we were here together. Just us. We had that. Something calm and perfect and just before the coming of some storm we would only endure.

Every day was a battle.

For Awee, it could be his constant battle with what came out of his butt.

For me, the battle was the city. My contact with white culture is always turbulent.

The first thing that comes to me at night are the sounds. The sirens. The wailing like a wounded animal. The traffic. The trucks. The buses. The people above you. The people below you. The bottles breaking on the street. The shots from guns. The woman in the next room screaming while she is being fucked. All of this going on at the same time was enough for Awee and me to hide our heads under our blankets and our pillows.

Our world was shrinking more and more into the context of a bed. It was hard to get Awee to go to sleep on a good night. He might miss something.

The characters at the Whore Hotel intrigued Awee, and they scared him a little bit, too. They could overwhelm you with their problems. The problems they carried on their shoulders, on the tips of their tongues. You knew who they were, and what they were about. You wanted to watch, but like a stove you didn't want to touch.

Awee and I would be in bed. Ostensibly asleep. But I was not asleep, and he was not asleep. There was no sleep.

"Dad."

"What."

"I didn't ask to be born."

"No one does. We just find ourselves born is all."

"But what if we don't want to be born."

"It doesn't always matter what we want, honey. I guess what matters is what we do with what we have."

"I have AIDS."

"I know. But look at the other things you have. You have a heritage. You come from a bunch of very tough people. Some of them were warriors like you. You have me, too."

"I don't want AIDS, Daddy. I never asked for it. To be like this."

"Awee, it's late, and you sound a little angry."

"I think I am mad."

"At who?"

"I don't know. I wish I did."

"Go to sleep."

"Dad."

"What, Awee."

"What if you are born with something, and then you don't want to be born with it, and you don't want to live no more. Then what."

"Then you try and get some sleep so you feel better in the morning."

"Dad."

"What."

"I don't want to live no more."

"Awee, you have to stay with us."

"Why."

"Because I said so. Because I need you to hug me."

"Dad. Let me go."

There was always a steady silence here. He would say this— we had these conversations a thousand times, ten thousand times—and there was always the same cool stone silence when we arrived at this place where he wanted me to let him go. The antelope herd I had been chasing stopped.

"No. I will not do it. I don't care what you want. *I* want you with us. It's about what I want. Go to sleep."

"Dad."

"What."

"Hold me."

"Why?"

"I'm lost."

Awee was no different from anyone else who lived here.

Everyone here was lost. You checked in to fucking die.

Everyone who checked in had given up.

Awee had given up. It happens slowly. Over time. In increments.

He allowed the doctors to torture him for me. He put up with it. For me. If he gave me these things, I would love him, I would not leave him. Awee was one of the loneliest people who had ever lived.

AIDS is loneliness. There are no pills for that.

Part of the Whore Hotel was a hospice. Public health nurses walked softly down the hall room to room. You could always tell them by their shoes. Providing comfort to the low-rent dead.

The separation between the folks who lived just outside the Whore Hotel on the street and the folks dying inside the Whore Hotel was a fragile one. The people on the inside and the people on the outside did not appear to be all that different.

What brings you here? Divorce. The end of marriage. Cancer. Poverty. Addiction. Scraping bottom is relative. The residents with bowel cancer saved their pills under their tongues, and spit them out when the nurse was gone. Pain pills in a jar.

You were careful about where you hid them. You needed more than a few to die. You wanted to do it right. You did not want to linger in a coma.

Your cab ride from the train station to the Whore Hotel had been a blur of lights. The cabdriver could not shut the fuck up. Why were you in town? Staying long?

You had come here to hang yourself from a rope.

You told him this. Silence.

The rooms in the Whore Hotel had once had chandeliers. They had been removed. You could still tell from the plaster patches in the ceiling where the chandeliers had been. Too many chandeliers had crashed on to too many people who were hanging from them nude and masturbating.

The marginal in America are everywhere. Living life out of their Safeway grocery sacks.

We are unclean. We piss in doorways. We leave behind the rags we use to wipe ourselves. We are rough. We smell. Most of us have thrown up in at least one concrete gutter somewhere. We have ascended from the subway. We wear long, heavy, warm, gray coats, for sale, fifty cents, at the Salvation Army used-clothing store. We live in clothes someone else used to own. Our eyes are drawn and our heads are bowed and our spirits were broken years ago and it's hopelessness that feeds us like a feast of rats.

We were the lucky ones.

You met people in the hallway. You met people in the elevator (Awee liked playing Elevator Man with the drag queens, who adored him). You met people in the lobby. There was no way you could not know them.

People seemed to sigh inwardly as Awee left them. As he walked away, their eyes would linger on him like *what is it about this kid*. Something. He was soft, dark, beautiful.

Most of Awee's friends lived down the hall, or for tomorrow, or lost yet somewhere in a past of sniffing glue, or they lived upstairs, and down the hall by the fire escape that descended down to basement structures no one knew.

Gruff lived down the hall where tomorrow smelled like cigars, or dust that comes in through the yellow window, and tonight and tomorrow night are nothing but long legacies of sleepless leaves. Gruff explained that when he moved into the Whore Hotel he did not know how long he would be staying there.

Most people kept one bag packed. Some people had kept that one bag packed for over twenty years.

The clothes in the bag had disintegrated and so had you.

Gruff would not be staying long. Forever is tomorrow night. Most of us did not plan to be there for any length of time. Most of us would die there tied to filaments of light.

"Just a box," Gruff said, describing the apartment he lived in.

When Awee asked Gruff where he was from, Gruff bit his lip and said the Big War. The one we won. "It was a long time ago, kid."

Some men were their wars. Awee understood. He had compassion.

Gruff hardly ever moved from his chair. He smoked cigars by the window that was never open. The disabled move slowly if at all. The sun came in like a yellow stain.

Gruff's apartment would become too crowded with all the cigar boxes. They were made from wood. Not the cheap cardboard kind. But the kind you buy in tobacco shops.

Gruff paid Awee to take away stacks and stacks of old newspapers and the cigar boxes. Some of them had been in the apartment since "before Korea."

Awee brought some of the cigar boxes home. He set them on the table.

"Do we have a shovel?" he asked.

Not exactly.

"Awee, why do you need a shovel?"

"To bury some of the boxes, please."

I said something *sane* about just putting them in the Dumpster. But no. Awee was intent on burying them.

A drag queen down the hall had a shovel.

"To bury the bodies," she explained, "of the people I do not like."

The drag queens had the best tools in the building.

We buried the cigar boxes in the field in the back. The one littered with the rusted hulks of cars, beer cans, tires, old dead condoms, snakes, broken bottles.

I had no idea what was in those cigar boxes.

But Gruff knew. He was throwing his greasy grocery bag down the trash shoot in the hall when he pulled me aside.

"Everybody has to bury something. Your boy has more to bury than most. Just let him."

It took a long time before we could talk about it. Awee could only do it in the dark. At night.

"I want to bury everything," he said.

"What do you mean?" I asked. I knew what he meant. He meant his life.

"I don't like nurses," he said.

This had been a bone of contention between us. I wanted him to be nice to them although I wasn't always nice to them. I disliked them as much as he did. But we could not escape having to deal with their rigid rules and their unfeeling authority.

Nurses in clinics were always telling him that he was going to die. Unless he peed into their plastic cups, and did what he was told. Awee would turn to me and tell me he had already peed.

Already peed was not acceptable.

They would squeeze it from him.

How dare you pee without the cup.

Essentially, he was being told to be helpless. When they dealt with him, they were usually exasperated. You pee on schedule. You piss on appointment.

He would bury them, too.

"I keep people in boxes so they don't come out."

I would say nothing. Our silences were acceptable.

I understood now that those of us in the boxes he kept around were like the plastic soldiers of a younger boy.

Although Awee was eleven, and bursting at the seams to be fifteen, he did not fool me. We'd be in Wal-Mart walking through the toy department and his eyes would dart left and right and then linger.

"No, I'm too old for toys," he said.

No kid whose world was shrinking to the size of a bed was too old for toys. They still have minds and imaginations.

I bought Awee a box of tiny plastic Indians.

He would play with his plastic men under the covers. I would turn to my writing, and sit at the table by the window that overlooked the fire escape, with my back to him, and he would play for hours.

A box of tiny plastic cowboys. Another box of soldiers. He would line them up, and crash into everyone with small plastic dump trucks. When I crawled into bed at night, there were always one or two plastic people in there to poke me. The plastic people were small enough for him to put some of them into cigar boxes.

He would bury the people who had tortured him.

There was a list. Most people on the list were authority figures who had failed him.

I had failed him. I had dragged him from AIDS clinic to AIDS clinic. I did not know if there was a box for me. There probably was. I didn't ask.

He kept his biological dad in a box. "It's not the hurting box," Awee explained.

"Oh," I said.

"He can't hurt you in the box. He didn't mean to."

You could taste the blackness then. The storms. The waters in the sky. The turbulence.

"I'm sorry your body got hurt," I said. I did not differentiate between times he had been abused and times when he may have simply been receiving medical care. To him, it was all abuse.

"It's a bad, bad thing."

"Yes. It's a bad, bad thing, honey. But no one is hurting your body anymore. You are safe now." Inside the box I had constructed for us to hide in. This room. This bed. This hotel of ghosts.

"You don't hurt my body."

"No. Your body has been through a lot of hurt. No one is going to hurt you again. I promise."

"Do you promise?"

"Yes. I promise."

It was a lie. He knew it. I knew it. Some doctor somewhere was going to hurt him.

He put his face into my shoulder, and he seemed to deeply breathe in my blue pajamas.

"You can keep him in the box. I will help you make him stay there."

"He doesn't want me. He is afraid people will find out I'm sick, and then they will think he is sick, too."

"He is sick," I said.

"I know. But if people find out, it will be bad for him, and for my mother. So I came to live with you."

Yes. Just yes.

Awee needed to make sense of his life. What sense there was that could be made of it.

"I don't want him to come out of the box," he said.

"You don't want him to come out and hurt you."

"He kept saying over and over that he was sorry."

My shoulder was growing wet in the dark. It was like being bled.

One of his teachers had whipped him. "He made me stay after school, and no one cared, and no one would have believed me anyway."

That stone of silence now between us.

"Do you believe me? I need you to."

I turned to him. "Yes. I believe you. Let me tell you something, okay. You might not like hearing it. It's hard."

"Okay."

"You are what is called a very pretty little boy. And you're smart. You're articulate. It's sort of like a curse. You don't even know it, but you make men have feelings that they would rather not have. All they have to do is look at you. It's okay for men to put those feelings away. Some men, not many, are brave enough to acknowledge them, and move on. It's okay to smother the feelings, too, if you have to. Society needs men to do that. Men should do that. It's called impulse control. It's not okay under any circumstances for any man to hurt your body."

"But I'm *not* a girl."

"No. You are not a girl. It's not okay to hurt girls either. But people are people. Some of us are not beautiful. Some of us are too beautiful. Some of us will want to touch it."

"Men did touch me."

"I am beginning to understand that."

I was beginning to understand the depth of it. Like some blackness of the pit.

"But when you touch me it is not in hurting ways."

I had touched him, too. That was just the way of it. I had wiped the shit from his bleeding rectum when he had been too weak to wipe himself. Times when he had been so weak, I had had to hold him up on the toilet—he was always tilting or sliding off.

"No. I hope not. I hope that when I touch you, I am helping to take care of you. There is a difference."

"I want to ask you something, Dad."

"Okay."

"Some people say asshole."

"I know. Words are important things. Sometimes they are weapons. Why turn them against us?"

"Okay, rectum. But how come I can't feel it when it's coming out of me?"

"You have extensive nerve damage."

"How did I get extensive nerve damage, please?"

"Some of it is from trauma from disease. Some of it is from reaction to the medicine that was used to treat the disease. Like Zerit. I think you were on Zerit for far too long. And inconsistently. The treatment was sporadic. You developed neuropathy. Remember, I got you off the Zerit as soon as I understood what was going on. I had only just come into your life then; you were beginning to fall apart. I suspected the Zerit immediately, but by then a lot of the nerve damage had been done. No one understood how it was destroying your nerves. It's a lot of guess work, and, honey, we're wrong a lot. Sometimes we make you take drugs that end up hurting you. For instance, the prednisone. Prednisone is a steroid. It is a powerful drug. You take it so you can breathe. But it has a side effect that could affect you later on. It is known to destroy bone tissue. But if you don't take it, you won't be able to breathe. You want the truth. That is the truth. We don't mean to hurt you. We don't want that to happen. But sometimes it happens, and then it's too late. And sometimes we can't find the right people who know what they're doing. That is the truth, too. Often, you're just a number, honey. We've gone to a lot of doctors. I know. I sound like the people at the hospitals who tell you to do this. Do that. It's for your own good. I get tired of hearing it, too. After awhile the whole litany of doing things for your own good becomes as much of an abstraction as the life we are living here. Am I losing you, Awee?"

"No. I understand. There are always people who say they don't want to hurt you and then they hurt you. You don't want to be like them but . . ."

"But what, honey?"

"But you make me do what the doctors say to do and it doesn't always work. So now I don't feel it when I have to go to the bathroom, and I don't like my life much anymore. Am I losing *you*?"

"No. I understand."

"You want me to live. But it's hard wanting to."

"I know."

"I want to bury everything and everyone."

"Okay."

"I don't like shit. Aren't you disgusted?"

"Sometimes. But you don't disgust me."

"I am so embarrassed to be like this. I want you to like me. And I am afraid you won't like me no more if you have to clean my rectum. I don't want to be like this. To be someone who needs so much help."

"I wish I were half as strong as you."

"I don't feel strong. I just feel mad. I want to bury my life."

There was no pity in the room. Life comes down to struggle and the smell of shit.

His nose had nuzzled down into that crack between my shoulder and the bed. He was my baby in his blue pajamas. He smelled like clouds.

I was in love with him.

I would have died for him. Enduring the Whore Hotel, the hookers and the sirens, the gunshots, the sewers in the fog, the smell of urine on the bricks at noon, the traffic jams, the tired anonymity, was nothing.

I could love someone and do it. Awee was my teacher.

We were standing around at the funeral of a bunch of cigar boxes (contents undisclosed). His attempt to construct a symbolism of passage. Down. Down through the immense. With outcry. Stars and pearls washed up onto shores of earth. Deep buried numbness from which he had been trying to awaken to tell the secrets of his nights and days. His blindness was the buried midnight, his noon, the cooling haze.

He really wanted to believe that the man who had abused him—I was not entirely sure how, I did not want to know—had been a nice man, just another man who didn't mean to.

Hurt him.

There were others. All locked away in boxes.

How could anyone hurt him?

"I'm not sure I understand my life," he said.

"People who think they understand their lives," I explained, "don't."

We returned the shovel to the drag queen who had lent it to us.

I did not want to be one of the plastic people who got laid to rest in a cigar box. I did not want to be one of the ordinary ones who got buried in a hole of his forgiveness.

I wanted him to know me. Perhaps I could make him live a little longer if I could infuse my strength into him.

I wanted him to know that I was there in the middle of the

night even as he descended down into the depth of his Sustiva dreams. Down deep. Down through the immense with outcry where his words have broken free at last from his stoic teeth and the grinding of them while he was being tortured with the insertion of yet another scope up into his rectum and being told to breathe deep.

I would hold him between examinations while he vomited into clinic toilets.

I wanted him to know me even through everything that was thrown at us and all the fires blazing around us and that I would hold his hand even though our only weapons were our words.

I wanted him to know me not in some buried box but with his new clothes all laid out nice and crisp upon the bed and I would help him dress. I wanted him to know me in all the deeper places that I have and we would eat cinnamon rolls and raisins and buy more blue jeans than we needed and I wanted him to know me as our arms touched at basketball games and we would jump up and yell and jump up and down and root for teams whose exploits and messes (of lives) we would read about in papers. I wanted him to know me way down deep where no other ordinary men are allowed to go—this place is reserved for him, my son. I wanted him to know that I would drag this travois with him tied to it across broken plains and rocks and desert arroyos filled with snakes and we would get there to some land of peaches and oranges and sugar and melons and sweet things in our gourds to drink in this oasis more fragile than the boy tied to his despair.

We would talk for hours about my walks through deserts. He was living through me, through my stories, and my eyes. It was necessary for him to do this. I wanted him to know me as more than just the man who got him from one institution to the next.

One examination to another.

One pee cup to another pee cup.

We would go into the bathroom and close the door. I would hold the cup. It would grow warm.

I wanted him to know me for the deepness of the secrets that I hold. I wanted him to know me for the summers I could bring him. I wanted him to know I could catapult the two of us together through moment after moment, sitting in the sunlight, fallow, as the weeds sing echoes of their journey to the wind that comes pouring down as if it were a thing of faith sent windswept from the sky.

I was beginning to see that Awee's mind was agile, mercurial, swifter than an arrow from a warrior's bow. It would fly until it dropped. There was a beauty to the way it danced. To the way the air seemed to hold it somnambulant in transit. The world around his mind was closing in. Awee was a pilgrim. A bird of passage. All I could do to calm Awee was to hold him tight, let him melt into me, surround him with something of the softness of my darker places.

Let him see into the deep. Soothe him. Reassure him. Baby, Awee, go to sleep. Go to sleep.

10. Kissing Buddha

"Do you think I'm ready to shave yet?"

Awee wanted to shave more than anything even if there was nothing there to really shave yet. He stood on the verge of puberty as if it were some vast, breathless abyss. But he had not spread his wings and jumped. He wanted to shave because he wanted to be like me.

I wanted to protect him.

He wrote things because he wanted to be like me (all my boys eventually do that). He wanted to shave at least as much as he wanted to play baseball, and that was a lot.

He was afraid he might die and miss all the male rituals.

His face was flawless and brown. He was grinning at me. It was his version of a joke.

Yet we would do that, too. Together. Shaving at the sink. Nude. Standing there in small puddles on the bathroom floor.

"Don't cut yourself," he said.

The things I wanted for and from Awee were different from the things Awee wanted for and from himself. Awee wanted to shave and play baseball.

I wanted him to know the power of giving back.

"Daddy, you cut yourself."

It happens.

Him, horrified. Me, still waking up.

He consulted the new image of himself (shaved now) in the mirror. He wanted people to like him. Tons and tons of aftershave.

He was dressed up, and going away today.

Off to work with him.

I helped him find a *job*.

I did not have Awee in school. I know, I am a rotten person. It was an issue I avoided because I could.

No school wanted him.

There were no truant officers banging on our door. Every school wants a kid with AIDS.

Please.

He was every school district's nightmare. Was his teacher going to change his shitty pants? Not every teacher is Tina.

We could have arranged for a teacher to come to us. Public health nurses did. You just brave the gauntlet of junkies and whores in the lobby, and you're there.

Delay. Delay. Delay. Delay works just fine. I forged doctor's signatures on forms and then threw them away. I bought time.

That is what AIDS is. Buying time.

We were people who did not exist.

Finding him a job was easy. He was free.

There was a Head Start program in a church down the street from the Whore Hotel. I asked them if he could volunteer a few hours a couple of times a week. They were absolutely delighted to have him. Did I tell them he had AIDS?

No. I definitely did not. Disclosure can be dangerous. It has real social and legal consequences. People with HIV have to live with the fact that insurance companies always want their names. Corporations compile lists of the names of people with HIV that insurers such as Blue Cross can deny health insurance to as a preexisting condition. No one wants their name on these lists. And revealing the names of people with HIV is against the law. The law is there to protect them and their privacy.

The Head Start children were far more dangerous to *him* than he was to *them*. Those little runny noses. Those grimy hands that just returned from the bathroom.

But he needed to be *in* the world. And the world needed him whether the world knew it or not.

He looked handsome. He shone. He was fabulous.

It worked. The mix was right. The four-year-olds ate him up. They were all over him. They were a little afraid of him, too. After all, this is one of the big boys who never play with you, and who will hold you upside down with your head in the toilet.

Here was one who would read to you, who would perform for you, who was better than Big Bird. Here was one who could teach you numbers, who would show you how to paint. How to write your name. Here was one who would let you sit on his lap, who smelled nice (they sniffed him), who became the characters in the books and the stories he read. Here was one who *wrote* the stories in the books he read. Here was one who encouraged you.

I would sort of lurk in the back of the room. This was his gig. I was there in case he had to make a mad dash for the bathroom. But it never happened. Unlike school, this was not a setup for failure.

"Awee! Awee! Awee!"

Twenty four-year-olds jumping up and down.

He had to plan his activities. This giving back. Awee was alive.

"The other teenagers would never think to come here," the Head Start teacher said.

I smiled and said nothing. I made him do it. I bribed him.

Clothes.

Shoes.

New fancy razor.

"They really *like* me!"

They adored him. They hung from him like Christmas tree ornaments. It shook him. He came home and cried. Softly like the sun comes in the room.

A four-year-old had kissed him.

I am thinking: germs.

Mend him who can. Kids from the projects. Mongrel kids who had nothing to give him but perhaps a kiss.

That night, asleep, he reminded me of Buddha.

He was my prince. A glooming peace that morning with it brings the sun, for sorrow will not and did not show its head or run. Go hence to talk of these sad things in kisses for some shall be pardoned, and some punished, for love in stories is more heartfelt than is woe, than this of tongues and sons and Romeo.

11. Jack Knife

Our bike broke down. Eventually everything wears out. Goes brittle. Comes apart. Even good people, the toughened ones who have healed, and glued themselves back together, scarred, become unglued, dissolve, and snap like bones at the stronger places you once thought of as impenitent as stone.

"Tell me why everything goes . . ."

"Bad, you mean," I said.

"No. Not bad, Daddy. Why does everything just have to end? I wanted our bike to be forever. Why can't something be forever?"

"Some things are forever," I explained. Because I am the idiot of the cathedral tower with my humps and my pulling ropes and resounding bells. The idiot hunchback of the Whore Hotel where mass is conducted hourly.

We were in bed.

Sleeping.

"Name one thing."

"One thing what."

"One thing that lasts forever, and don't say no love shit. Not to me."

Duhhhhhhhhh.

There are cracks in the ceiling. You can see them even in the dark.

"Stupidity."

"Stupidity what?"

"Stupidity. There is no end to it. Stupidity is a vast cosmic phenomenon. There is gravity. There is the speed of light. There is subatomic structure. All of these things are laws and absolutes. And then there is the only law that is more absolute than even these."

I knew when he was trying not to laugh.

"Stupidity?"

"Stupidity transcends entire galaxies. Scientists wonder why we do not hear from other galactic species."

"Stupidity?"

"Yes. It is entirely probable that other galactic species are as stupid as we are, which is pretty stupid. God said: *And let there be light. And make everyone in the universe take a stupid pill.* Have you had yours?"

"What, my stupid pill?"

"Yaaaaa."

"I don't know. Is it time for fucking pills?"

"Yaaaaa."

"Am I going to have to take these pills *forever*, Dad?"

"Yaaaaa. Until there's a cure."

"For AIDS?"

I smiled. "As soon as we cure stupidity, we'll cure AIDS the next day. Trust me. I promise."

He is gulping pills. Gulping water. In the dark.

I am sitting by him on the bed.

He will have to pee soon.

"If you have to pee, can you do it, or are you going to need help?"

He had to think.

"Will you check my toes, please?"

I turn the light on. He is in his pajamas under the sheet. I lift the sheet off him. Awee looks down at his legs.

I move them a bit. I gently squeeze his toes.

If he doesn't scream, it means he will be okay. It means the pain medication is working. It means he can get up, and do things on his own. Without falling.

He does not scream.

"Just needles," he says.

This is good. Needles are not the ice picks. Needles are not the razor blades. Needles, he tolerates.

I turn the light off, and lay down beside him. In a couple of minutes he will be up again. To pee.

I hear him in there. Whimpering. Trying not to wake me.

As if I sleep in this apartment. In this bed. Looking out the window where the light comes in, and the shadow of the fire escape is a path to nowhere except perhaps up to the stars that dance up on the roof.

He is whimpering because it hurts to pee.

The scar tissue that has formed in his urethra is a result of all the catheters that have been shoved unskillfully into him.

There are people who can do it. There are people who do not do it well. There are people who glance nervously at the hospital room door when he screams his guts out.

He gets back in bed. Curls hard. Protects the part of him that hurts.

By himself. He is a rock.

Okay. I wasn't going to do it. I am glad he has his pajamas on. With that wet warm spot where he leaks. I hold him and he slowly unfolds and falls to sleep even as the travel clock ticks the minutes off like drops fall on an old tin roof.

.   .   .

There were two places that he lived. There was the empty house where he knew nothing. There was the furnished house where he knew everything and could not be hurt.

In the morning, we would push the bike to be repaired. The Harley, too, was a wounded animal. We pushed the heavy corpse together. Uphill. It is always uphill. Never down. No way life was about to give us that. Awee was smiling because he could remember when just a few short weeks ago he could not have pushed anything.

My helper. I loved to watch his muscles strain like some pony jumping fences. Awee sets his jaw, and grinds his teeth.

We push and sweat.

There were bikes outside the garage all lined up in a row on the sidewalk. There was a sense of order here imbued with attentive arrogance. The smell of concrete, old rags, gasoline, leather boots, and oil in dirt. There are fan belts on the wall (they fixed hot rods here as well as bikes).

Rebels do not own Harley-Davidsons. Only old wrecks like myself who are easily reminded of our mortality when perfection comes apart.

When perfection comes apart, we reach for our credit cards.

I did a lot of parenting that way, too.

Awee looks around. The eyes half-lids. The golden calf at graven images (there is a naked woman on a calendar on the wall that he pretends not to see). Every waiting bike is quiet.

"Can I help you guys?" The smile as straightforward as the coveralls. Everything is costume performance art. Wipes his hands with rags.

His name embroidered in red on his pocket.

Jack.

"Our bike broke down," I explained. I did not know what particular part had worn itself out. Probably all of them.

"Well, you're in the right place."

"Good."

The difference between twelve and fifty is that at fifty you have been both the garage mechanic and the younger boy with the broken bike. One out of breath. One who wears black and hears confessions.

When bikes like this break down, it is usually the fault of the person who owns it.

Guilty.

"We rode it pretty hard," Awee said.

"People do that. Let me look at it."

At fifty, I know this: *Let me look at it* is where it all begins.

It is forbidden among the males of the species to speak of it. To bring it up. But the reality is that most preadolescent boys fall in love (however briefly) with someone.

Usually a friend.

Sometimes it is a teacher.

Or the older girl who rides your bus but never, ever sits by you.

You fear for your life that someone will find out, and someone usually does, and often enough it's the person you have the crush on. They know.

At twelve I fell hopelessly in love with a priest. A priest who came to perform mass in the migrant camps. What he performed on me was nothing less than an exorcism. He made me promise I would never tell. I never have. I have though gone back and forth for almost forty years of hating him and then not hating him and then forgiving him for me. Father, I forgive you. I forgive you for me. Not for you. I loved him for a year, and then the Church sent him away. He was all of twenty-six, and straight from Mexico. At twelve I had been loved and left. Both things hurt. At twelve you want everything to be forever.

If only for a day. If only for fifteen minutes. The boy who fixed things. And the boy who needed fixing.

Measure with your instruments the immediate space between them. There is none.

The soft silencing of any son is easy. I can do it with my eyes. I could not separate them with horses. It was that fast.

Apotheosis. Call it what you want. Bewitchment. The twelve-year-old and the sixteen-year-old connected like some malicious magnetism of Circean hypnosis. Apparitions. For a moment, I wasn't even there.

"I think the cylinder cracked," Awee said. "We were riding back from the reservation."

This to say: *I'm Indian.*

He looked Indian. I do not.

Awee knowing it can go one of two ways here.

The reservation is a place of beauty and of pain.

Awee watched Jack's eyes intently. Like some intergalactic species scan.

Jack quietly, privately drank him in. Honey and water. He knew when a thing was dark and sweet.

"I think the cylinder is cracked."

The twelve-year-old repeated himself because he did not know what else to do, and he was not confident. In fact, he had yet to change a lightbulb.

I had so much to do. So much to teach him. I wanted more *time*. That *motherfucker*. I wanted to teach Awee to be decent. To not fall for the lies of priests. I wanted to teach him to stop trusting everyone. To not give them his eyes like that. Not that Awee was going to listen to a word of it.

"We'll have to take it apart and look inside the engine. It's a major job."

Take the thing apart. Touch it.

"Can I help? I won't get in the way."

He was already in the way. It is what twelve does.

. . .

The rest of us tolerate them (for as long as we can) because we love them. Then we lose our patience.

Sixteen isn't stupid. Jack looks at me. "Are you his dad?"

Yaaaaa.

"It has to be okay with you."

I am a recreant misfit and can see the future. I have danced down mountains with the Chiricahua.

Really, I have.

I can see the future because I have known the past for the lament it is. There is no way Awee had my permission to do this. I wanted to forbid him to even contemplate it. My job was to protect him.

From life.

Sometimes I get kisses. But I have to *earn* them. I don't care what anyone says. There are no free kisses.

"Can I stay?" Awee asked.

It was ill-advised.

"Yaaaaa. You can stay. Just don't be annoying."

"He won't be," Jack said.

Oh, yes, he would.

I leave them to their ministry. I do not look back. The older one is a Jesuit. The younger one *hooooooooovering*, a choir boy, a moth.

Reduced to the level of a trudge, I know my secular place is temporal, and go back to where I came from. I cannot believe (believe it) I have lost him to a sixteen-year-old grease monkey. Were you to look at me you would see a soothsayer at the College of the Cardinals, busy, with something important to do, some deep question to ponder among the dust and books.

I had nothing more exotic to do than the laundry. I sit in a chair by the window of our room with a shot of gin. How dare he leave his underpants on the floor like that.

It occurs to me he is not wearing them.

This romance could be over soon enough. What romance. They would both deny it. *My imagination.*

I ought to pick his underpants up with tongs and take them back to the garage and demand that he put them on.

Meanness goes well with gin.

I picked them up. His underpants. They do feel soft against my face, and the smell of him, and medicine, makes more things in heaven and earth, Horatio, than are dreamt of in exorcism. All his unclean sins were mine.

"You always call me when you need me," she said. "I'm glad you do that. How is Awee?"

"Getting the bike fixed."

"By himself?"

That was why I only called her when I needed her.

I would like to have been able to call her when I didn't really need her, but was simply calling her to call her, and take some comfort in her wisdom and her voice. I would have liked to just call her. For nothing.

But we had this disconnect.

With Awee. It was as hard as it was fundamental.

She was a woman, and would have surrounded him with her protective wings.

I did not blame her for any of this.

It only was.

There was this disconnect with how we saw him. Me: *willing to risk things in allowing him to taste perhaps too much.* Her: *grinding on the training wheels of his bike because he might fall and he would fall because he would.*

I had resolved to do this alone.

My way.

Pulling ropes and bells. The hunchback of the reservation.

I called and gave her updates.

It usually did not take too long for us to get to the part of the conversation where she said: *What do you MEAN, all by himself?*

I did not do training wheels.

There was no time.

"He's never spent the day in a garage with a mechanic before. He'll have fun."

There was a silence between us on the phone. Tina grinding teeth.

"He's so vulnerable."

"Yaaaaa. Well, I'm the one who knows him, okay. He's been doing just . . ."

"So, that stupid bike broke down, I knew it would. Did he get hurt or something?"

"No, he did not get hurt. We were almost home. We pushed it."

"He's twelve years old, and he has AIDS, and you've got him *out there* pushing motorcycles."

"When the bike breaks down, you push it."

"I knew that bike was a bad idea."

"That bike was a great idea." I loved that bike.

"You and your adventures, Nasdijj. *When* are you going to grow up?"

"Don't hate me too much, okay."

"I love you. That's the problem. I'm in love with a cowboy who won't grow up, who thinks children are like dogs who just hop in the truck and come along for the ride. And they're not. They're just not. I have to go. I can't talk to you about that bike. When you fall off a cliff somewhere don't call me, okay."

"Okay."

"I did not mean that. You better call me, Nasdijj."

"I just did."

"When are you coming home?"

"I am home. Are you asking me when is he going to die? I don't know. No one knows. We all die. Everybody. You. Me. Him. There was a hooker down the hall who got hit by a truck just the other day when she . . ."

"I don't want to know. How come you won't bring him here? To be with me? Us?"

"Because I'm afraid. I'm afraid if someone puts the screws to him—really lets him know that he has arrived at this place where there is no or little exploration—he will internalize that, and then he really will die. Do you understand?"

"No. He's a baby."

"He's not. He really isn't. He is making every moment he has count. Even if he is easily lost in the moments as they descend on him, and they do. He gets up every day, and tries to put his pants on. He wants to know about things. Like what does it mean to love and be loved. He is not a baby to face that. To ask those questions. Most adults never even get close. He is not an adult. I am there to protect him if I feel it's necessary. I do fuck up. I do. That is when I call you, and ask for your forgiveness. I need you to forgive me. I need to do this. I'll be in touch."

"I forgive you. I think it's wrong. Some baby living in a place like that."

"He's getting care."

"He needs a woman in his life. So do you. You require supervision, you do. I am going to whack that bike with a sledgehammer."

"This is not about the bike."

"This is so much about that bike I could wring your Navajo neck. *No twelve-year-old* . . ."

"He's fifteen . . ."

It went on like this for another twenty minutes. It usually did. I did not tell her the part about being barely able to hold the bike up at all. My bones would scream the hurly-burly, hags, witches, toads, steam, wars.

She wanted us to come live with her.

She would not have let Awee stay at the garage with Jack.

There would have been no garage. No Harley-Davidson. No underpants on the floor. No Jack.

No gin.

It was almost dark by the time Awee came home. Time had escaped him.

Awee was enervated. He fairly bubbled over with talk and wisdom. Things he did not know that he knew now.

His monkhood.

He eats his cold food voraciously. I am glad to see this. He is much too thin, and holy water is not nutritional, nor is the sin of gin.

"So I said it was okay to put on a new starter."

"Oh, you did."

"Yeah, because we need one."

"I guess if we need one."

"We do."

"Okay." I deny him nothing.

I wish he would kiss me but shit. I am such an idiot.

"And Jack is coming over soon as he's done, and we'll ride around the block."

I say nothing.

"I promise not to be late, okay?"

I smiled like I would at communion if I believed in it.

The twelve-year-old pops into the bathroom to make himself presentable.

"I washed your underpants," I say loudly.

He ought to wear them.

He emerges and accuses *me* of worrying about *him*.

Yaaaaa. I do do that.

You bet I worry about him. I have custody.

Knocks at the door.

Jack.

The two of them off into the sunset.

No one kisses me. No one.

It would rain. The bike would break. The mechanic felt he had failed. He had. They had gone into the country. Way off the map. I probably would have done it, too. Which is no excuse. Cold night rain. They would have to fix the bike in what I had defined as a downpour (Awee said drizzle). At the side of the road. Using what tools I had in the saddlebag. Their fingers in the warmness of the crankcase. I keep the batteries in the flashlight new. Touching oil in the dark. Me, waiting by the clock waiting for them to come.

I am *pisssssssssed* off.

Jack delivers him late, drenched, and shivering.

I am obviously *a nut*.

They say some sort of secret, stiff good-byes almost in the hall. Jack is in agony.

The fifteen-year-old (in his dreams) goes into the bathroom. Jack lingers. Dripping. What they have done is serious.

"Take care of him," Jack says. Yaaaaa. I say nothing. I am too angry for words.

I considered spanking Awee.

I stick him in the bath. I feed him hot soup. I dry him and dress him in his pajamas.

"I'm sorry, Dad."

"I was scared. Can you understand that? I need to know if you can understand that, Awee."

We are both sitting on the bed.

"It was raining. We had to fix the bike. I was so close to him. He started touching me. I liked it. I wanted to. It was dark. And then I told him. About me."

I had to sit on the floor now. Sliding down. I didn't want to see him. Be seduced by him. I had not protected him. I had failed him, too.

"Did you have sex?"

A silence a lot like church.

"Yeah. In the rain. He said I was beautiful."

I did not accept this.

"Awee, what did he do with his penis?"

Awee was crying now.

"He let me touch it."

"And what did he do with your penis?"

"Nothing. He was afraid. It doesn't go hard anymore, but you know that. You read my journal. I know you did. I think I came anyway. I think. I always tell you everything."

Eventually, he always did.

Two boys touching in the rain. "We did kissing," Awee said.

"Awee, this is serious."

What was serious—I think now, looking back—was my ability to slide into something hysterical.

I did not think it was really sex. To a twelve-year-old, a sixteen-year-old represents many things, some of those things are sexual in context, but not overtly over-the-top when, in fact, what would have touched Awee was not Jack's flesh so much as the fact that he thought Awee was beautiful. They kissed. They did some touching. They were late in coming home. It was still raining outside. You could hear the cars splashing through the puddles by the sidewalk. Awee was asleep. He was so determined.

I called the police department back.

"No, they came home," I said. So much for missing persons.

I was sitting in the dark when there was a knock at the door. It was very late. Awee stayed asleep.

Jack.

I did not let him in. We sat against the wall in the hallway.

He had not been home. He was soaked and the carpeting was wet. He was quite upset.

"I didn't even know him until today," he said.

He would hurt him. This was going to hurt Awee.

Sex was just the thing like electricity that drove the beast. But it was not the beast.

The beast is always loneliness. How we tame it. How we let it go.

"I want to see him," Jack said.

"When?"

"Tomorrow."

That quick.

If I were to say *no* there would be some great crusade, and everyone would hate everyone. I would have rules.

No sex.

No touching. I meant it.

They were to observe my curfews. Period. Or I would end it.

Their new adolescent masquerades would astonish both of them eastward toward the moon, who hangs her yellowed superficial head like a potato and I would move Awee away. I was prepared to fight for him.

I was so glad to not be sixteen, I would have danced with hookers in the halls.

Jack stood up. "I'm glad you're not against it."

I wasn't for it either.

"Awee has AIDS, boy."

"I know."

At sixteen, you don't know shit.

Jack took Awee bowling. I had neglected it.

Home on the fucking dot.

Jack's parents were a little bewildered. Imagine that. Awee went to dinner.

Meat loaf. Green beans. Potatoes.

Awee went on and on about Jack's room. Jack had his own room. With posters and a desk that was all his.

There was an exchange of pillows.

I would owe the hotel five bucks.

Awee slept on the smell of Jack. It was his first cause.

Jack would come around. He pretends not to love (Awee or anyone).

I am always just the watchman on his rounds. All is well.

I never get kissed.

It never really ended. After we left that town, Jack continued to write to Awee. He would write back to Jack. Like they had been deep and desperate lovers from some motorcycle universe, which is something they never were and something they were never going to be. I do not think they ever touched like that again.

"What do you want?" I asked Awee.

It would get me into trouble. He smiled. He was wicked. He was not fifteen.

"I want to ride the bike naked with you at night."

That bike kept getting bigger. Heavier. Nonetheless, I could keep it upright. For now. The dark hard against our balls. His arms around my belly. Fast on top of blacktop. Hang thou hard upon the tomb of rain and blood's the spot on hands that melts. Holds fathers to their sons like fans and the growling humming of the belts.

12. Jesus Is a Statue

It was Awee's idea that we would go to church. We would dress up.

I don't dress up. It doesn't work for me.

"We will buy suits," he said.

Yaaaaa. The tooth fairy lives down the hall, and when you lose your teeth, she sneaks into your room at night, and leaves hundred-dollar bills under your pillow, or in your underwear.

He made hurt and articulate remarks about my sarcasm. He was often the adult.

My sarcasm.

"Look," I said. "I don't wear suits. You can't dress me up and make it something it's not. I don't go to church. Let's just stay home, and read comic books, and get drunk."

He just stared at me. "I need a nice shirt, okay."

Okay. Church.

"But no ties or dressing up."

Okay. Clean socks.

The twelve-year-olds (Awee was still eleven, but I was not allowed to tell) are either lawyers or priests. Or both. The twelve-year-olds can be clotheshorses, too. They understand the notion of costume.

"Do we have to go in?"

"You look *nice*," he said. He brushed toast crumbs off my T-shirt. But it was a *new* T-shirt. Fruit of the Loom.

"Why don't I stay out here, and *you* go in. I'll wait out here."

I would sit out here by the fence. Eat a sandwich or something. Behave myself.

"No. You're going in with me, remember. We do things together. Please."

Yaaaaa. Yaaaaa. Yaaaaa. Fucking church. He sort of pulled me up the steps.

I will tell you why I don't like church. It's like walking into myself. That lurking emptiness. That echo off the stone. I can smell the sweat. The burning of the candles. The light sneaks in. Someone else's suffering. Sums due for voyages you have taken. Church will find you out. And from that room where you have been put in prison, all the sorrowful issues condemn me for a hypocrite.

"We'll pray," he said.

Aww *shit*.

"Where did you learn about this stuff? You've never been to church."

"I saw it in the movies," he explained. "It's almost church."

There was no one there. It wasn't even Sunday. I don't know *why* we had to be dressed up, or *why* it mattered what we looked like. The place was empty. You could hear the traffic outside. We sat in the back in the pews.

"We have to get down on our knees," he said.

Awwwwww.

Like in the movies.

"What are we supposed to pray about," I asked him.

He sighed deeply like I am such a stupid idiot.

It was one of our better times. Everything was good. Awee wanted to thank someone or something for it.

"We're supposed to pray that I *live*, that I don't die, okay? I don't *want* to die. I want to live. I want to be alive. I want to be with *you*. Can't you pray for it? Is there something wrong with you? Is it too much to ask from you?"

Some things are.

Down on my knees.

Okay, God. Now what?

Father, please make me well again. This being sick is very hard. I am so tired, Father. Father, I'm worried about him if I die. What he might do. How will he get along. Father, he is going to miss me so much.

I looked over at him in . . .

Shock.

Or something like that. Close anyway. He was praying *for me*.

"Stop it," I said.

We sat in the pew at the back of the empty church in silence for a long time. I was angry with him. I do not know why.

"You don't have to pout," he said.

"I'm not pouting."

"Yes, you are. I know you when you're pouting. You're pouting now."

"I'm not pouting. I'm just pissed off is all."

"I'm gonna die, you know, and when I'm gone I want you to take care of yourself. I worry about you. I am allowed to love you."

"For one thing, Awee, you're *not* going to die—and nobody has to worry about *my* taking care of myself."

"I'm allowed to worry. About you. You will probably kill yourself."

"No, you're *not allowed* to worry. I'm the one who worries about *you*."

"You're gonna have to face it. I have this disease."

"I know that."

"Sometimes I wonder."

I hate God. I hate church. I hate praying. I wanted to get up, and run, and scream.

He was looking up at the ceiling. Someone had painted stars up there.

"My mom used to take me outdoors, and we'd look up at the stars, sometimes when it was really cold," he said.

"Yaaaaa. My mom, too."

"She did?"

"Yaaaaa. So we could learn the stories."

"I didn't know you did that."

The problem with being twelve is that he thinks it's so unique.

"What's your favorite story?" he asked.

"Sa."

"Sa?"

"Yaaaaa. Sa. I liked her. She was old age. When the War Twins came to slay her, she talked them out of it."

"I never liked her. I thought they should do it."

"Why?"

"Then no one would grow old."

"We all grow old."

"I won't," Awee said. Awee was eleven. Age is relative. So is religion.

"What is it with you. You *will* grow old. We'll be old together."

"When you're really old will you remember me, please?"

"Awee, stop it. You're hurting me."

"I want you to remember me. I want you to remember this. This coming here. We did things together. We slew Sa."

"How did we do that?"

"You do that when you write it down. Then someone else might know we existed. You and me. I want everyone to know."

"Know what?"

"That I loved you soooooooooo much. I want you to write it. It's going to be really hard. You probably won't be able to until I'm gone."

"You're not going anywhere."

"You know I am. I want you to write it."

"I can't write it. Please, it's hurting me so much."

"You have to. You have to try. I want people to know we had this *huge*, *huge* thing. Us. People don't have that. They try. But we have it. I want you to tell them about how to have it."

"Why?"

Everything is swimming now. Awee is looking up.

"It's a lot like God."

There was a statue in the church. I am a *criminal*. I allowed him to steal it. I didn't say a goddamn thing. We just walked out with Jesus.

He made a shrine in our hotel room. I let him get away with too much.

"I think we should pray every day," he said.

Aw shit.

"Pray for what?"

Now he gives me the evil eye.

I couldn't do it. But I could bring him to the roof. It was blacktop covered in broken gin bottles.

But you could see the stars.

It took time to find the things we shared. You have to understand the constellations. And how at night they become the stories, too. Like sleeping on the slopes of an extinct volcano. The night so Bible-black, the light from the stars will cast a shadow on the ground. The stars will take your breath away. You may touch them.

Be careful. They will burn your fingers. They will put dogs inside your eyes. They will make the bears dance. Our mothers gave them to us.

I do not know where our fathers were.

Spider Woman. Sa. Changing Woman.

I kissed his cheek. He did not pull away.

He pointed out the constellations. The bear. The coyote. All the flying ghosts like bats. We could hear the beating of their wings and see them fly into the mouth of the volcano.

Our lives sat on a fault line that earthquakes shake and lurch. In the morning, we put Jesus back in his place in church.

13. Two Dying Boys Dancing in Pajamas

Young men laugh, and young men go. The sun. The moon. The rain. The snow. Their music was always much too loud. For a hospital.

Pediatric AIDS is this whirling roller coaster: one day you're out of the hospital, and the next day you're back at the hospital. There is no escape from this. PCP pneumonia has killed a lot of kids with AIDS.

Science has made enormous strides in dealing with this kind of ravaging pneumonia. Bactrim works wonders although Awee found intravenous Bactrim to be quite painful and he complained bitterly that it burned him where the needle went in. The HAART antiretroviral therapy has improved AIDS treatment immensely. Mortality rates are way down. Unfortunately, the drugs don't work for every child.

The more drugs the child has been on, the less options you have.

Awee always had a roommate during hospital stays. The closer in age to twelve the roommate was, the better the hospital stay was. Jon was sixteen. Emotionally . . .

Well, what the hell. Give a kid with AIDS a break. Awee and Jon shared an awful lot.

They had lived all their lives with HIV. There was always a lot to talk about.

Jon would make the point (without being asked) that it was no way to live.

Jon was often suicidal.

You walk into their room. Jon is in his bed by the window. Pretending to be asleep. Awee is in his bed by the bathroom.

Blankets pulled up.

Both boys were mischievous as hell. They have just jumped back into bed. That look of guilt.

Busted.

They were not supposed to be *out* of bed. Let alone have wheelchair races in the hall.

They hated nurses. They hated hospitals. And sometimes they hated me. Sometimes I felt so guilty that they were being tortured so unnecessarily I would buy them stuff.

I bought them a compact disc player but they had to promise not to play it loud, and to use earphones as much as possible.

I bought them CDs. They had to promise not to dance.

No dancing.

Jon had avascular necrosis. It is becoming more and more common in people with HIV. It is common, too, among asthmatics who have been treated with drugs such as prednisone. Environmental causes are to blame. No one is born with avascular necrosis. Jon's bones were dying. Inch by inch. The blood supply does not reach the bone. This is a progressive disease that can be caused by many things. Injury. A history of broken bones. Exposure to steroids. Jon was in enormous (untreated) pain. There would be no dancing.

At least the music kept them in their room.

PCP pneumonia is commonly treated with steroids to keep the lungs open. The side effects can cripple you. It does not take a *lot* of prednisone, a powerful steroid, to begin the process of bone decay. Avascular necrosis is not well understood.

At sixteen, Jon had a little more experience at subverting nurses and institutions than Awee did. You could easily bust Awee. You could never bust Jon. Never.

You could humiliate him though.

You could be a young nurse's aide, not that much older than Jon, and you could come into his room, and in front of his friends, you could ask him about his bowel movement, and if he hadn't had one you could give him an enema.

Can you guys leave the room, please. Jon is going to have his enema.

There isn't much you could do to a sixteen-year-old boy to humiliate him more than this.

Jon just didn't care anymore. He would fight them.

When Jon wasn't sick, he lived with his dad. He had only recently been placed with his dad by social services, which had taken custody away from Jon's mom, who also had AIDS.

The kinds of social dramas teenage boys with AIDS shared, teenage boys who had lived all those years with that virus, and had survived . . .

A litany of drugs . . .

The experience of losing their parents and their friends . . .

The long-term things that toxic chemicals (antiretroviral drugs are highly toxic) had done to their livers . . .

These experiences compelled them, drove them into the arms of a brotherhood difficult for anyone not a member of the group to understand, swept them up, and embraced them like a sharing of your brother's arms, and only he could hug you quite like that.

You're sixteen. Girls (you should but you do not refer to them as women) come into your room and chart the progress of your bowel movements. Girls who in any other environment would be the kind of females you would want to like you—they are the kind of girls you went to school with—now give you enemas, and make you shit in bedpans, and they clean you up, and wipe you, and there was a part of you that wanted to die in the rituals of humiliation that clashed sorely with the rituals of development, and you would always be just a thing to them that had either shit or had not shit, and had left a paper trail like a long roll of toilet paper attached to you that followed you everywhere. You were *sixteen*. At sixteen you were shy even if you laughed out loud with the other guys who came after school to see you. There was not too much hope that any of this invasiveness was going to change. You would never learn to drive, and if you did, you would find the highest cliff you could to roll the car from.

Jon's dad was well, and had been divorced from his mother for some years. I liked Jon a lot. Awee adored him. When you are twelve, a sixteen-year-old (who likes you) is a gift from God.

I walked into their room once, and the nursing staff had tied them down.

Their legs were tied down to the bed, and their wrists were tied down to the sides of the railing.

Catheters stuck out of each boy's penis.

I hit the fucking roof. I could not *believe* I had to deal with this *shit* again!

"We cannot be held responsible for their behavior if they leave their room," I was told.

Wheelchair races. Just getting outside. To breathe real air.

How many times had I been told by Jon that there were two kinds of air: real air and hospital air.

I was informed by the head nurse that the catheters were perfectly legal. Society gives the medical profession more leeway than it deserves, and fighting this (single-handedly) is pointless.

Jon is pulling at the restraints and screaming about his rights.

Awee is silent and simply crying.

No one has the right to play baseball in the hall.

Again, they were totally humiliated. I saw it then, and I see it now, as punishment. Jon had no rights. A catheter is *not* a medically acceptable form of behavior management.

"Jon bit them," I was told. *But he didn't break no skin*, I was also told.

I don't think I hated AIDS as much as I hated nurses.

That night, Jon took *both* of their Foley catheters out. He had figured out how to do it. He had stolen a syringe (easy), and simply sucked the liquid out of the balloon. Then you pull the snake out of the pee hole of your penis. You can suck the liquid from the balloon from your mouth, too. It reaches.

This pissed the nursing staff into Kingdom Come. More restraint as punishment. I called Jon's dad and we both threatened lawyers. The nurses backed down. Not quietly.

I think maybe I hated medicine more than the boys did. I wanted Awee *out* of there. But the pneumonia scared me.

Each boy helped the other boy into the bathroom.

The boy not using the bathroom guarded the door. The lock did not work and nurses always barged in. It was nice to have a friend.

I would sneak Awee in his wheelchair out to places like a small garden in a courtyard. We were not supposed to go there.

Awee in his pajamas.

"Jon's gonna run away," he said.

"Really."

"Yeah. Soon."

They had been hatching plots. "That might not be such a good idea."

"He wants to die."

"I might feel that way, too, if I had to be tied down. I hope you don't feel that way."

Awee looked away. Sometimes he felt like he would be better off dead.

Jon was more of an enigma. Jon was more rebellious. It was difficult for Awee to talk to me about things like wanting to die. I wanted Awee to live.

For me.

Jon did run away. He ended up coughing blood into a bucket at the county jail. I am afraid Awee was his willing accomplice. Guilt by association and planning.

You never knew what to expect as you rounded the corner in the hospital hall to their room.

The CD player was on. Not loud. Just nice. I had goodies. My arms were filled with junk. I did not want to be one of the bad guys. The life-at-any-cost guys. The you-have-to-do-this-even-if-you-hate-it brigade. I stopped dead in my tracks.

They were so alive. I am the one who is with the dead. The invisible.

They didn't notice me.

Jon was, of course, the taller one. Awee was the little guy.

I did not want to move. Frozen. Standing just outside their door. Looking in.

I am rarely stunned by life. But I am stunned now.

I am bearing silent witness.

Two barefoot boys in pajamas with their arms around each other's waist. Barefoot toes. The music sets its song and loving pace. Two barefoot boys in pajamas touching cheek-to-cheek. Two barefoot boys in pajamas not knowing what the hell they seek. Two barefoot boys in pajamas only now advancing.

Two dying barefoot boys in pajamas laughing as they're dancing.

14. Dances with Girls

We had a birthday coming up. I was as pleased as punch.

Maybe now I would be allowed to tell the truth about his age.

"Yeah," he said. "I'm really fifteen."

He was such a flirt. I had worked with lots of boys his age who had developed crushes on me. Silly things. It is quite normal. But I had never worked with one I had a crush on. I wanted to hug him tight and buy him everything.

I just wanted him to be happy.

I loved Awee for all the things he loved. At twelve, the things boys love can be downright strange. Twelve is twisted.

Not in a sinister way. Twelve wants you to like it. Twelve is afraid of many things, but the thing that terrifies twelve down into its bowels is the thought that you (as parent) have the power to yank it back. To childhood.

I lied to him. I told him time and time again that what I wanted was for him to grow up. I did want him to grow up. But there was a part of me that also wanted the little boy in him. I did not want him to lose that. So soon. So soon. The pressure on them to be adults is so real. *To be a man*. But I have to admit in this writing place—even if it hurts, and it does—that I wanted

him to be that child he *was*. Even if he only had fragments of it
to hang on to. I would settle for fragments.

I did not know him for those first ten years. I had not been
there when he had taken his first step. I missed so much! I
missed him losing teeth. I missed his first time on a horse. I did
not carry him on my back in a Navajo cradleboard. I wanted
small important moments. What little I could have. I watched his
eyes. I saw them linger once on a set of Lincoln Logs in a toy
store, and I bought the set. He told me not to. That Lincoln
Logs were for babies.

We played with those Lincoln Logs for days. Making forts
and cabins.

We were at war with so many *other* things. AIDS. The medical, in-
stitutional ropes he wore around his neck. Indifference. We battled
huge dragons: insurance companies, nursing staffs, even the federal
government (Awee wrote letters urging them to find a cure for
AIDS, they were never answered), and publishing. But we were not
at war with each other. Not real war. The real kinds of war that destroyed things. Our skirmishes always ended in smoke and hugs.

Now I have this bad habit of buying Lincoln Logs for kids. In
the (usually futile) hope that they will play forts with me.

Or I buy them fishing tackle boxes.

The ones I am allowed to know—I buy both.

I had this gift, this twelve-year-old who worshiped me, who
trusted me, who thought I was something special.

He wanted to share the things he loved with me, the electric
jolts he felt—the ones far more powerful than the ice picks that
stabbed his feet and legs—when he made extraordinary discov-
eries, always coming back in some circumfluent navigation, to
me, to show me breathlessly where he had been.

I see, now, from this removed distance I live in, so many fathers and their sons encased in the armor that protects them from ever really knowing one of the most profound connections any man can ever have. My male friends talk about it constantly.

Awee and I avoided that. It would have bored us straight to tears. We were lucky. Even with AIDS. Even with the microorganisms that attacked him. Even with all the frustrations and the pain. We could change our eyes—to see things differently—the way other people changed their shoes. New eyes, *yes!*

Awee had eyes the likes of which would melt the frozen mountains of the moon into oceanic pools of pyrotechnic blush. Deep, black, midnight eyes, the prince of devils, liquid ebony, from which nocturnal light was viridescent at the bottom of the well, a smoldering, like smoke. Black is never really black, it is a mix of colors, as Awee was a mix of thought and sparkle, a snapdragon who put new eyes in his head, and changed his colors, and the paradox of who he was every day.

Life was never ordinary to him. Even something as dull as a turtle stirred him. He wanted to taste the underbelly of the turtle.

With his tongue.

"No tasting turtles," I would say. He would shrug and laugh.

He could be dangerous in a pet store.

We did not miss television.

I hear moms and dads and kids fighting about television. What to watch. The same moms and dads who have programs that monitor their children on computers. You need *software* to do that?

I am taken aback, and wonder what they are talking, fighting about. We did not have a television, and we did not miss it.

I did not miss it.

Awee did not miss it, but he had to explore not missing it. To know the thing, such as what it was like to have fire-engine red toenails.

I am curious to see my friends who are parents impose rules on the watching of TV. What shows their kids can and cannot see. What websites their kids can and cannot click into. "Just throw the TV out," I say.

Whenever I say that, there is usually a moment of short but profound silence. A nice silence. Silence can be good.

"Well, we could never just throw it out . . ."

"Yes, you could."

Just throw the TV out.

Out into the snow.

All his silly secrets. "I used to like 'Spiderman,' " Awee said. "The cartoon." He threw his head back and then he laughed.

I can hear him now. The *reason* I was born, the *reason* I exist, was to hear Awee laugh like some errant goodness had escaped the evil, the clutching of the claws that is life within the universe. He could laugh *at* himself. It saved him many times.

"I thought I missed TV," he said. "But if we had one we wouldn't have our talks, I don't think we would. And I would miss them more than I miss TV. I love our talks so much. I feel good when we do them, and everything slows down, you know. I have a secret, too. And I'll bet you can't guess it."

We played guessing games a lot. I was supposed to guess the secrets. I would make a stab at it three, maybe four times, then he would crack the code for us stupid people.

"You liked cartoons."

"Warm."

"Your girlfriend is Natasha on 'Rocky and Bullwinkle.' "

"Cold."

"I give up."

"I *was* Spiderman."

More laughter. This time, outrageous laughter. Kid laughter. Kick up your feet in your pajamas laughter. Twelve looking back at itself—even as far back a lifetime as the age of ten—is the kind of laughter that can crack the night with light.

"You were Spiderman?"

"Yeah, and I used to play in the trees with ropes, and climb up real, real high. I was *really, really stupid, huh*!"

Well . . .

Maybe not as stupid as being Howdy Doodie.

"Did you ever hear of a guy on TV named Howdy Doodie?" I asked him.

"Who?"

"Never mind."

"Howdy Whodie?"

"I said never mind."

"*You were Howdy Whoodies!*"

"I was not."

"You *were*! I was Spiderman, and you were Whodee Doodies!"

"*Howdy* Doodie."

Twelve looking back as far into the deep, dark past as 1954 is screaming hilarity.

When twelve says *I have a secret*, it means it wants to know your secrets.

I was Howdy Doodie. He was a cowboy puppet. He did not leap over buildings. He did not capture bad guys. But he sang songs with Buffalo Bob, and he was nice.

"I won't tell anyone your stupid shame," Awee promised. "Your secret is safe with me. *My own dad was Dowdee Whoodie.*"

"Howdy Doodie."

Never tell a twelve-year-old you owned a Davy Crockett hat either. The Davy Crockett hats had raccoon tails. Then there was the Mickey Mouse Club. But even migrant children (fifty barefoot children in a migrant shack and one black and white TV) would *not* wear those nerd mouse hats. I was Zorro for a year, commandante. I did not tell him about my crush on Annette Funicello. He would have laughed the entire night, and I was trying my best to get him to go to sleep.

Awee, go to sleep, please.

I never liked going to sleep, Daddy.

I know.

It was the Sustiva.

I know. All those dreams. Sleeping was one of our bigger dragons. We never did slay that thing. A couple of hours here. A couple of hours there. You slept when you were exhausted, and sleep just sucked you up. I used to hold you while you struggled in the dreams, honey. I never took LSD. Tell me about the dreaming.

Everything was colors. But you couldn't look down. If you looked down, you would fall.

In your dreams, you lost your sense of balance.

"Did you have a *dad*?" he asked.

We were in bed. Many of our conversations occurred here.

It was intimate. It was where he lived.

That bed.

I told myself for a long time that I took the little apartment with the one bed at the fleabag of a hotel we lived in because it was cheap. There was some truth to that, but not the whole truth. I took the little apartment with the one bed at the fleabag hotel we lived in because I could *feel* him next to me. Breathing. Or not breathing. I was *there*. Whatever happened to him I would know. There were times when he stopped breathing. There were times when I had to pick him up like some limp, wet rag doll and get him to an emergency room. There were times when I did

CPR. There were times when I simply got him on a toilet *in time*. I think I took that dusty room with the one window by the fire escape with the *one* bed because I knew my own dad would have let me die. His skills at *being there* were not finely crafted.

"Yaaaaa. Most people have one—a dad."

Most people meant a sense of balance. There was me. And then there was this *other thing*: *Other People*. As a Navajo child you are taught from day one that you are not by any stretch of no imagination *alone* in this world. Whoever you are, however you are, your existence is balanced by the existence of Other People. In Navajo medicine, we refer to this as *hozo*.

An enigma not confined to medicine, *hozo* is a way of living.

To find balance in a universe of balance is to move your center of gravity from once place to another. This is essentially what the universe does. The stars. You.

You are the stars.

Ask any Navajo what hozo *is. He will walk away.*

That is what hozo *is.*

He is finding balance.

Life is about finding balance. That is all it is. Shifting and reshifting the center of your gravity. You are the stars.

"I had another dad. The one who had me."

Awee was examining his toes here. Pulling them apart. Counting them. Babies do that, too. But at twelve you are mischievous. He put his toes in my face. Wiggled them.

"Do you want to kiss my feet?"

Then he laughed again. When you are twelve, the idea that someone might kiss your feet is too outrageous for words.

I grabbed his toes and started biting them. They were fat little nibbles. He screamed, of course, and we wrestled.

This was *not* going to sleep. I am a bad, bad parent.

Even his funny toes were yummy.

"You hurt me! You bit my little toe!" He pretended to pout.

Awee, go to sleep, please.

No. No. No. I want to talk about this dad stuff. Your dad. My dad. I wish I was going to be a dad but I never will be.

You would have been a wonderful dad. Someday.

"Do you think about your other dad?" I asked him.

"Yeah. Sometimes. Like when I dream, and he is chasing me. I don't like that dream too much. He did hurt me, not like biting my toes, but like really. I am sorry he is sick. I wonder about them, and I think about them being sick. I feel bad for them. It makes me almost cry so I try not to think about it. Like I am bad cuz I left them to be sick all by themselves. When everyone in your house is sick then there is nobody who is making you food. Nobody chops wood. I got so hungry so I used to hitchhike to the store. I had my quarters. I would buy beans, you know, the kind in cans with sausages. If you eat all the beans in the can then you are not hungry but I was. You know, he would be drinking when he was sick a lot. And throwing up. I would try to help him, and then he would hit me. Did your daddy ever hit you? I don't like it when he is hitting me."

"My dad was a little rough, yaaaaa. It happens."

"I do not like it to happen."

"No. It hurts. It hurts to think about, too."

Awee would sigh, and snuggle down against me.

"Do you have lips?"

"Do I have lips? Yaaaaa. Most people have them. Lips."

He pinched my lips and then he pinched my nose, which did not come off.

To see if I was real, I think.

He had to know if it might all disappear.

Everything you think you know could turn out to be the landscape of Sustiva.

"I'll still be here tomorrow. For you. Okay?"

"Tomorrow is my birthday."

"Yaaaaa."

"What am I going to get, a present?"

He smiles.

"Do you want a present?"

"Yes. Very much."

My belly button does not come off even if you stick a finger in it and try to unscrew it. I gently remove his finger.

"I want candles."

I was afraid he might want to drip hot wax on me. To see if I would disappear or melt.

"Why do boys have tits?"

He was pinching his.

I would pin him down and bite his ear until he screamed into his pillow, laughing.

We never slept.

Sleep was for the sane.

He wanted us to buy birthday cupcakes so we could pass them out to the whores up and down the hall.

One of his favorite whores on the floor below us went by the name of Cupcake. He thought it hilarious.

I did not have either the stamina or the heart to tell him that Cupcake was not a female. It was not a door I really wanted to open, although eventually he would fling it open himself, and walk straight into the room.

He liked first-grade cupcakes. I think because he had never had them. I do not make them, but Safeway did. He liked cupcakes with huge red gobs of frosting, and sprinkles of junk that glittered. His friends, all whores, were not unlike his cupcakes.

Sometimes he got upset when he thought I thought him ridiculous. Nevertheless, there was a big part of him that understood I loved him the most when he *was* ridiculous.

Now when he told people he was twelve, it would be the truth.

The entire year he was eleven, he told everyone he was twelve.

It was his birthday. He was alive. No one really knew except the two of us the extent to which becoming *really* twelve was an accomplishment. He was beautiful in his pajamas. We had these little victories that meant so much. I reached under his pajama top. Touching his tender tummy. I pressed it just a little. He smiled. He had not shit the bed. No mess in the pajamas.

You take victories over dragons where you can find them.

Awee was learning to listen to his body. In new ways. In ways no one else could teach him, really. Most twelve-year-olds have settled comfortably into their bodies like that balanced, warm spot the cat sleeps in illuminated by the sun. And then they jump, their bodies reeling, breathlessly to run. But most twelve-year-olds do not have AIDS.

I saw his small body as heroic. Twelve whole years of war. Twelve whole years of fighting AIDS. This was an awesome body. A strong body. A beautiful body that would not give up. It wanted to grow and live. The mind was not always quite in alignment with the battles of the body. The mind of the child could be— and was—depressed. Just the pain from the peripheral neuropathy alone was enough to make a lot of folks take a long hard look at giving up. The mind of the boy was growing tired. I could see that. I know how to measure things like sadness. But the body of the boy had not given up. I am not sure it knew how. It was the body of a warrior.

Awee, I would have given you mine. My body. Once it was the body of a dancer. Now it's used and old. But you could have it. Awee, just give me all that pain, honey. I don't want you to have to live in all that pain. The razor blades, and the ice picks, and the swollen tongues, and when you pee it hurts, and, honey, please forgive me for allowing them to put those tubes in your penis, I am so sorry, Awee, that they did that. I know it hurt you. I know no one believed you about the pain. Honey, I believed you. I really did. I still do. If we could make a trade, I would exchange bodies with you in a minute. I know you hated your body, and you would get so mad at it. But it was perhaps the most extraordinary, fierce, fighting body I have ever seen. It was so determined to live. No matter what. No matter what the next challenge was. Tumors. Temporary blindness. Blood. It stood there at the top of the cliff you lived on, honey, and I could see the flashing glint of light bouncing off the sword you waged and raged your battles with.

Athletes get trophies, and scholarships, and awards for what their bodies do. They do not give awards to bodies that take on the dragon that is AIDS. Pneumocystis pneumonia. Countless fungal infections. Aspergilosis. Horrible reactions to the latex catheters that had been inserted, forced into his penis where his urethra had wept blood and had formed scar tissue. The onslaught of what science had done to him. The reactions to Zerit. Chicken pox. Shingles. Intestinal microorganisms that would wring him dry. Thrush. Herpes.

Drenched in shit.

"I don't want us to say that *bad WORD* like that *NO more!*" he said.

Shit.

The words we use are important.

I nodded. "Okay."

"Can we call it something else so it doesn't sound so . . . *disgusting?*"

We could do that. "What do you want us to call it? Hey, we don't have to call it anything. It's okay."

He sighed deeply. You did not push. You let him lead the way.

"We have to call it something. I need help. I need you. I can't do everything by myself. So we have to call it something. When we have to talk about it. In words. Why do all the words have to be bad words? Can't we just say pottie? I know it sounds like baby talk or something. But I am so tired of hearing shit-shit-shit. It makes me feel like I am horrible, and dirty, and a bad sickening thing. *Am I, Daddy?*"

"No, you're not. I know it upsets you. Awee, you have to have a bath after you're done, or the fungal infections eat the flesh right off your skin. You can't just run in there, do your business, and rush out. I know other guys your age handle it like that. I wish you could, too. But some of the things that come out of you are organisms that we have to be really careful to not leave anywhere on your skin. And then we have to put the antifungals on you to make sure. If we don't do these things, we start going down a road you don't want to go down. I know you don't. I know it embarrasses you and depresses you so if we can call it something to make it softer, let's do that."

"I know I keep asking you this, but, *Dad*, isn't it making you sick to clean it up all down my legs and everywhere? How come it disgusts me and not you?"

"You have taught me so much, guy. About myself. I never thought I could do this. I never thought I would be the kind of person strong enough to clean up someone's . . . shit. I thought I might run the other way. I wish I could tell you why everything has changed for me in the time we've been together. I am not the same guy who took you in. There is nothing, Awee, nothing you could do that would come out of your body that would disgust me. I am not that person anymore. Your body just astounds me all the time. It is such a fighter, warrior body. I want to keep it as strong as we can. I want us to give it a chance. I want us to take really good care of it. I want us to find ways that make it feel good, and ways that make it want to stay with us. I'm on your side. If we are using words that hurt you when you hear them, then, please, let us change that."

"Can't it just be pottie for us? No one else has to know how bad it is. Or that you have to help clean me. We could just say *going pottie* even if it is like some little kid thing to say. But there has got to be something nicer to say than fucking *shit*!"

There was a spot on the bathroom wall where his head had made an indentation. Always pounding.

This is where he had had to lean while I wiped his legs down. I asked him to stop it—the pounding—but it was one of those things he could not do. I had tried backing off. Huge open sores would form on the skin of his butt. He could not sit down. He would ask for help again.

"What do you want," I would ask.

"I want to be the kind of guy who says words like *going to the bathroom*. Even saying pottie is like a kid thing. But I need it to be a kid thing. For now. Like I am a kid. I'm *not* though. I'm *not* a kid. I'm *not*. But sometimes it's easier if you can be like a kid again. So if I am like a kid again, you can just clean me up, okay?"

"Okay. So we call it pottie for now. And maybe next week we'll call it *going to the bathroom*. Does that sound okay? Is that what you want?"

"Yes, please."

We drove the Harley to an intertribal powwow. Intertribal pow-wows are events where many tribes and clans come together and hold ceremonies and perform. Hoops. Feathers. Sheep. Drums. And hot dogs. We stayed in a place called the El Rancho Hotel and Motel. Old Route #66. The place is famous. John Wayne stayed there once. We saw his picture in the lobby. The day was desert dry, blue, and warm. We took a walk and bought Awee a headband and some moccasins. He could turn the head of any girl. I knew something he did not know yet. No one can teach it to you.

Girls are shy. Like he was.

We walked around the powwow. It was exciting.

Then, there was that almost startled look on his face.

I squeezed his hand, and we quickly found a bathroom. It was a State Park campground bathroom. We went to the far stall where we would be anonymous.

He sat down and held my hand.

It gets complicated with AIDS. It could be diarrhea. Or (and this was actually far worse) he could be constipated, which would really tear him up.

The narcotics he was on constipated him severely. But the parasites that could get into him (as he had almost no defense against them) could wring him like a sponge. We never knew.

His eyes are closed. I am afraid it might be blood this time. But no. Another father with a much smaller son, a toddler, goes into the toilet stall next to us. Awee was aware of them. The boy kept kicking. Daddy had to help. Awee could only grin and shake his head. Almost laughing. Laughing. At them. At himself.

We found the dances.

Shy girls in Indian skirts holding hands.

A circle of Indian people in a baseball field.

"I can't dance," he whispered. That look of sheer panic.

I was going to tell him that he would be terrific as a dancer when I spotted someone I knew.

Across the baseball field. Leaning up against a pickup truck. Drunk as shit and laughing with the other men. The bad men. The loud men. The men everyone ignores.

The man who had signed Awee away to me. The one with all his secrets.

The one Awee had dreams about. In my bed.

The one who was sick. The one Awee still protected. The one Awee was afraid of. Still.

I realized I was holding Awee's hand so hard, I was hurting him.

"If he sees me, he's going to come over here."

He did.

I am an old hand at talking to drunks. They will not remember.

The three of us walked over to the red rocks and away from the dancers.

The girls dancing in their scarves. We could hear the drums. We could smell the whiskey on his breath.

There was a lot that hung between them like the pow-wow dust.

Awee asked him if they were sick.

"Yeah, we're sick." He spat. "So what." Then to me: "You said you wouldn't *tell* anyone."

I had told no one. To this day, I have told no one.

"If people from our village find out, we will be *shunned*."

I knew what it meant. It could be life and death for them. Being shunned means no one picks you up—trips to town, food, and to the doctor—all of this is over. Shunned. They would be worse than lepers. No one would even look at them. Even relatives who had known them all their lives would stare past them.

"What are you two *doing here*!?!"

Dancing.

His red eyes flashed like wounds. "I'm drunk," he said.

Awee hugged him, or tried to.

He pushed Awee away.

It was an awkward moment. I am standing with the dead.

He had given Awee to me. He had asked me to take Awee even when he knew I would probably say no, and I did say no, at first. Drunks do one thing almost better than anybody else. They will wear you down to bone. His word was good. He had signed custody away to me. It had been an act of courage. It had been an act of selflessness.

You give people what they are due. He was due this.

He knew that he could no longer give Awee *anything*. AIDS had been enough.

"I don't want people to talk about me."

He did not want to be seen with us. It hurt Awee. It seemed to crush him like a bug.

We returned to the dances.

Awee had new moccasins. A girl gently held his hand. Both the girl and the boy were delicate.

Twelve is rarely hard, and if it is, it is usually an act.

I held his other hand. We danced round and round the tribal circle.

That night we put twelve candles on a pizza from Pizza Hut. Awee blew them out before they melted. We ate pizza in bed. In our blue pajamas.

"Can you guess what I wished for?"

I thought about it. "You wished for a visit from Spiderman."

He rolled his eyes. "*No.* I don't like Spiderman no more. I'm *twelve*, now."

Oh. My mistake. Forgive me.

"You wished that Natasha on 'Rocky and Bullwinkle' was your girlfriend."

"*Cold!*"

I gave up.

"I wished that nobody never never never finds out he is sick so I don't have to live with his fucking goddamn secret no more!"

We toasted the wish with Pepsi-Cola.

He slept in his sweat that night in my sky-blue arms, and I cuddled him, and kept him safe.

The room smelled like candles and pepperoni.

In the morning, he went pottie by himself.

I got a big, big hug. He thanked me for remembering his birthday. His other father had not remembered.

I was all ready to feel superior and smug.

"I forgive him," Awee said. "I am sorry for him to not remember me."

On the way home we stopped at Safeway and bought enough chocolate cupcakes with red frosting sprinkled with some kind of blue sugar glitter to feed all the whores up and down the hall.

Forgiveness. Awee would forgive us all for a cupcake. Whores. Poverty. AIDS. Fathers. Doctors. Everyone who had failed him. We were forgiven. *Hwiih* is the Navajo word for the idea: inside him, satisfaction.

Forgiveness. *Diildooh*. It is about to burst. Forgiveness like the flood. Tenderness and holding hands with silence and the girls. Twirls. In circles with the boys, and every warrior stud.

All of us who are engaged to this loss knew we had ventured out into such choked and wanton coyote deserts where our victories and the tyrants would be filled with wrongs. Attend him here in blue pajamas. It is the earth that sings his wreckage and his songs.

15. Jimmy Dog Is Building Houses

Imagine: You live in a Navajo hogan.

Out among the red rocks and the coyotes. Light comes in from the smoke hole at the top of the hogan. Or through the door (which always faces east). In a traditional hogan no windows face north. North is where the ghosts come from on the wind across the mesa.

It can get a little crazy in a small Navajo hogan. Families are crazy things.

Big houses in the suburbs where everyone has their own room to go to—to be alone—can still house families who are crazy.

Every family I know has a crazy cousin somewhere. Crazy Verna. Crazy Norbert. Crazy Wilma. Crazy is as crazy does. My crazy cousin has always been Jimmy Dog. Jimmy lives on the Navajo Rez. We call it the Big Rez. It's remote, and bigger than a lot of states. There are very few Navajo who have even seen the whole thing. Everyone in my family was worried about what would happen to Jimmy Dog when it was time for him to be out there on his own.

In the world.

My old aunts would sit around and cluck.

Jimmy isn't crazy. It's just how an awful lot of folks both on and off the Navajo reservation see him.

When we were little boys, only slightly younger than Awee was now, Jimmy Dog and I (and sometimes my brother) would hide at night under a thick pile of our Navajo rugs and blankets. So no one would find us and snatch us. It seemed that when the adults got together, there was always drinking.

Drinking was one of the great mysteries of our lives.

Drinking had been one of the first things Awee had asked me about, too. "Do you do drinking?"

I did.

Not *Do you drink* and then I could slide out of it and say only a little bit.

No. Do you do drinking.

Okay. I knew I was going to have to give it up. Tina did not approve either.

When we were children, it smelled bad, too. So many lives we knew revolved around it. Drinking could go on for days. It was loud. It was mean. People you loved screaming at each other. It was violent.

Folks got knocked around. Drinking was hungry. When the adults went on binges, no one made too much food. We hated drinking. Yet we were intrigued by it. People walked funny, and they never slept. They passed out right where they were. When we played *drinking*, someone always had to be the baby, someone had to be the mom, someone had to be the dad, and someone usually played grandma. All of these characters in our *play* family (including the baby) woozed around, and fell a lot, and passed out. We never referred to *sleeping* as *sleeping*. To us it was *passing out*. That was what we knew of drinking.

That, and people would vomit on you.

So Jimmy Dog and I would hide.

There is a whole universe of darker places where the spirit people lived underneath the shadows of a Navajo rug. If we curled up hard enough inside this place, chances were good we would not get snatched.

Getting snatched could mean anything from tolerating being slathered and mauled in whiskey kisses, to being thrown up against the wall. One was about as awful as the other. When people talk about Jimmy Dog, people always say: *Drinking did it.*

People will nod.

People said Jimmy Dog was slow. People said Jimmy Dog had FAS—fetal alcohol syndrome. The more fashionable thing nowadays is to say "fetal alcohol involvement." Whatever. I did not know then, and I do not know now what *slow* is. When we ran outside with the goats and sheep across the mesa, Jimmy Dog kept up. As best he could anyway. It was enough.

Jimmy always gave me presents. Sometimes it was embarrassing. Anyone who has *never ever* over the years forgotten my stupid birthday (not even once) cannot possibly be crazy. And Jimmy Dog can't even count. He makes a lot of notches in trees though. He's got his day tree, his week tree, and his year tree. The older I get, the fewer trees there are. Jimmy's presents are always the same. He does not surprise you. Even today, now that I am a long way from childhood, Jimmy makes the exact same thing.

The Navajo call them kachinas. They are made from wood. Carved mainly. Most of them look like warriors in masks. Children are not supposed to play with them. But Jimmy and I shared a secret (one of many). Kachinas were wonderful and exotic toys. Jimmy carved his from piñon pine. They are intricate. To a boy (like I was), they were highly valued. We did not have too many toys as kids. But we had kachinas, statues of the warrior gods. It does not come much better than that.

Our toys made the world.

Not the other way around.

Everyone knew Auntie Merlinda was a heavy drinker. Still is. When Auntie Merlinda woozed around the house, you did not want her to sit on you, or snatch you. When she had Jimmy Dog, he was tiny. Jimmy Dog is still thin as snakes, and limps when he walks somewhere, which is most of the time.

As a kid I was out of breath, and looking back, always looking back, at Jimmy Dog running to keep up, limping. He kept pace with all the boys. It was very hard, but Jimmy was determined.

Jimmy Dog owns a circa 1950 pickup truck. I would say Ford, but most of the things once in it from Ford are gone. Replaced by a corporate mix of junk found in junkyards.

When Jimmy moved out of his mom and dad's hogan, the news traveled like the Navajo wind flies across a sheep camp. His dad gave him goats and sheep. Jimmy has taken care of sheep most of his life. He herded them. Sheared them. Wormed them. Sold them. Sold their wool. And sometimes he ate them.

But Jimmy needed his own house to live in. When I heard that Jimmy planned to build his own hogan, I knew that Awee and I would go there. To help Jimmy Dog. We would bring some tools. Awee liked to pound things.

Jimmy Dog never saw Awee as anything other than absolutely perfect. He never treated him as anything less.

But this was not play.

This was real. This was building houses.

A Navajo hogan is usually round, or it has eight sides. The roof is often made of earth or sod. There is always a smoke hole in the middle of the hogan so the smoke (from your fire) can rise and escape the house. It would take us about two weeks to build a hogan. Jimmy collected his wood from the slopes of an extinct volcano called Ak'i Dah Nast'ani.

White people thinking: Well, if they all live in the same room, that means they can see each other bare-naked.

Yaaaaa.

The shiest folks anywhere in the universe are the Navajo. You will never seen one bare-naked. It will never happen.

Navajo who are raised in a hogan know this: The things you see are not necessarily the things you acknowledge. The divisions that exist between us that mean anything are the divisions we build from such notions as respect. Respect does not come from the construction of a wall. It comes from the construction of a family and a child from the ground up.

Jimmy lived in a canyon that can only be described as remote. Awee smiled broadly to see it. It was hours and hours from any town at all. Jimmy Dog could have lived in White People Town if he had wanted (there were residential programs for the disabled that would have taken him), but Jimmy could not see himself in White People Town. "Where would I keep my sheep?" he asked.

The sun and the fresh air and building houses (with the men) was going to do a world of good for Awee, who kept checking his muscles to make sure he had some.

T'aatsoh (May) is what we call the eighth month of the year. The heart of T'aatsoh is *ayehheeidiniyodi*, which means a mixture of rain and spring snow. *Nilch'ihdifhil*, the black wind, is its feather. The grass becomes a darker green. The antelope drop their young. *Nilch'iltsooii*, the yellow wind, shakes the earth, and there will be thunder. The flowers push up and open their petals.

It is the time to plant. Jimmy Dog would have corn. It comes in many colors. Jimmy Dog believes that people are not unlike the corn he grows.

It is a good time to build a house.

But what if Jimmy Dog got sick? What if Jimmy Dog got snowed in? What if Jimmy Dog was lonely?

All of this would come in time. It is only life.

But what if is not how Jimmy Dog lived his life.

Jimmy Dog remembers the Bad Winter when the People got snowed in and had to eat the ponies. Nothing could be worse than that.

Jimmy Dog did not eat his pony the winter of the Big Snow. He refused to do so.

Jimmy Dog and his mom and dad (and the pony) lived on piñon nuts Jimmy Dog brought home.

Jimmy Dog out there in the drifts among the piñon trees. And they say Jimmy Dog is dumb.

Jimmy Dog has two things.

Jimmy Dog has opinions. Most folks have them (Auntie Verna does). Jimmy Dog is of the opinion that drinking is bad. Just bad. No two ways about it. I refrained from even beer in his presence. In his world, up there on the high slopes of an extinct volcano, deep inside a canyon, many things are black and white.

The other thing Jimmy Dog has (that few people have) is a loom.

This is unusual. Even for a Navajo. Men do not weave. Women weave. It is not considered to be manly.

It is not reading or writing. But it is another way to see the world.

Jimmy Dog loves to weave.

He finds patterns in the clouds.

How many times have we herded sheep up the canyon so we could lie in weeds. To do nothing more complicated than watch the patterns in the clouds going by. Jimmy Dog is always weaving something in his head. Jimmy Dog measures the dimensions of the universe with his fingers, his tongue, his nose, his eyes.

Jimmy Dog gave up learning how to read. He gave up on learning how to write. He still maintains that (in time) he could learn to do it, but not when his teachers get so frustrated with him.

Still, what Jimmy does is unique. Grandma Yazzie down the dirt road takes Jimmy's rugs and blankets to the weavers' market in Crownpoint. Where she fetches Jimmy cash from the rugs she sells there. Grandma Yazzie with her cane, nodding to the tourists and the dealers from the boutiques in Santa Fe, as if she made the weavings that she sells. Collectors come to Crownpoint to buy what they think are Grandma Yazzie's rugs. I still think of Grandma Yazzi as a wily goddess. Grandma Yazzie has too many grandchildren rolling around her hogan to make a rug on a loom. You need time and patience. You need skill. There is artistry involved. The tourists do not know that the rugs they think are so special and intricate come from a man a lot of them would see as retarded. You are more than the sum of your diagnoses.

No indoor toilet. No phone. Jimmy Dog has never seen MTV. Auntie Verna thinks Jimmy Dog ought to move into the group home in White People Town and stop being a burden to society.

She worries.

Cluck. Cluck. Cluck.

She will never be invited (with her six-packs) up the hill to Jimmy Dog's new hogan. For one thing, old Auntie Verna is so fat she'd never make it up the hill.

Awee spent two weeks with his shirt off. His titties turned to ripe plums in the sun. Brown and pounding nails.

Building houses is heavy work. Sometimes what Awee pounded was his thumb.

Building something that is fundamentally round (and has a hole in the middle) is harder than it looks. But you could say that about Jimmy Dog, too. He is harder than he looks.

Awee and I would be dead tired near sunset, and Jimmy Dog would trot off to plant his corn.

"Is he always so . . ." Awee was looking for the word. "Busy?"

"I don't think Jimmy Dog has been bored for a single moment of his life," I said.

There is nothing worse in Awee's book than being bored. It is a great and incomprehensible agony.

Jimmy Dog was Awee's new hero. I was glad. Jimmy had never been admired.

By anyone. With the possible exception of Grandma Yazzi, who is probably Changing Woman.

"He knows so much," Awee observed.

Anyone who allowed Awee to pound nails and saw logs with the men and build houses had to be admired.

We were almost asleep on the ground in our Navajo blankets in the not-yet-finished hogan. Awee was beyond exhausted. I do not think I had ever seen him sleep quite so well or quite so deeply.

"You have a son," Jimmy Dog said.

In the dark.

His observations can be rather basic. This one had to do with loneliness.

"Yes, I adopted him."

There are many things Jimmy Dog does not know. There are many things about the world that he does not understand. But there are many things Jimmy Dog understands intimately.

"You love a woman, too."

Just a statement.

"Yaaaaa."

"It must be hard. Most women wouldn't want him being as free out here as you have let him be."

"He needs to know what it means to build something. Something important."

"A hogan is important."

"Yaaaaa."

"Like sacrifice."

Jimmy Dog was something of a sage.

There is no *self-determination* without sacrifice. Not for nations. Not for individuals. There is no history without the fragments of us who came before.

Our gods and ancestors and our masks.

Even old Auntie Verna had sacrificed when she did not have much (a few sheep). Three of the sheep from Jimmy Dog's new flock were from her. When we were little boys, and scared to death of the darkness on the way to the outhouse, it had been old Auntie Verna who had held our hand.

"What's adopted?" Jimmy asked.

"Well, you take another man's son, and you love him as your own, and in time he becomes your son, too."

"This boy loves you."

"It is nice you can see that. It's a nice thing, you know, being loved."

Jimmy sighed. "I will never have a son."

"Probably not. But you like your life."

"I like my life up here. I have my own hogan."

"And your own cornfield, and your own loom, and your own weavings, and your own goats, and your own sheep."

"And my own dogs, too."

"And your own dogs, too."

"Auntie Verna thinks I'm stupid."

"Yeah, well, Auntie Verna couldn't bend over to plant a kernel of the corn you are gonna pick."

"Remember, we used to hide from her inside the rugs."

Jimmy Dog was laughing in the dark.

"Yeah, she'd sit on us."

"And snatch us."

"And snatch us."

"And slobber us with all her drinking kisses."

"*Yuck!*" We both said it.

We had loved her, too.

Each child has what can only be his own, unique, singular childhood. The things I remember are not necessarily the things Jimmy Dog remembers yet both of us were there.

Each hogan measures about twenty to thirty feet in diameter. Yet we spent most of our time outdoors. Old Auntie Verna kept things where they belonged. Children learned where things go.

We as boys were very concerned, overly concerned, really, with where things *went*.

This is what got us out of diapers.

And quickly.

We boys were toilet trained (by guess who: old Auntie Verna) well before the age of two. I am amused when white pediatricians tell parents it's okay if kids wait until they're four.

This is a failure of parenting.

Bite the bullet.

It was harder for Auntie Verna to let Jimmy Dog go (not that far) to build his own hogan. She had had to walk (again, not that far) the path into the woods weeping so she could do it.

Handicapped is a cultural phenomena.

By four, we were herding sheep.

It was responsibility.

"I have something I want you to have," Jimmy Dog said to me.

Jimmy Dog got up and found a flashlight. He went over to his stuff and retrieved a yellowed cigar box.

"Here. When you have a son, it costs money. I have some. I want you to have it."

I took my own flashlight out and shined it on the cigar box.

It was an old cigar box with the image of an Indian headdress on it.

I counted over twenty thousand dollars in there. I was a little overwhelmed.

"I can't take this Jimmy. Just being here, you allowing us to help, that is more than enough."

I said it softly. I knew my refusal would insult him some.

This was his weaving money. His rugs.

Enough is relative on the slopes of an extinct volcano.

We would say prayers for the new hogan.

The Navajo are always emerging from yet another world. It is their history. Like the Insect People who crawled up through a reed. Letting go of what they knew before. It is the self-determination of *bi yeel*, sacrifice. Sacrifice is an internal space not unlike the darkness of a hogan.

Jimmy Dog was determined there would be a gift.

The intricately carved image of a kachina.

To Jimmy, Awee had been perfect. Awee had never asked to be treated like he was. But he was. By this man whose house was built from logs and sod. Behind the masks we wear, we are the warriors, and a little bit like a god.

16. The Trembler

We passed the old uranium mines after we left Jimmy Dog's new hogan.

There is a sign north of Church Rock where the road splits. The sign says: "Uranium Mine."

If you go one way (north), you run into one of the most god-forsaken places on earth.

If you go the other way (east), you end up at Smith Lake.

You cannot go west.

It's a little rocky.

South is the Church Rock chapter house, and west of that is Gallup, New Mexico.

That yellow you see stratified in the rock . . . that's uranium.

That is why they call the stuff that gets processed into pluto-nium yellowcake.

There is more yellowcake in this area than anywhere else on earth.

If the federal government had known that, in a hundred years, the land they were giving—as if it was theirs to "give"—to the Indians would turn out to be some of the richest mineral deposits anywhere on the planet, is there anyone out there who really thinks the Navajo would have been offered one single postage stamp–size piece of it?

No.

If the federal government had even suspected that the land had anything to offer at all, the Navajo would be living on twenty acres of insects on the Pecos River, not anywhere near such energy-rich deposits of uranium. The uranium has made many people rich.

All of them are white.

All of them.

The uranium miners are mostly dead.

Dead Indians.

Indians were worked to death as slaves by the Spanish for hundreds of years in mines that made Spain a wealthy country.

Indians, too, were worked to death in mines owned by Americans.

We call the Americans *stockholders*.

They abandoned their mines when they realized that the damage they had done to the environment—and the thousands of people they had murdered making yellowcake—was damage they were liable for. Liability means cash.

Some of the largest corporations in America simply declared bankruptcy in the early 1990s and walked away. If you're bankrupt, you're not liable for environmental damage, nor can you be sued. So they just packed up and left the reservation.

With the mess still there.

It is all still there.

Now, how are the Navajo going to clean up an environmental disaster that eludes even the resources of the Environmental Protection Agency? Easy. They're not. Where would they begin?

How many nuclear physicists are there among the Navajo?

This is a place where the wind kicks up the radiation in the dust.

The Russians have Chernobyl. We have Church Rock, but you've never heard about Church Rock or the radioactive accident that occurred there. An accidental spill released more radioactivity in the water table, and into the land, than was released at Three Mile Island.

It was a nonevent.

That is because to this day it is not considered to be *newsworthy*. They were only Indians.

It is, however, a matter of public record.

This place where the road ends also happens to be a great place to stop on a motorcycle. There is a chill to the air here. It is a place of coyotes, arroyos, dust devils, big jackrabbits, wild horses, and the wind plays voices on the rocks. Down the dirt road that goes south toward the caves there is a group of fine hogans where the Doyah boys live, and they have never once missed a day of school at Mariano Lake. They are fine, fine young men.

If you stop—and you should because there are few places on the earth that sing with such clarity—you will hear the Doyah boys playing on their bikes, up and down the old dirt road.

The shadows of the mines pulls history itself into a vortex of crevasse and sage. I climb to the top of an old yellow rock.

The mines themselves are like silent scars upon the earth. Landmarks among the Navajo sheep camps. The Navajo believe that the earth is their mother. Anyone who has ever lived on the Navajo Nation knows about the old uranium mines. If you want to climb fences, and trespass, you can walk around them. Many of them have been declared EPA Superfund sites, yet nothing has been done. Nothing has been cleaned up. No one comes here. It is a landscape of agony and ghosts. The carcasses of mining equipment are rusted everywhere. Like dead elephants. Artifacts from the past.

Even today, Navajo children who live anywhere near the abandoned mines suffer from conditions such as acute asthma and continuous nose bleeds.

I have tried teaching such children to read.

They must learn to read.

Just ignore the blood, okay. Sop it up, and suck it in.

And people wonder why such at-risk children—who typically live in inner cities, such as African-American children—do not learn their letters and their numbers.

Because they are trying just to breathe.

How hard can it be to understand that.

Acute and chronic asthma on the reservation is epidemic. The kind of asthma that at the Indian hospital (like the one in Crownpoint that you rush your not-breathing baby to) is treated with prednisone, which, in turn, cuts off the blood supply to bone. You can breathe again. But your bones die.

You exchange one kind of damage for another.

Just ask any grandmother (hardly a scientific study, but viable nonetheless) from Church Rock, Pinedale, Mariano Lake, Coyote Canyon (these are small Navajo villages the Navajo call chapters). Ask any number of doctors at the Indian hospital in Crownpoint, and you will be given a litany of horror stories about the old uranium mines. The doctors are adamant. The mines must not be allowed to reopen.

I have received anonymous letters from people who claim they will blow my head off if I oppose (in print) the reopening of the mines. For some people, mining jobs are all they know. You take away the work, you take away the man. To date, the Navajo have resisted extraordinary economic pressure.

Jobs.

The Navajo are used to being offered jobs.

Like driving trucks of yellowcake for minimum wage.

The mining companies (they all have new names now) want back in, now that uranium is profitable again, with Mexican breeder reactors going on-line, and they have spent tens of millions of dollars in an attempt to convince the Navajo that it can be safe. To mine uranium. Again.

Public relations experts have been called in from New York, Houston, Dallas.

To date, this public relations mumbo jumbo has failed.

Because it assumes that grandmother, while scenic, is a stupid soul. This is a mistake.

Grandmother Doyah wants to know why, if it's safe to resume the mining of uranium now, they don't just clean up the mess they left before.

Before . . .

They begin again.

Grandmother shrugs. They have never answered her question.

They have sent scientists (white men in suits). To explain to the Navajo how mining uranium is safe now. Grandmother is not entirely convinced these white men in suits know how to do anything except maybe lie to the Navajo.

Grandmother has consulted the Trembler.

His old hands still shake.

Not too unlike his voice. The Trembler was born into the Black Sheep People Clan (Dibelizhinii Dine) for the Bitter Water People Clan (Todich'ii nii Dine) many years ago — before grandmother. He had a name once — Curly Tso — but no one calls him that anymore, now they just call him the Trembler.

The Trembler's hands told him no. No to more uranium mines.

Even the Trembler wonders why, if children can be told that they must clean up the old mess before they begin a new one, why can't international mining conglomerates be told essentially the same thing.

To clean up the old mine sites would be to admit that what was left behind was nothing less than a disaster.

These stockholders will not admit to anything. Trust me. They all have lawyers, and their lawyers say: *Do not admit anything to grandmother, and if she continues with this line of questioning we'll file a motion to dismiss.*

Have you ever tried to dismiss a Navajo grandmother who wants to know why her grandchildren, who ride their bikes up and down the dirt road, have had continuous nosebleeds since the day that dust storm came?

It cannot be done.

And now you want her permission to construct *newer, safer* mines in her backyard. You *should* have tens of millions of dollars for a public relations campaign. You'll need it.

You might even want to take grandmother (and the Trembler, but his hogan is hard to find) to lunch at the Holiday Inn in Gallup. She likes the buffet table and the free toothpicks. She would like a glass of wine, too. That good stuff from France.

She will note that she makes better bread than this.

You could offer to give her a brand-new pickup truck. A nice one from Japan.

She could use a vacation in Maui, too.

She would like a room by the pool, please, and some of those drinks with the umbrellas in the glass.

You wanna build a what?

Oh, another uranium mine in her backyard, well, why didn't you just tell her that?

Grandmother likes the ice they use in water glasses at the Holiday Inn in Gallup. The ice reminds her of hell when it freezes over.

Deesk'aaz. It is cold.

In hell.

Many Navajo grandmothers had husbands who worked in those mines.

Grandmother does something not too many people do too well or too often.

She remembers.

Awee ate an apple as I surveyed the landscape of the Trembler on the top of my very yellow rock. Everyone in Pinedale knows that rock.

The Rio Puerco runs through here. I stood on this very rock when the radiation spill occurred. It was an accident. White people were sorry.

There were dead animals everywhere. I saw them. Dead cows. Dead sheep. Dead horses. Many grandmothers had to be removed and relocated.

Have you ever tried to move a grandmother whose final goal was to die, here, in her own hogan? She had lived a good life, a life of balance, and she owned many sheep.

How do you explain to grandmother that the water was poisoned now; the dust was poisoned, too; the animals were dead; and she was going to have to move to the Evergreen Nursing Home in Farmington.

There is no word or even phrase in Navajo that expresses the idea of poisoned water because who would poison their own water? It was beyond comprehension. And *who has done this horror to her sheep?*

There are still Navajo who drink the water from the Rio Puerco.

The idea that it is radioactive makes no sense to many traditional Navajo who have never traveled even as far as the Acoma Casino.

Which, as the Navajo will tell you (if you are stupid enough to ask), is *not* Navajo. It is owned by the Acoma. The Navajo have never, ever allowed gambling on their sovereign nation.

Many Navajo think of Gallup as far, far away.

Which it is if you are walking there.

Who *is* that old woman walking all the way to town?

We call her our grandmother. Because that is what she is. We will stop, and give her a ride because it is only right, and her feet are tired, and the night gets cold.

Why is her hair in a tight bun?

So no witches get her.

What if a witch gets in her hair? She will consult the Trembler.

His trembles have scared many, many witches back into their caves.

The Trembler lives in an old hogan in a sheep camp on the Rio Puerco. Awee knew of him, too. Everyone knows the Trembler. You can only reach him on a horse. Awee looked magnificent on a horse.

Everyone from all around knew we had come to see the Trembler. Many people do, although less and less.

Awee sat in front of the Trembler on the dirt floor of his hogan.

The twelve-year-old facing the ancient man.

Eyes shut. Touching fingertips. The Trembler trembled, and he sang some songs that trembled, too. The Trembler would know the future.

We live.

We die.

That is the future.

Awee smiled, and he cracked his eyes just a bit to peek at me to see if I was watching.

Yaaaaa. I was.

It took awhile to get there. To leave the bike behind. To rent the horses. It took even longer to do all that trembling.

It was growing dark. We would spend the night at the sheep camp.

It is hard for white folks to imagine that there are still places like this. But there are.

Like the Bedouin.

A sheep camp is nomadic. There is the coming and the going of the sheep. The movement to grazing land. The sound of bells on goats.

There was a family at the sheep camp with a boy not too unlike Awee. It was decided we would stay with them.

It is only fair to pay.

Grandmother took us in.

"We came to see the Trembler," Awee explained.

"I have trembled, too," the boy, a little younger than Awee, said. "I tremble when the sheep walk on me. It hurts."

They laughed. Like boys. This one slept with his sheep.

Outside.

It is hard for Americans to understand that many tribal peoples were assigned their names, and many Indians forget that that was once the case.

You needed a name to get food rations.

The names stuck. This one was called Cowboy.

Ray Cowboy. He was maybe ten.

He had never been to school. Ray did not exist. On paper anyway. Grandmother did not believe in paper.

They could neither read nor write. I asked Ray about his mom—parents—but grandmother gave Ray the eye. There were some things you didn't ask. Or talk about.

Much of the child rearing now is done by grandmothers.

Sometimes it seems that an entire generation is missing. I wonder where they went?

I envision some cocaine island in the Galapagos. Rocky. Barren. Great drugs. Crowded with walrus and failed parents.

Ray Cowboy runs around up here with the prairie dogs, the cottontails, the jackrabbits, the bobcats, the coyotes, the red fox, the rattlesnakes, the piñon jays, the bluebirds, the ravens, the house sparrows, the starlings, the red-shafted flickers, the rock wrens, the sparrow hawks, the red-tailed hawks, the mourning doves, the Grama grass, the Indian rice grass, the rabbit brush, the saltbrush, the juniper, and the Trembler.

Who only shook, really, at the fingertips.

I had heard that when the Trembler was young, more than one female had trembled in her moccasins at the suggestion of his trembled touch.

Many grandmothers brought him food. And trembled.

Grandmother Cowboy cuts off a sheep from the herd, holds it by the neck, cuts its throat, collects the blood in a pan, and proceeds to butcher the animal. Both boys watch intently.

They are sad.

But the Navajo dare not see their sheep as pets. Sheep are a measurement of wealth. Sheep are food. The sheepskins hang from trees so coyotes and dogs don't get them; the skins will fetch a price.

The blood is used for cooking. The old ways are almost gone. But not quite.

Yet.

There are no electric lights up here. You are with the sheep, and in the world. Stars do spit from other stars.

Ray knows the starway song, and sings it. He has never been outside the universe of the sheep camp.

Supper was potatoes, chiles, mutton, sheep fat, cornmeal. Boiled together in the stomach of the sheep.

Kneeldown bread. Decades and decades of kneeldown bread. Ray and Awee play and bathe in water from the sheep trough. I ask Ray if he will go to school. He glances at grandmother. Probably not. Who can blame her.

She is a lioness.

She has done well by the standards she knows. Ray is not obnoxious. He is not disturbed. He is polite, likable, smart, responsible, and he herds a lot of sheep.

Later, Ray Cowboy looks into the darkness of the mesa. A landscape unbroken by any structure or road. *"Eehodooziil."* I will know many things.

He will.

We sleep with our dreamcatchers beside us (not above us as is the usual way). My dreamcatcher is on overload. So many dreams to haul across the cosmos. Take my dreams away. My dreamcatcher works hard, sweats, and strains to do this work. To filter out the good things from the bad. It is not enough. Just take my dreams away. My dreams of squaws heavy under furs and ripe tits for baby boys to suck the milk from. Deep black-liquid baby eyes. Him kicking naked. I chew his toes. He smiles at me. To be here in this place with us. He touches me and I tremble. This universe that made him. Dream baby. From her. From me. From dreams. The dreamcatcher asks me to stop. No. You must do this work. For me. Catching dreams like grandmother catches the blood from yet another sheep into the pan. It has no choice. This one is made from string, old leather from a dead buffalo, and war feathers. It catches my dreams. Filters. I have no idea what it does with them. Only that I exhaust it. The dreamcatcher in my bed sees all my naked squaws who come here with their songs in their throat, and pin me down. And why is it I pick the ones who like to be on top? Who come with their necks thrust back, and Chiricahua lips wide open to stare straight into the abyss of, what else, a dreamcatcher.

"Daaaaaaaaaad. Daaaaaaaaaad. Are you okay? You're dreaming."

Must be my bones out here sleeping on the ground.

"*Yoo 'iiya,*" I say. I came here to see who or what was dying, and what I find is life trembling to what it knows.

Now I am the one who is lost in time as if it were a need. What boys who grow from soil as this, and watered like a seed.

17. Motel

Motels are nocturnal creatures.

Maybe we would stay the week. There is something about living in motels that turns everything into maybe. It would depend.

We had a rule. Do not decide anything until morning. The ice machine worked. The bed was soft. There is something that comforts us about motels.

Our favorite motel was the Motel Six in Tucumcari. Everything there was anonymous. The neon cowboys out by the road riding their flickering bulls hang tight. Just like the rest of us.

The gas station next door sells wind chimes in their asphalt parking lot, and the wind chimes play an all-night orchestration pushed to discontent by the desert wind that screams across the mesa not too unlike a wild herd of horses shaking the ground with blood and thunder.

Tucumcari is a place of hunger. Your stomach twists, cuts around that coffee knot, the waffles and the biscuits steaming grease and hot, the gum stuck to tables is always under, we have arrived to rob the bank, terrorize the town, and plunder.

We would sit in restaurants and concoct secret plots.

Whispers. Furtive glances. We were the bad guys.

Awee loved this.

Pretending to study our menus with the plastic pictures of frozen home fries.

"We could rob the bank and put our money in a pillowcase."

"Yaaaaa," I said. "Just hand it to the teller and tell 'er to fill it up, sister."

"Yeah. And then we drive our getaway car really fast and squeal out of there burning rubber cuz I'm the driver."

"You don't have a driver's license."

"Too bad. Twelve-year-old criminal scares the diarrhea out of Tucumcari."

"How about: Twelve-year-old with diarrhea scares Tucumcari Denny's during Thursday morning breakfast?"

"Do they got a bathroom?"

"Over by the pay phones. Do you need help?"

"I think I might."

"It's not a problem."

"It *is* a problem, Dad."

This is not good news. I carry a small, black backpack. I really value the bathrooms that are clean. Big towns rarely have bathrooms that are clean. Small towns sometimes have bathrooms that are clean. We were desperadoes. But we liked our bathrooms clean.

Sometimes the handicapped toilet worked best. It might be big enough for two. There might be room to hang the backpack on the door, and help him change. I had learned to carry an extra plastic trash bag for him to stand on in his socks if the floor was soaked in urine. We put a lot of ruined underpants in plastic bags, and threw them away. We stopped using those paper covers for the toilet seats because Awee could be in such temporary agony that they just got messed up. We had baby wipes. We had clean underpants. We had clean socks. Stuff. We hated floors that were wet, had never been mopped, and we carried our own disinfectant to wash our hands with.

We no longer used rest areas.

"You know what," he said to me as he was washing his hands in the Denny's broken sink. "White people look at us sometimes like we are the *dirty* ones. Dirty people. How come?"

"I don't know, honey."

"Daddy, I don't write words on walls."

"No. You are a nice person, Awee. You would never do that."

"Why do they write bad words on walls?"

"I guess it might be the same reason they leave the bathroom a mess. It's a public place. People need to use it. I guess they feel some kind of secret contempt for other people. They would never do these things in their own bathrooms at home. But it's like spitting on other people. And they're titillated."

"What's titillated?"

"Excited. That they can do private things in a public place. They can't make the adjustment. They feel like they can see other people and other people can see them. So the private rules don't apply."

"Like what private rules, please."

"Like we don't pee on the bathroom floor. We pee in the toilet. But they pee on the floor because it amuses them that someone else has to clean it up. They are never waited on at home. They don't have maids. So when there is, indeed, someone somewhere who has this job of cleaning up after them, they abuse the privilege."

"I don't think some of them had good dads."

We would head back to our table.

Slide in.

"Like you."

"Like me, what?"

"You are a good dad to me."

"Thank you."

I would touch his hand. He always ordered pancakes.

No one knew us here or anywhere. We drifted through the night like frost. Like an empty song in diminution, succinct, credit cards, and registration. Got a room for a sick boy, and his dad? I loved him, and the TV worked. We often turned the sound off. We were like fireflies in the bushes by a river.

Everything was blue. The neon by the door outside. No vacancy. The glitter on the gas tank of the Harley, painted there in flames. Our pajamas. The pool. Even the ice from the ice machine was blue. Having been perfectly chipped into perfect iceberg chips by ice gnomes from icebergland.

We vowed someday to buy an ice machine. Sometimes we bought champagne from the liquor store across the street. We limited ourselves to *one sip* and laughed as the bubbles hit our lips like tiny bullets. We laughed and laughed and played games with our toes.

He liked to read the signs posted behind motel doors. The fine print, too. He wondered what eviction was.

One motel had a laundry, and it was a nice motel, so nice that you didn't have to stand guard while your laundry dried. You could even leave it, and go play games. We played a lot of games. We would buy them in the toy department at Wal-Mart. I do not remember the names of the games. I lost anyway. All the games. All the spinning needles. All the spaces where you were supposed to move, and you could jump the other person's men. He knew all the rules because he studied them. Like law. He was a lawyer. The rules came in the box. On thin paper. You had to unfold the rules carefully, and study them. That was his job. My job was to spin the needle.

We both forgot the laundry in the laundry room.

I had no business letting him drink champagne. I had no business letting him buy his potato chips in the little yellow bags from the machines in the motel lobby.

He wanted to play a game where the person who lost had to strip in stages.

I was his dad. Not some guy he got naked with. His curiosity was the normal curiosity of a boy his age. But the nudity was too vulnerable. He pouted. He would not win.

"Well, I might get an erection anyways, and I don't want you to see it!"

The chances he would get an erection were not good.

This child was a conduit of pills. I had seen his erection once. Enough.

"Well, I don't want to see it. It's private. It's your private business, Awee."

Awee was not sure he had anything left that was his private business.

"Well, I don't want to see your erection either!"

I guessed he told me.

We drove to Wal-Mart.

Where I bought him a robe.

Buying him a robe was really not too unlike explaining to him why men urinate on the floor in a public rest room.

Trust me. There's a connection.

He turns around in front of a mirror. "It feels like a dress," he said.

I would make him wear it anyway.

He took great delight in my getting lost.

I do stop and ask for directions.

After five thousand miles. Of being lost.

He was never lost.

He knew the directions anywhere from just about every town.

He studied maps. He always knew where the parking lots were near an AIDS clinic. Sometimes I would drop him off in front of big hospitals where he would wait for me to go park the bike, and find him. Sometimes the hike from the parking lot to the clinic was too much for him. It can be blocks. We were going from clinic to clinic. One place might have a specialist who could deal with this. Another hospital or clinic might have a specialist who could deal with that. It was a blur of clinics and motels.

He found directions to the zoo in the phone book.

I packed our lunch (nice sandwiches from a deli), and his medication in the backpack. I was never comfortable leaving it in motels. If it had ever been stolen, we would have been up a creek. We are at the zoo. We are sitting in chairs and drinking pop. We both agree: The bubbles in champagne are better bullets. I hand him his pills, and he takes them. Classrooms of children run by. Children who do not take pills. Hundreds and hundreds of pills. I know he hates them.

Sometimes we hold hands. But not if boys his age are walking by.

Then, when he begins to tire, we hold hands again, and he doesn't care who sees us.

Sometimes I simply make him hold my hand so he does not wander off.

He had never done this. But I am fearful of things like AIDS dementia.

So I hold his hand, and not too many people look at us strangely.

Today will be a day without a nap. We take lots of naps. Today will be one of those all-day things.

Bedtime is not up to me anymore, and he does not fight me on it (he used to). Now his body just unfolds.

The ritual is that by midnight, I get him up again. I set him on the toilet, aim his penis down, and he pees. He never remem-

bers this. He is less likely to wet the bed. I have never understood why this upsets him to the extent that it does. It just does.
Wetting the bed can mean crying jags of such agony you might
think the world has ended. Or he refuses to speak to anyone the
entire next day. All he will do is hate his life and spin the needle
on some game. My job. He is so hard on himself.

We watch the elephants for a long time. He likes them. One is a
female with a baby. He watches them intently, but he doesn't
want to talk about it. His mother is an enigma to him. Whenever
he attempts to discuss her, something hard gets caught in his
throat, he literally gags, and his eyes fill up.

He is in enough pain. Most adult men could not cope with the
pain he copes with every day.

"Do you think animals love their parents?" he asked.

I know him now too well.

"Do you mean: Do animals who are parents love their
offspring?"

"Yeah."

I sort of drag him to see the coyotes. We have seen coyotes
before. But not in captivity.

"They love their puppies," he noted. "They really do."

Yaaaaa.

But it was the seals that did it.

Barking. Cavorting. Diving. We were there for hours. He
could not get enough of them.

The seals were sensual, curious, playful. A lot like him.

"The seals are in their bodies," he observed.

Fast through the water twisting. Showing off.

I got him now. In ways I had never seen before. I saw him so
absorbed by the behavior of the seals.

When he was naked, Awee was showing off. It was not, in

fact, sexual behavior at all. It *was* a showing off. Awee was in his body. I had taught him that it was beautiful. Now I needed him to cover it up sometimes. In his new robe. I am sure it did feel like a dress. I needed him to do it for me.

He was getting tired now. The schoolchildren were getting on their buses. We were climbing on our big motherfucker bike. He let them stare at him from the windows of their bus. Awee *in* his body. Showing off.

We made it home to our motel. The lights at night to blue. Blueness is the glow of ice, and blueness is the moon. Playing games, and spinning the needles. He stays asleep till noon.

18. Secrets of the Mountain Gods

No one is supposed to tell the tribal secrets.

It is forbidden.

That is why you see only one name here—Nasdijj—I do not use my last name, or what is called my "white name" in my writing because the consequences (to my soul) would be dire. I do believe that, but I do not ask anyone else to believe it. I do, however, ask them to respect the fact that I do. I would be exiled from my world. I do not say that my world is the world exclusive to the Navajo. My world is the world of the high mountain desert. I would be banished by the gods I believe in.

From the earth.

I left that white name long ago. I am a mongrel. Not unlike the wild ponies that run around here like they own the place. Like them, I have no pedigree. I belong to a fraternity of coyotes. Nothing more. Not only am I *not* him, I don't remember him.

The person who tells you about the things I love—like dawn's first light into the door facing east of a Navajo hogan—is not the person who had that name. I would be destroyed. My loved ones would be destroyed.

That is how the Holy People see it. That is how I see it, too.

There are many powerful songs that should only be heard by those who sing them. There are songs (the Navajo would say "sings" not songs) that are not meant for an audience. There are sings that require participation.

Where you are *in* the thing.

For the Navajo, being *in* the thing is a fundamental concept required for correct living.

Wellness.

This is why a Navajo sandpainting is usually made with a Navajo *person* physically *in* the thing. The sandpainting is constructed all around you as you sit inside of it.

Not like being in church.

You are the church.

You are thinking: *I understand.*

No. You do not understand.

You do not understand the *power* of a sandpainting.

If you are white, you have never seen one. Those things you can buy in stores that sell Indian trinkets are *not* sandpaintings.

Traditional Navajo roll on the ground in laughter (this is an internal place, too, not an external one) at the *notion* that you could hang a sandpainting on the wall.

Of your house.

Like: *Oh, look at what we own.*

Like: *Your name is who you are.*

Your name is external. Who you are is somewhere on the inside.

I am Nasdijj. To become again. I cannot own it. I can only *be* the thing.

You cannot own wellness. You can only be open to it.

A *hataalii* (there are many ways to spell it) is a Navajo medicine man who performs healing ceremonies. The sick person sits

on the floor of a hogan, and a painting made from sand is constructed around him. There are songs.

Often there is a sweat before the song.

Awee enjoyed these. He would be shirtless. The water would
come pouring out of him.

Then we would be ready for the sandpainting.

This kind of ceremony is called a sing.

It is very complicated. It takes decades to learn how to become a *hataalii*. There is a rigorous training. It is an extraordinary path.

Do I, a modern person, believe in this mumbo jumbo stuff?

More than you can ever know.

Why?

Because I have been there. I have seen it, felt it, tasted it,
been carried away by it, saved by it, tested by it, and I have heard
the songs. It goes far, far beyond anything I could ever write in
words.

The Long Body Gods speak to me. Me, a mongrel. A mix of
cultures.

There.

You see.

I am doing it. Again. I am telling the secrets of the tribe. I
hang my head in shame. I do.

But you need to hear this.

Dad!

What, Awee?

Tell them about the Navajo way in medicine.

Tell them what?

Like with handshakes. All that *stuff*. You know, Navajo stuff,
Daddy.

You mean if they were to sort of *know* us?

Try, Dad.

But I am only a coyote out here howling.

Try, Dad.

HANDSHAKES: We touch hands but it is only a touching of hands. We find a firm grasping of the hand, and pumping up and down, to be quite disconcerting.

EYE CONTACT: We find direct eye contact with white people to be rude. Please. Our souls live in there. You do not automatically have permission to just stare into us. It's intrusive.

TIME: In physical matters we often refer to time (like when you ask us when something started) by the lunar cycle, not the white calendar.

TAKING A MEDICAL HISTORY: We are suspicious of this. If you are a healer and at all intuitive, don't you *just know*?

TOUCHING US: It would help if you would respect us enough to inform us you want to touch us in intimate places and why, and you need our permission to do it. Do not *plunge* ahead assuming we have given you our consent when we have not. Our response to this kind of arrogant invasion will be to simply not come back.

POINTING: We do not point with our fingers or our arms. It is considered barbarian to do so. We point with our lips and our noses.

RELIGION: Do not assume anything. Some of us use peyote. Some of us are Christians. Some of us have been born again and born again and born again.

RACE: Do not assume anything. We might have Spanish blood in our veins. We might not know who our parents are or were. We might only know who raised us. We do not think it is your business to probe, or to hold us up to the ridicule of being someone's bastard.

WE WANT OUR THINGS BACK: Scalp hair, even placentas. We think it is our right to properly dispose of these things. So they are not used by witches against us.

WE DELAY DECISIONS: We consult our families before we decide on things like surgery. It is not always easy to assemble the family. It takes time. But we do.

WE WILL TRY TRADITIONAL HEALING FIRST: We will go to a ceremony first. Then we will try the white way.

PRIVACY: Please understand that we do not want you to share our X rays and pictures with people who do not have to see these things. We find this invasion of our privacy to be beyond abhorrent.

OUR HOMES: Our homes typically have no running water, no indoor toilets, and no electricity. So please take this into consideration when you design treatment plans that require medicines to be kept cold and things to be kept sterile, and please do not look down on us for not having these things.

COURTESIES: Phrases like thank you and excuse me are infrequently heard in our culture, but please do not assume that we are not thankful. Usually we need time to get to know you.

REFERENCES TO THE FUTURE: Please be aware that when you say things like "if a man does not wear a condom when he has intercourse, he stands at risk of acquiring HIV"—to many men this statement means it is going to happen. And why should he change what cannot be changed? Be careful how you discuss future events and their consequences.

TRADITIONAL HEALERS: Crystal gazers, herbalists, stargazers, and hand tremblers are not New Age, cosmic enigmas to us. We have lived with these things for thousands of years and in harmony with the earth. When you belittle these things, you are only exhibiting your own stupidity, and why should we entrust our care to someone ignorant enough to belittle something far, far bigger than his own knowledge probably extends?

Awee understood. Awee was the only one who understood my nightmare and my struggle.

How to paint a picture of something that is mostly veiled.

I am now going to tell you something you will not like and you will not understand. But I am going to tell it to you anyway.

If a biomolecular scientist from UCLA were to come to you and explain exactly how an antiretroviral medicine works on the protein molecules of the virus we call HIV, would you believe him?

You would be wise to.

Would you understand everything he told you about how this virus invades cells and replicates?

Probably not everything. But maybe some. The rest you would take on faith.

That is what I am going to do here. I am going to tell you about a world you do not know. You will not understand all of it. Maybe some. The rest you will have to take on faith.

Awee comes to me. His voice is a little different here. It is not twelve. It is more fifteen. Deeper than the voice I used to know when Awee was, let's say, eleven (my favorite age, when my nighttime stories can still scare them).

Sometimes the voice breaks. I am so pleased to hear it.

"These secrets are from the Mountain-Top-Way," he said.

"Yes. I am afraid."

"You are afraid to tell the secrets."

"Yes."

"But if you don't, how will anyone understand what we have been through together?"

"I want them to know," I say.

"Why?" he asks.

"This going back and forth you and I do between the Navajo way and the white way—in medicine—if I don't articulate some of that, all I am left with is a screaming rant, and the rant is just a lie. In the rant, all I am left with is my rage with white people, and how horribly indifferent they are. All I'm left with is going to the top of the mountain at night in the rain, during an electric storm, and shaking my fists and screaming at lightning until I have no voice. White people turn off the rant. I do not know why. But the rant is only half the truth. I want them to know the whole truth. That there is earthshaking power to the Navajo way. I do not say that as a Navajo. I say that simply as someone who has been around it. That it is as real as anything Anglos have created with their molecular medicine. It is only another way of seeing things. The white way does not have a monopoly on reality. My whole life is about taking one arm and pulling the ways of the people to me, and taking the other arm and pulling the modern world to me, and when I do this, it's like confronting matter with antimatter, and the thing . . ."

"Explodes."

"Usually."

"I can help."

"How, Awee?"

"You write. Then, you will read it to me. I will sit and listen like I do when we do the Mountain-Top-Way. With my eyes closed. If the words you use are pulling the Navajo way into a bad place, I will know it. I will tell you to not go there. Or if the words you use are just the rant, I will know that, too. I will tell you to not go there. Then we will do the thing together."

"You will do this for me, honey."

"Dad, we do everything together."

The Mountain-Top-Way is a nine-night chant. The last night is the Fire Dance. The Mountain-Top-Way treats the infectious diseases from bear, porcupine, or snake. Bear sickness is mental balance. Porcupine sickness involves kidney, bladder, or stomach trouble. The main symbols used in the sandpaintings are the Mountain Gods (or their hero, who they call the Prophet), the Long Bodies, Changing Bear Maiden (or her home), the Great Plumed Arrows, the Bears, the dens of bears, the Porcupines, the Snakes, the Feathers, and the Rainbow People.

All of these gods speak to me. A mongrel.

I take Awee to them. To the mountaintop.

The Prophet escaped from his captivity. He visited the homes of the Beings to accumulate the ceremonial knowledge. The Prophet came to the home of the Mountain Gods at Chokecherry. The Mountain Gods gave him the Great Plumed Arrows and taught him the dance which I will not speak of here. The shaft of the arrows is made in two parts. Half wood, and half hollow weed. In the Fire Dance, the Mountain Gods swallow the arrows. They teach the Hero to use the bow for hunting and defense. There are two male gods, and two female gods. The Long Body Gods hold a quiver and four arrows. They stand to protect the Rainbow God. The East is guarded by Big Black Fly Gods.

For nine consecutive nights you are brought into this world.

You hear them, see them, smell them, touch them, and you are pulled into a place that you will be told (by sane white people) does not exist.

But you were there. You know.

His fingers touch my face. My eyes. My lips. He is telling me to write about the healing ways. I am not betraying anyone or anything. The tree still stands.

Our world is filled with Holy People and with the gods.

These beings are represented by everything—animate and inanimate. The Holy People are the colors, desert winds, the

San Juan River, animals, men, children, women, directions to Shiprock, sky, earth, the clouds to weave.

This is the spiritual world, and it, too, has devils, taboos, evil spirits.

I see them come alive inside a sandpainting. That is why I say a sandpainting is a thing of power.

Many medicine people wonder (and I wonder deeply about this, too) if humans should even make sandpaintings. They are that powerful.

When a Navajo is sick, it is because a deity has been offended.

He must regain his balance with nature.

This philosophy is not at all at odds with another philosophy that says: *To regain his balance with nature, the patient must be able to produce helper T-cells, and in order to do that, the HIV virus must lose its ability to replicate so easily.*

There is no contradiction.

In Navajo medicine, as in Western medicine, the patient "submits."

Today I go up to a mountaintop. There are people who want to help me—I am now a man who lives on crutches, who walks slowly—but I tell them softly I must go alone. I leave them to their world.

I go into mine.

I submit to it.

It is January. Yasnilt'ees, the fourth month of the year (melting snow). Its heart is *tin* (ice). *Akiisda'hi*, which awaits the dawn, is its feather. That is the milky way. The young men hear the sacred stories, and learn to become the singers and the shamans. Grandmothers prepare to grow corn. There are many ceremonies in January. The women cook the food and take part in the women's rituals. The coyotes breed. The mongrels howl.

I have a cradleboard on my back. It is clumsy going with the crutches.

I never made Awee his cradleboard. He was too big. Then, *time*. There was no *time* to make a cradleboard.

We submit to time.

I made a cradleboard. I have a workroom in my cabin with my tools. I like to touch them.

I like building things. I like to use my tools.

Daddy, you are making me a cradleboard.

Yaaaaa. For you.

We will bury it in the leaves!

Yaaaaa. At the top of the mountain.

I want to be in it.

You can be in it. You are a whisper now. Such a little boy.

I take him in his cradleboard to the mountaintop.

I stumble in the mud. It is okay.

The cradleboard blanket from grandmother is blue.

I am fastened to the earth with a rainbow. In the yellow world, there was no sun. I bring my *jish*. There is corn pollen in the *jish*. I blow this into the wind.

We dig a hole in the leaves to put the cradleboard in. To bury it forever.

Daddy, I submitted.

I know, honey. You did good. You were a good boy.

Daddy, I let the doctor do touching me. Like you said.

You did. You put up with a lot.

Daddy, I took all my pills every day.

I know. There was nothing more you could do.

Daddy, it was not all bad and mean and horrible. There were good things in what we had.

Tell me about them, honey. No one can banish you. No one can hurt you now. No one can exile you to some cold place. Tell me about those good places we went to, Awee.

We rarely left the bed, Dad. But you weren't afraid to sleep with me. Our tiny little universe was no bigger than a bed. I would get those fevers, and you were there to hold me. Sometimes you kissed me. No one ever did kissing me. You were not afraid. Daddy, you could pick me up! Daddy, we rocked and rocked and rocked and rocked. You were my daddy so much! You will always be him.

You bet I will.

Daddy, you hummed songs in my ear.

The summoning of the gods.

They came.

Yes.

You put me in the sandpainting. I know you did. I remember, Daddy.

What do you remember, honey?

Corn. Beans. Squash. Tobacco. White. Blue. Yellow. Black. There was White Shell Peak in the east. Mount Blanca in Colorado. It was the dawn. Blue Turquoise Mountain was in the south. Mount Taylor in New Mexico. It signaled the sky. Yellow Abalone Shell Mountain was in the west. It was San Francisco Peak in Arizona. That was the twilight. Darkness belonged to Black Coal Mountain in the north. Mount Hesperus in Colorado.

We could see it all.

Yes. We did see it all. In that little time we had.

Where are you now, baby?

Iikaah. Place where the gods come and go. You touch me when you touch the sand. Put some on your forehead, Daddy.

Awee, what happens now, please.

You know.

The sandpainting must be returned to earth. It is not a thing for walls.

When can we be together again, Awee? Please, I have to know.

We are together now.

When can I hold you again, honey? I need to hold you, please.

Just touch the sand. I am there.

When will I be able to hear you? I need to hear you. I never got enough *kisses*!

My songs are in the sings.

I lost you in the dreams when you slept to shake and shiver.

You find me, Daddy, in the dancing voices of the river.

19. That Swallowed Us

It was this huge place that had swallowed us. He was just a boy. I was just a dad. That was all we were. We were waiting in this huge place that had swallowed us.

We were sitting in a waiting room.

I was trying to be patient. Quiet. Well-behaved.

At first, Awee was silent, and he sat there like a nice boy with his hands folded politely in his lap.

From time to time he would wring his hands as if there were insects in his head, and they were trying to get out through the sockets of his eyes.

His legs dangled. They almost touched the floor. But not quite. Or maybe it was just the way he was sitting. But he would swing his legs like they were pendulums that kept record of time as only he defined it.

Then, he would cross his arms. Head down. Looking at his shoes like there was some small speck of dust there that held his attention like nothing else could.

"Why don't you read?"

"I can't read."

"Why?"

"Dunno."

He curled up like a ball in his chair. The other people in the waiting room, flipping through magazines, did not take any special note of us. "Daddy," he whispered into my ear.

"What, honey."

"I don't want them to see me. Only you see me, okay."

I did not understand.

Then, I understood.

He meant naked. He did not want people (especially girls) to see him naked. I admit I had made him worse. I had told him that *no one* was to touch him, and *no one* was to see him naked.

I wanted him to be safe.

I was unsure. I did not want to sit in this hospital waiting room that had swallowed us, and negotiate deals with Awee I could not keep. I knew better than to pat him gently on the head and say something stupid like: *Nobody is going to hurt you, or see you, or touch you, or dehumanize you.*

These were things I could not negotiate. I did not have that power or authority. We were here to try and take what we could, and then if there was any luck involved, we'd try and leave before the beast that was this place crushed us completely.

"We just have to do the best we can, honey. Now, sit down, and be patient."

He did not sit down. He was on his knees and sideways in his waiting room chair, and whispering with his hand cupped to my ear.

"Daddy, I don't want them to do touching me."

This is where I am supposed to say: *It will be okay.*

But we have been through this too many times in too many places.

"Daddy, I want to go home. I feel okay."

He gave my cheek a kiss. This is where I am supposed to melt. I do. Melt. On the inside. On the outside, I want him to see a doctor. I want his blood checked for viral load. He did not feel okay.

Sometimes he had trouble breathing.

When he slept, I could actually hear the crackling deep inside his lungs.

I was glad I slept with him, or I might not know about it.

Sometimes the razor blades he walked on were too much, regardless of the pain medication.

The morphine was becoming less and less effective. He had been bugging me about allowing him to play baseball. I knew that if I allowed him to play baseball he would eat a lot of his pain and say nothing. I did not want Awee to be in pain because it just made it that much more difficult to get him *out* of pain.

His rectum bled. It was raw and sore and eaten up by fungal infections. No matter what we did. *Oh, just buy that over-the-counter cream, that ought to help.*

But it didn't help, and they didn't care.

He could not sit still in some waiting room chair for very long.

There are always walls to climb.

The reason I write about it over and over and over again is because all of this stuff would kick up over and over and over again.

Like a jackass out in the barn that really does not like you, and no matter what you do, it just isn't going to like you. *Ever.*

It was not a onetime deal. It was his life. It was my life. It was over and over and over again. The good periods would last for a while.

Then it would all descend again.   ·

The fungal infection had crept up and now involved his testicles and his groin.

He was having trouble urinating. When he did urinate, it hurt. He cried a lot.

There was blood in his stool.

There was blood in the junk he coughed up.

There was thrush like cottage cheese in his esophagus. I was afraid it probably went all the way down into his stomach.

The chances they were not going to want to touch him or see him naked were not good.

And I was supposed to allow him to play baseball?

We both knew I would.

The nurses often yelled at him. When they did this, it would take everything I could do to control myself. It made me shake. It made me literally have to back up against some wall, leaning on it for support, so I would not fall down. Please, don't yell at him. They did not need to yell at him. He could be reasoned with. You had to take time to do it. You had to go gently.

It is as if you are driving some old rickety truck on some wet and rocky road where treacherous is no abstraction. And you take it one very careful inch at a time so the vehicle will stay together.

"Daddy, I have to go to the bathroom."

You do not say: *Can it wait?* It cannot wait.

We find the bathroom. He makes sure I have locked the door. It takes awhile. In there.

We return to the waiting room. To wait. It has swallowed us completely.

I am holding his hand and I see that he is losing it. He has grown hot.

I go to the window.

The window where the magic nurses live.

"I'm sorry, sir. We're very busy today. And we're doing the best that we can."

So were we.

"Daddy, everything is going wrong."

"No. It's not."

I scratched my head.

"Awee, I want you to tell me what you want to happen. You're a very informed guy. You know more about HIV than most of us. What's going on?"

We kept our voices low. There was a TV placed on a shelf near the ceiling of the waiting room. People were pretending to watch the soaps.

"I might need an antiretroviral change. My viral load is probably way up, and my CD4 count is probably dropping."

He felt the lymph glands in his neck. They were tender and they were swollen.

He sighed. "They will have to take my blood to know . . ."

He winces.

". . . but I already know. And then there will be a long wait to get the test results back. And then you have to hope that whoever makes the decisions here is smart enough to match the genome testing to the right drug, and just doesn't reach into their bag of tricks and take out any old drug that comes to mind. If they were smart they would just do the genome testing now, but we don't always get a smart one, and they don't like it when you know more than they do. They get all nasty. You never know. But they are gonna make me be naked. The girl ones are gonna see me. They're gonna touch me. And it's gonna hurt. I wish I was dead."

"Let's talk a little bit about what's right."

"Nothing is right. Nothing."

"What do you want?"

"I want to sit on your lap and you hold me, and then we will just wait until we go in, and then don't go anywhere, okay."

I could do this.

Even swallowed.

By the time we got into the examination room, his fever was worse. The Minnie Mouse hospital gown did not help. He did not care about Minnie Mouse anymore. They yelled at him. Poked around inside his rectum. Took his fluids. Made him weep. Looked down into his esophagus.

It would be better if they kept him.

But it was up to me.

Always.

They are impatient. They know we have been through all of this before.

I go slowly here. With them.

For all their gruff toughness, for all their seeming indifference, their clipboards, for all the hostility they exude, I decide (I do not know why) that it is all a cover-up. In the face of evidence that would indicate otherwise, I decide that they are only people who do not want to get too involved with a child who could die, and if he died, it was going to hurt a lot.

If Awee died, I could go fishing.

But they had to care for the next child.

They were not yelling at him to get his clothes off. They were yelling at him not to die.

I bite my tongue. I am curt with medical personnel. I do not want them to know the depth of my contempt for them and these places.

I need them.

I need them to do the right tests. I need them to prescribe the right drugs. I do not need them to wash their hands of us because we are beneath them. They would never comprehend the enormity of my contempt. What I need them to understand is that we have been here many times before, and that the dividing line (for us) where they get to keep him is that dividing line that separates life from death. We were not there. Everything that was wrong with him could be treated. They wouldn't like it. But we would be willing to come back (we were always coming back anyway) if they were willing to write us the scripts we needed, and let us go.

Doctor's scripts make a particular unique sound when they're ripped off one after the other.

If the bleeding continued or got worse . . .

Yaaaaa. Yaaaaa. Yaaaaa.

I listen intently. Smile. Shake my head a lot. What nice, smart, caring people. Just don't touch me. Yes. I do know exactly how serious it is. I live with it.

I clean it up.

I rock it to sleep.

I cook for it and feed it soup.

I bathe it and soothe it.

I pay for it.

I give it much better care than it gets in your hospital.

And they know that. They know that in their bones. Because this huge beast they tend to has swallowed them, too. Swallowed them, but it does not fool them. There is a difference. Swallowed them a long time ago. Swallowed them whole. There is no *them* outside their skin of what has swallowed them.

Tissues. He blows his nose. A nurse will help him dress. His underpants have blood on them. I have clean ones in the backpack.

"No," he tells her. "My dad will help me."

He does not want her to touch him. He feels betrayed.

I dress him. He limps down the hall. I pay.

The scripts are in my pocket. We will have to stop and get them filled. There will be another wait.

It is dark by the time I put him to bed. I figure out all the new pills. We will get through this one.

He decides what kind of soup he wants. It is important that some things be left to him. That not everything be removed. Taken from his person.

Turkey noodle.

He slurps it.

"Do you want some?" he asks.

Yaaaaa.

He holds the spoon to my lips.

He pinches my lips.

I have fish lips.

I slurp some with his big soup spoon.

He laughs. He knows I hate this stuff.

That is not what is important. What is important is that some things *are* right, and not everything has gone wrong. An awful lot. But not everything. What is important is that not everything has been swallowed by some snarling beast of hate. Some things still belong to us.

Like turkey noodle soup and fate.

20. Baseball

I do not know what it is about Navajo boys and baseball. Every Navajo boy I have ever known has had a love affair with baseball.

Even the little ones. The tiny runts in the back of the field. So far back no one knows they're there. Specks. Out there in the heat with the jackrabbits. Hoping against sanity and hope that someday the ball will come to them. It never does.

You are seven years old, and you do not have a mitt. No way in hell your mom is spending money on a mitt. It does not matter how badly you want one.

"Baby, you wanna mitt," your mama says. "Go get a job."

You go out on the back porch and pout. No mitt. You'll show her. You'll go play baseball without a mitt.

The seven-year-olds would show up without mitts. All they had was this desire, really. It was the first time you had really left the sanctuary of the house to *show her* you could do it. Someday some wayward pop fly was going to make its wayward way to you. You. You would catch that ball—looking up squinting into the ball of fire that was the sun—your lungs filled with the smell of dust and sweat, and the sting from it, the sheer hurt that rang through you would stay with you forever. You did not know (or care) if she had seen you. For the first time in seven years, you didn't need her. You were doing this for you.

Do not drop the ball.

People were screaming. Do not drop the ball. You stood there with the ball in the thing that had been your hand.

Now, if you ran fast enough, they were going to let you bat.

I do not know how Awee found the team of boys who were playing baseball in the city park. I'm not sure I was listening. Okay, I pretend a lot. I smile. I'm nice. I nod my head.

"You're *not* listening to me!"

"Huh?"

"*DAD!* I said I found a baseball team and they want me to play with them. You don't listen to me—*Daaaaaaaaaad . . .*"

Play baseball. What baseball. What team. What city park. And why?

"*Daaaaaaaaaad. Pleeeeeeeeeeze.*"

Baseball? Shit.

Who *told him* he could walk around the neighborhood like he was feeling better?

"*You did.*"

Oh.

Him. Me.

I was ready for a lot of things. Disaster. Volcanoes. Hurricanes. Earthquakes. War. Tina.

But not baseball.

Some normal thing. "It's only baseball," he said. "And I really want to."

There are four answers to the questions kids ask.

Yes.

No.

Maybe.

I'll think about it.

I would have to think about it.

I wondered if we could do this and get away without saying anything about You Know What.

Awee took me to a baseball practice. We watched from the bleachers. The other boys knew better than to bug us. They knew what this was. I saw those little waves they gave him like they were wishing him good luck. This was a dad out *thinking about it*.

This was one of the good periods. For however long it lasted.

We were having our dinner. He could sit at the table now. Nothing bled. He could breathe (it helps if you want to play baseball). The neuropathy was being kept at bay.

"Okay," I said. "But I don't think we should tell them. I know that sometimes it just comes out. And we've even bumped into people from the hospital who know. But I think you've got to understand that if people find out—there's a lot of fear out there—it isn't always rational, but that doesn't mean it isn't real, and people can do hurtful things."

"Like what?"

"Like you get real close to some boy your age, and his parent pulls him from the team because they don't want him around you."

"People would do that?"

"Yeah, honey. People would do that, and lots worse."

"Then we won't tell them. It's not their business, is it? It's our business."

"Yaaaaa. But maybe we could just go watch."

Now there was an idea. I thought a good one.

But no.

He wanted to be one of those specks out there in the outfield. Waiting for that wayward pop fly to make its wayward way to him.

"I want to play baseball with my friends, please."

It was the world to him.

He was supposed to have a physical. I forged a doctor's signature. It was like being back in high school when you needed a bathroom pass. Sue me.

I sit in the stands with the other parents who have arrived in their SUVs. I sit with a can of Coke. In terror.

What do I do if he bleeds?

I am so nervous my hands tremble. I have to clench my Coke. He steps fearlessly right up into the balls. Swings. That crack. Home runs win him a lot of friends.

What if . . .

Fuck.

What if he gets invited to his friend's house—other boys his age have sleepovers, and camp in backyards in their tents. What if all his secrets are found out. *Can I? Can I?* He wants everything.

I do say no.

Just no. Sometimes I am the bad guy, too.

"But everyone will be there."

Not everyone.

John's house: *Where John and his brothers sleep with their friends in the basement in their sleeping bags. And stay up late. And eat chips. And cookies made by John's mother. And shine their flashlights on their dicks like look at mine.*

I know John.

I know his brothers.

I know the basement. I know the friends. I know the cookies. I know the flashlights. I know the laughing squeals of boys. All of it is normal. All of it is fine. You let them live their lives.

It wasn't spending the night at John's I objected to. It wasn't

John's mother and her cookies. It wasn't the basement with the boys. It wasn't sex or flashlights.

It was chaos. Anywhere.

AIDS is chaos imposed on time.

Awee would go (if I let him, and I would not) and lose himself in those quickly running moments in the wind where he was just a boy again, and essentially like them.

But he was not like them.

"But I want to go," Awee begged.

A basement with sleeping bags.

A mom. Cookies.

Now, who was going to give him his medication? Would he remember it? Not likely. Mom? With her cookies? Dispenses the antiretrovirals.

I think not.

This is where he crawls up onto my lap again. Cries. I am his rock. His wetness is touching me.

I see them, too, the boys. Coming in at night off the baseball field with its electric lights. The mitts. The balls. The bats. Their arms around one another.

Touching.

Awee was something like a thief. Stealing bases. Sliding into third. Skinning everything. His knee.

Him screaming in the bathroom as I spray him in antiseptic.

All that hurt should steal such gentle shapes as this until such time as the boy becomes a hurtful thing himself.

Baseball ended.

We still had sunsets from the window. I could still make him smile like no one else on earth.

He liked it when I washed his hair and we spoke quietly in whispers. Soapy head. He would dunk himself down in the water of the bath and emerge more beautiful than God.

When I think about touching him I remember how he hugged me. Hard at the baseball field—his arms around my neck. We got on the big bike and drove it slowly home. His arms around me like the Acropolis clings to the burden of the cliff. If it's true that good boys need no blush upon their cheeks, it's true, too, that men do not need epilogues. Come sit behind me, son, and touch me here and here. To wake the soul by tender roaring strokes of bikes, and touching me through fear. To touch the ball as it descends to earth from soaring suns of flame. To grin at me pretending there is no such thing as pain. He forgets I was once a boy, for it's not a me he knows. I'm just a dad to him in summer wind whichever way it blows.

21. Crow Dog

He came right in. He did not knock. He was *pissed off*. I had it coming. Awee was thrilled to see him.

You have not really had anyone angry with you until Crow Dog has been angry with you.

The first time Crow got really angry with me was when he was about the same age as Awee, and I found him at night dangling in a tree with a rope around his neck. I cut him down. *Breathe.* My lips against his lips. My breath into his lungs.

Why did you DO that?

I want you to live.

What if I don't want to, and you . . . you can't MAKE me!

But I could.

Crow took the hotel room in. The tiny kitchen with the midget fridge. The window. The fire escape. The table. Awee's new laptop. The pictures on the wall from Awee's Head Start. The baseball mitt. It took Crow some time to cool down.

Navajo steam.

Awee and I had not been in touch with him. I am not too good at communication.

"That is no goddamn excuse, Nasdijj, and you know it! I *love* you. I *love* Awee. I did not know where you were! I was *worried*."

I knew what he meant.

There had been a time when I had been worried sick about him, too.

Even then, he had always worn those cowboy boots.

Daddy.

What is it, Awee?

When you blew life into him that time—that time you found him hanging in the tree—did it feel like kissing? I want to know.

Yaaaaa. Kissing? In a way. I guess. I was only blowing air into his lungs. You don't think of it like kissing, honey. You just want them to wake up.

Crow Dog sits on the hotel bed. He puts his head in his hands. And weeps.

Awee went to him. "I'm sorry, Crow."

"You're just a kid."

He looked at me. I felt horrible.

"Nasdijj is the adult. Or he's supposed to be. He can be *such* an asshole."

There were no excuses. I had put off calling him. I do not know why. Crow thought he did.

"You always have to do it your way. You always think you are imposing. You always think nobody can do it but you. You always think you are alone. You are *not* alone. I am *person*! Isn't that what you always taught me? Isn't that what you wrote on blackboard in sixth grade? You made us think like *persons*! Isn't that what you said? Or was it just your teacher bullshit? I am *person*! And you left me. To be by myself. To wonder where you were. To wonder how Awee was. I looked everywhere for you. I even thought about calling Tina—but my voice sucks. Finally, Jimmy Dog tells me. He is my cousin, too. Why do you do this to me? *Me!*"

"I thought I would handle things without messing up some-one else's—"

"*Life?*"

"Yeah, *life*. I didn't mean to hurt you, Crow."

"But you *did* hurt me! You hurt me by shutting me out. It is *my* life. *My* persons. *I* decide if something is intrusion. *Not you!* I decide if I want to do this or if I do not want to do this with my life. To *be* with you and Awee. Nasdijjs, you *cannot* just push me out. You *are* my life. I was *learning* to love Awee, and I am not just going to sit around while you walk out the door to go be some big man and do everything alone, cuz you are *not* alone even if you wish you were. There are *other people* you have to thinks about, not just you, you, you. I am *person* who loves you, and wants to be in struggle *with* you, not sitting in some trailer by myself with the dog waiting and waiting and waiting. Do you *understand*? You are *not* getting rid of me so easily."

"What can I do, Crow?"

"Do I have to ask for every fucking thing? *Hug me.* I need you to hug me, Nasdijj. Please."

I got up. I went to him. I hugged him. He cried and cried.

It had been too long.

Awee had gone to get the dog. Usually I don't let him out there in the dark by himself with the hookers and the pimps. Crow had parked out front. I could see Awee from the window. I needed a minute alone with Crow.

"You're limping," he said.

Shakes that long head of dark Navajo hair.

"My bones," I said, "are not too good. I'm getting old, Crow. It ain't what it used to be."

Awee came in with Navajo.

She was insane to see us.

Kisses.

She will lick my tears. She has loved all my boys.

Crow looks around. Like where is the other bed?

One bed. The three of us.

And the cattle dog.

Crow Dog went and got his stuff. His one bag of clothes. His basketball.

He threw it to Awee. "There's a hoop in the parking lot in the back," Awee said (hopefully). "But it looks pretty old and rusty."

"Old and rusty is how I learned to play," Crow Dog said.

"Where did you learn to play basketball?"

Crow looks at me and smiles. "Oh, back in the sixth grade someone taught me. Some mean teacher I had said if I learned to read he would play basketball with me."

"Didn't you have nobody to play basketball with you?" Awee asked.

"My dad was in prison. The other boys in my class thought I talked funny. I had a teacher. Did you ever have a teacher?"

"I got one now."

They laughed.

"Is he mean to you like he was mean to me?"

"He makes me take pills and he makes me go to doctors."

"That's because he loves you."

"*I played baseball!*" Awee glowed like a lightbulb.

"Was it fun?"

"Oh, I wish you could see me hit home runs, Crow."

"He was terrific," I said.

"Nobody invited me."

"Are you going to forgive me?" I asked Crow Dog. "Or is this open season on saints?"

"*Saints?*"

They both said it.

Crow got up off the bed and sat in the rocking chair. The chair itself was out of place. I had purchased it.

"Hey, I like this chair."

"He rocks me sometimes," Awee explained. "When I don't feel too good."

"How have you been doing, Little Feather? Come over here. He's not the only one who knows how to rock."

Awee was not too sure just yet.

Crow moved his legs and opened his arms in an almost imperceptible way that seemed to say he was big enough to accommodate the child. Awee went to him. But he was shy.

Crow just wrapped him up in who the bigger brother was.

He was big enough to hold me, Daddy.

Yaaaaa. He was. You were very good for him. You gave him something valuable to protect.

Crow has strong muscles.

Yaaaaa. You liked that.

Awee put his head on Crow Dog's chest.

"Tell me all about it," Crow said. "Tell me everything."

In Navajo there is a phrase: *yi'ash, yil*. He is walking with him. This is the literal translation. It can mean far more than that.

He was walking with him.

This was my big son's way of doing two things.

He was lifting the burden of being alone with it *off* my shoulders. When I said "it ain't what it used to be," I was not kidding. I felt like every bone in my body was about to snap. We were not taking too many trips on the Harley. I just couldn't hold it up anymore.

But Crow Dog was with me now. I had been such an asshole to keep him away.

It was also his way of getting to know what this challenge was going to be like. The battles that would find their way to us. Not unlike the battle of language versus sign, and the reality that sometimes Crow uses both his voice and his hands.

I once sent Crow to the San Francisco Hearing and Speech Center on Divisadero in the Western Addition where Crow learned within the context of his speech therapy *how to listen*. Those were good people, and they dramatically increased the quality of our lives.

In Indian sign, the word for listen is made with the right hand as a cup, cupped near the right ear, you turn the hand back and forth slightly with your wrist action.

Listen.

Awee told him everything. How it hurt when they took his blood. How he did not like the *girl ones* (female doctors, nurses) to *see him* (naked). How he did not like their fingers in his rectum (Crow would nod). How the doctor who lived upstairs was good for pain but not much else. How being inside an MRI tube scared him. How walking on the razor blades was horrible. How the razor blades could come and go. How it was hard to always have diarrhea, and then you had to take a bath because the fungal infections were so bad.

Crow Dog just pats Awee's tiny butt.

How the catheters hurt him and made his penis bleed.

How he was allergic now to so many things (like latex) that you only knew about by bumping into them. How he was mad because so many medications had tortured him with side effects. How the nurses yelled at him. How frustrating it was to have to always explain things they should know but didn't. Such as how anything less than 800 mg of acyclovir was not effective (against the horrible attacks of herpes in his mouth that were so bad he could not eat), but doctors would typically *have to see*. That meant he would have to suffer an attack. How it was the same with the antifungals. He would have to suffer an attack before they would believe him. How nobody believed him because he was just a kid.

How it was hard to sleep with the ice picks in his feet. How it was hard to find places that could do genome viral testing. How sometimes he was fine and wanted to be twelve. How sometimes he was not fine—he would sweat with fevers—and wanted to be dead.

It was a lot of hows.

Crow Dog did not interrupt. He never said: *No, don't feel that.* He never told Awee not to be angry. He respected the little one. His feather. He rocked him. He ran his fingers through Awee's hair. He patted Awee on the back.

I think he will be a father someday. To some kid. He will have had this extraordinary practice.

"Have I ever told you about Hwiina?" Crow asked Awee.

"What is Hwiina, please?"

"Hwiina is a Navajo place, a sacred place, a place alive, it is filled with animation, it is cheerful."

"Have you been there?" Awee asked.

"Yes. A man took me there a long time ago. I was your age then. A very arrogant man who had breathed life into me, who took me home, who told me about Hwiina."

"I want to go there, too."

All my boys get taken to Hwiina.

Hwiina is *na'iigeel nilinidi.* To dream where it flows.

By the time Crow Dog was done, Awee was asleep.

Crow looks at me. "What do I do now, Daddy?"

He calls me that when all the walls are down. "You hold him. I will get his pills. He will take them. But he will not remember."

Big silent blobs start welling up in Crow Dog's dark eyes. "He's dying."

Again and again.

"Slowly, honey. Very slowly."

Pills.

We took his clothes off. "Same drill as before," I said. "It doesn't change too much."

"He's smaller."

"Yaaaaa. Put him on the toilet. Let's hope he doesn't have diarrhea but he might."

"What happens if he does?"

"Then we have to bathe him, put antifungal cream on, dry him, put him to bed."

"Will he wake up?"

"No. He'll wake up around three. The ice picks in his feet will bother him. I have some antibiotics he has to take then anyway."

"What are the antibiotics for?"

"Bactrim for pneumonia. It will be pneumonia, you know, in the end."

"Pneumonia? I don't want him to have pneumonia."

You could hear the traffic outside the window. The coming and the going in the liquor store across the street. The barbershop would be closed.

"It's a blessing in a way," I said. "The pneumonia just slowly cuts off his ability to breathe. The oxygen does not get to his brain. It's the body's way to die without enormous pain."

He was a small naked thing in his bigger brother's stronger arms.

I was getting worn from lifting him. It hurt a lot.

Crow set him on the toilet. Awee's dinner just poured from him. Crow was lost.

"I will draw his bath," I said. "Just wipe him with toilet paper, okay. You'll get used to it. Don't be afraid to touch him. It is not a sex thing. I know how it feels at first. There are some rubber gloves in the cabinet. I will get them for you. Crow, look at me."

He did. His face was in agony. He was biting his lower lip. Hard.

"I want you to wear them."

"I'm not afraid."

"I want you to wear them anyway."

"I thought you said he is allergic to latex?"

"He is. And you are about to see how when we brush up against his skin, his skin is going to rash. But we won't wear them long. Only when we have to clean his pottie, okay, that's what he calls it. We try not to say shit in this house. It's important, okay?"

"Okay."

"We have to clean him well before we put him in the tub. One time I didn't do it too well, and the bacteria in the tub went just a tiny little bit into his pee hole, and the infection in his urethra almost did him in."

"Why the bath?"

"The fungal infections are almost constant now. They won't give us the medication until he has an outbreak. It starts around his rectum, creeps up, and his testicles turn the color of wet beets. Then it gets into his foreskin, and we don't want to go there. It's not pretty, and it leaves him in such pain he can't sit, he can't lie down, he can't stand himself. But we've worked out this routine. They have great soaps now. Then, we put him in his pajamas, and he'll be fine."

The twelve-year-old smells nice when we are done with him.

"I want cowboy pajamas like he has," Crow said.

"I'll buy you some. Wal-Mart sells them. They might not have extra-extra-large though."

We were exhausted.

"I just don't understand how you thought you were going to do this alone. I could not do this by myself. There is no way. I'm beat!"

Over the years I have taught Crow Dog many things. The importance of always wearing clean underwear was not one of those things.

"You call that clean underwear?"

"I've been busy looking for *you*. Laundry can wait."

"We do tons of it. Tons and tons of it. Did you see the Laundromat around the corner?"

"No."

"Well, I am there a lot."

"You're not alone anymore, okay?"

"Good. I need help."

It had arrived.

Awee slept between us. Navajo slept under the bed.

All my dogs are named Navajo. It's just something I want to keep. My first dog's name was Navajo when Tommy Nothing Fancy, my first adopted son, was with me. Tommy had FAS. That Navajo stood watch over him just like this Navajo stands watch over this son of mine. Sons and dogs. I am complete.

Awee was more relaxed than I had ever seen him. Curled like a bud worm and sound asleep.

"Do you think Awee can play basketball with me tomorrow?"

"I try not to overprotect him. It's hard. I want to keep him locked up in some pretty little box. But it doesn't work that way. Look at you."

"Look at me what?"

This is when they want you to tell them that you are proud of them. I have learned that it is important that they know. They want to know that you love them, but it is not enough. It *should* be, but it is not enough. They would never admit it, but they want to know you *approve* of them.

Tell him, Daddy. He needs to know. He needs to hear it. Especially from you. It means everything.

"Crow."

"What."

"I'm proud of you. I am so proud of you."

"For what? I didn't do anything."

"For being here. For doing this."

"Oh, that."

"Yaaaaa. That. And for loving him."

"You're such a romantic. How could I *not* love him? What's not to love? He's my feather. I want him to live."

"I'm proud of you when you sign. When you use Indian sign."

"I thought you wanted me to always speak? I have a lot to learn about sign. I thought you didn't want me to sign."

"I was wrong. I want you to sign. Will you teach me some more Indian sign?"

Awee was cuddled up hard against him. Crow turned to me.

"Give me your fingers."

"What?"

"Give me your fingers."

My fingers in the dark.

Sleep: lower the extended flat hands with a sweep into the following position: left hand in front of right breast pointing to the right. Right hand six inches to right of left, pointing to front and right. Head near hands. Then incline head to right.

Speaks with hands.

In darkness. Sight.

22. Barbershop

When he was a little guy, I used to cut Crow Dog's hair.

I was allowed.

Those days have been over for quite a while.

Sometimes I wish they would not feel so compelled to grow up.

I liked him in the sixth grade. Even when he had something of an attitude.

He was living with me then. He was *not* used to it. Yet. It was more structure than he really wanted.

I was a teacher at the middle school. I had arranged for him to attend my class. I knew the teacher well (me). And I could find Crow Dog when I wanted him to tend to homework.

Not being able to goof off was hard on him.

When I could, I rode my bike to school. It got your blood pumping early in the morning.

I bought him one. His bike was red. He didn't like the basket much. It wasn't *cool*.

I made him ride it anyway.

We rode together on our clunky bikes to school in the high-desert morning past the plaza in the sun. *No hands* down the moon hill, chasing mountain jackrabbits with their giant ears who had popped out of holes (sniffing, up on haunches) to see us skid around the corner by the post office where the shy white girls on their way to school played hopscotch with chalk, ignoring us on our bikes, our arms out like wings. Our solidarity was a crusade.

Our bike chains were new and oiled, and we only seemed to listen to the silence of the road in the face of unkept promises (both of us made them) screaming past when we came to Ball-Buster Rutted Road. Your handlebars come off, and the rattle in your dirt road teeth hurts to touch your Crow Dog tongue. I was your buddy then. Your independence was a song that had not been sung.

I like them when they're small, and you can cut their hair (and make mistakes), and they don't really notice. "Is it going to hurt?" he'd ask.

"No, honey, cutting hair doesn't hurt."

He knew that. But he had to ask anyway. Just in case.

He used to let me wash his hair before I cut it.

I told him it was "nice shampoo for big boys."

In reality it was insecticide shampoo for killing lice.

Knock knock. Who's there? Lice. Lice who? Have a lice day, Daaaaaaaaddddddeeeeeeeeeeeeee.

Even back then when he was small and vulnerable, I had to carefully edit the things I told Crow Dog.

Surprises. On the one hand, I wanted him to be able to deal spontaneously with life. Life is not a rigid thing (it would be if Crow were making the rules, but he is not). On the other hand, I wanted to cushion the surprises.

There have been a few surprises (not nice ones) in his life.

Dad being hauled off to prison was a surprise to a toddler who had only just learned how to walk.

Before Crow came to live with me, he lived in a series of trailers both on and off the reservation.

For a while Crow lived with his mom, and a series of men who came and went, outside of Grants, New Mexico.

I was a distant relative.

I did not want to get involved. I kept myself in the distance as much as I could.

It was when I realized that Crow seemed to be losing his hearing—his speech was almost unintelligible—that I began to get involved.

CROW DOG! CROW DOG! No response.

I would drive him into Grants for ice cream cones.

What kind do you want? No response.

There is no way in the world you can tell me that some lice-infested, snot-encrusted, shirtless, shoeless, skinny ratbone of a child fresh from Trailer Town *did not know* what kind of ice cream cone he wanted.

They know.

A big one or a little one? No response.

There is no way in the world that a child from this environment was going to pick *the little one.*

They want the big one. It could very well be the last time they ever see an ice cream cone. The big one, please.

No response.

As I cut his hair I would say things to him from behind.

Not a word of it.

Crow staring at some fly on the wall.

As he got older (right around first grade), I took him into Gallup where there was a real barbershop.

I made sure we had washed his hair with the lice shampoo beforehand.

A real barbershop.

They put a box-thing on the barber's chair for him to sit on.

All nice and handsome. Kid don't talk much. Not too much to say.

Crow Dog had never been to Gallup and he had never seen so many stores in his life. And all those people.

The only time his little hand left my bigger hand was in the barbershop.

Urban environments are still foreign to him.

Crow Dog had never lived in a city. The sound of people making love seeping in through the paper-thin walls drove him *insane*.

Awee and I had grown so used to noises, we just tuned them out.

"Do they have to do *that*!" Crow complained.

"Do what?" I was peeling potatoes.

I lead a vastly glamorous life as a internationally famous writer.

Who peels potatoes on a paper towel.

"You know."

"I do—what? Look, this one has a happy face with eyes and ears . . ."

"Daaaaaaaaaad!"

"What, Crow." Of all the things for him to hear—it would be this.

His lips to my ear. "They're fucking next door."

"Oh, you mean they're screaming when they're getting fucked," I said.

"Oh, yeah," Awee noted. "But only when they get fucked in the ass. You should hear him when *she* . . ."

"Daaaaaaaaaad! He listens to this, this . . ."

"Oh, we don't hear it anymore," Awee said. "Just turn your hearing aid down, but it might not help. They fuck really loud."

Awee started making schlooshing noises with his tongue. Crow

Dog (who had a very conservative streak, even at seventeen) just stared at him.

I don't think my older one had spent more than a few consecutive hours in a city. Even when I had him at the San Francisco Hearing and Speech Center—Crow getting everything from speech therapy to hearing aids—I had him staying overnight with friends who lived in the country in Marin. By late afternoon, Crow needs to see trees. Crow Dog would hit the city, and you could see his entire body tighten up. He reminded me of a skinny clam. Hauling that shell around to pop back into. Over the years, I have tried not to give him *all* of my urban phobias, but I think I have failed him in that respect.

Just walking down a city street with Crow is an eye-opener. He will not walk anywhere near a curb because it's too close to the moving cars. He stays close to the buildings. He abhors stepping on cracks. When he sees cracks in the sidewalk he wants to know when they will be repaired.

Crow likes things right. Fixed. In their place.

He used to think (he has become a bit more open-minded) all prostitutes should be arrested because prostitution is against the law.

Although his mother was a whore. Who sold Crow to men.

Crow has all these ironies and contradictions that haunt him.

But he is always honest.

He deals with his issues head-on. Fearlessly.

He went so far as to come to me with a problem when he was in high school. He was smoking dope with his friends in the bathroom and he did not know how to stop.

"Do you want to stop?" I asked.

But all I got were tears.

We nipped that one in the bud. Crow went from experimenting with it to proclaiming all drugs were bad.

Crow dropped out of high school. It had been one nightmare after another. But Crow Dog got his GED before his "buddies"
graduated.

Because Crow Dog is determined. Sort of like a pit bull.

His loyalty to me, and his love for me, is absolute.

He measures things like my sodium intake.

My blood pressure is often through the roof.

Crow Dog pecks at me. To be well. To not do bad things.

I do not sneak cigars (well, once) when he is around. I do not
sneak shots of gin.

After Crow got his GED, an aunt who loves him, and who I
love dearly, gave Crow Dog his little trailer.

Trouble was . . .

Loneliness.

Aunt Verna laughed and told me I was crazy. "Crow will
never be lonely," she maintained. "Every woman in three coun-
ties wants him."

Maybe. But loneliness takes many forms.

He would show up at my house, and practically beg Awee and
me to come over and spend the night in his trailer (just down the
dirt road from me), and Crow would arrive with a dozen rented
videos from the Pinedale Trading Post in the hope that Awee
would like maybe one, when, of course, Awee liked them all.

Crow would buy Awee that *horrible* disgusting red punch by
the gallon and enough popcorn to feed the balcony at the picture show.

Would we come over to his trailer, *please*.

For someone who wanted to live by himself . . .

Huge mounds of garbage bags piled on the street did not faze
either Awee or myself. We could pretend not to see rats.

But Crow wondered (out loud) how people could live like this.

This from a ratbone from Trailer Town.

He did not drive in San Francisco so he was not really aware of things like parking violations.

"You mean, they want me to put *money* in this machine?"

Crow's first encounter with a parking meter.

Awee just loved parking meters. He thought they were great fun.

"Oh, it's *fun*," he said. "You just put the money in and it makes a cool sound. I'll show you."

Machines that made cool sounds were right up Awee's alley.

Awee put the money in the meter. Crow stepped back, staring intently.

"What's wrong, Crow?" Awee asked. I have been through the *Crow Dog Urban Chronicles* before so I said nothing.

"What comes out?" Crow asked. (He refused to touch the parking meter or get too close to it.)

"Comes out, huh?"

"You're buying time," I said. "To park here."

Crow comes from a place where anyone and everyone can and does park anywhere on the mesa they want.

That you would put money, actual money, into a machine that made strange noises (and did not have so much as one gum ball) so you could park somewhere was about as stupid an idea (in the *Crow Dog Book of Stupid Things*) as childbirth.

Another idea I had had to explain to him some years ago.

He still suspects I made childbirth and parking meters up to tease him.

He is not quite sure.

He was about six.

"Okay," he said. "So after the man does this with the woman it must hurt her so she beats him up, right?"

In Crow's world there were things that got you beat up, and things that didn't.

Not too much in between.

Every time I thought I was getting through to the six-year-old, I realized it was just too much.

For Crow to articulate or absorb.

I also knew that in his world, the mechanisms of sex and sexuality were such that he had better learn the truth, or his ignorance and innocence would be used against him.

Eventually his innocence was used against him. Awee and I were the only people on the planet he would drop his guard with.

Even now.

Crow wants things to work and people to be nice.

If people had only followed the rules when he was about eight, he would never have been sold into a world of sexuality he did not want, his dad would never have gone to prison, and his life would not have been fucked up.

If people had followed the rules, he would never have been beaten. He would not have to wear hearing aids. He wouldn't stutter. And no sixth graders would have made fun of the way he talked.

We rode together on our clunky bikes to school in the high-desert morning past the burrito wagon, then we stopped, went back, caving in to hunger. Breakfast burrito juice dripped down his chin. He liked red chiles the best, and I said nothing when he had to run to the bathroom later on (during the pledge). *You mean you ride to school with your teacher?* they asked him in incredulous bewilderment. He was going to teach them sign (he only knew a little) but stopped when he realized they were not worth the work. We rode our bikes home, too, late in the afternoon when the burrito wagon was packing up, and the burrito man was going home. We made supper, did dishes together, argued about things like hearing aids, tired, losing our threads to each other, him: *stomping off to bed;* me: *good-night,*

Crow. Our bikes on the front porch in the dark waiting for tomorrow.

When he played basketball with Awee in the back of the hotel parking lot, he finally had to borrow a big broom from the hotel and sweep up all the broken glass and used condoms. Awee had gotten used to being in urban places. But Crow would stare (horrified) at homeless people and their shopping carts. Awee had seen so many of them, he just walked around them. I had protected Crow from the issue of the homeless in San Francisco. As a parent, you're always juggling what you want them to see, be exposed to, and what you don't want them to see.

Crow was the kind of kid who would have given all his clothes to some homeless guy who wore magazines for shoes. There go Crow Dog's boots.

Awee had seen it all in AIDS clinics. Everything. Having seen so many urban places from the back of a motorcycle—you are definitely *in* the thing. But Crow still finds the noise and the constant movement to be disorienting. Like me, he gets lost. Awee never got lost. Now, with his precious new laptop, he could study maps on the Internet.

With one click, he knew where we were, and where we were going.

Short cuts.

We could use the jeep now that Crow and Navajo had arrived in it. Crow would drive, and Awee liked to sit in the front with his laptop so he could show Crow where to go (as if Awee didn't know the way to Wal-Mart), which put me in the back with Navajo, who I keep safe in a dog harness (they're like doggie seat belts). I liked watching the two boys interact. My big one and my little one. I do not like to drive. I was sitting in the back of the jeep one day when I first noticed how the two Navajo boys had blended. Crow at the end of adolescence, and Awee just becoming one. It was a hands-on intimacy that both boys needed—in my own cowboy arrogance I had failed to see that.

But now I could give them this.

This time together where the adolescent whose inclination is internal now shares himself externally.

Grooming behaviors.

There was one bathroom.

They never saw themselves as strange. *All* adolescents are strange. It is a time of strangeness and soldiership.

The two of them alike.

They consulted on everything.

Hair. I wasn't supposed to know that in the bathroom Awee would help Crow with his hair, and Crow would help Awee with his hair.

They were not twins. But close enough.

With Awee, you could tell that Crow had done the hair. With Crow, you could tell that Awee had done the hair.

Perfectly.

I do not know where they got the thing about ships.

Smelling like ships.

Okay. I know.

They got it from me.

Old Spice aftershave is cheap.

When they were done in the bathroom, you could not go in there for about half an hour because the sprays and the soaps and the cologne smells had more alcohol floating on the air than a bowery bar on Saturday at midnight.

They had secrets.

"Now we smell like daddy," Awee would whisper to Crow Dog.

Then there was the silver.

When white people first come to the Navajo Reservation,

they are frequently knocked out by the silver jewelry. It isn't cheap, and the Navajo are not stupid. It is extremely artistic. Even the poorest grandmother with her sheep who has been no farther in her life than Bluewater Canyon has the most incredible silver jewelry with turquoise stones the size of goat testicles. Between the two boys, they had a few pieces of silver that they had made, and some stuff friends had made, and they shared everything.

Here's a tribal secret everyone knows: The Navajo keep their best jewelry for themselves.

Between the two of them they had enough rocks to qualify as a quarry.

Awee shows me a silver ring. Much too big for a finger.

"Crow wants to get his penis pierced so he can wear . . ."

"You what?"

That flash again. The look.

I don't want to know.

There are some things about my past *I wish I had not done.*

Do they have to imitate every mistake I made?

"Well, you . . ."

"I know that, Awee." I gave Crow my best *we are going to have to talk* look.

They would never in a million years imitate the way I cut my hair.

I buzz cut it. Real short. As in bald.

I told myself for a long time that it was because I simply don't have the same kind of time to put into grooming that an adolescent does.

These little lies we tell ourselves to keep our illusions alive.

Indian men frequently cut all their hair off as a traditional sign of mourning. I have kept mine almost bald ever since the day I buried my Tommy Nothing Fancy.

Who left me like the bird he was.

Tommy had the kind of fetal alcohol syndrome that came with rather significant grand mal seizures. Tom could have up to two hundred, three hundred seizures in a day.

I know. It's hard to visualize. But I counted them.

I swear to God this is true: There were doctors who suggested cutting out half of Tom's brain.

But Tommy died before they could get their hands on him.

Since then, I have had no hair.

The ring in my *peeeeeeeeeenisssssssss* (thank you, Awee) comes from some time I spent with the Sioux. In grief.

I still wear my grief. I do not know why. I think perhaps to simply remind me. That Tom existed. I am afraid of my internal irresponsibility. I am afraid I might forget.

The ring and the hair will not allow me to forget.

Both Awee and Crow understood the ring. I just didn't want them to even think about imitating it.

When Crow doesn't want to discuss something with me, he'll turn the volume on his hearing aids *way* down.

As his sixth-grade teacher, this was infuriating. As his *dad* . . .

I had to find other strategies. Being infuriated was ridiculous.

Crow and I have always had a certain tension between us.

I wanted him to have speech. I paid a *lot* of money at Hearing and Speech so Crow could have speech.

The kind of speech people understood.

I fought him about the use of sign.

I *have* given up that struggle. I even have him teaching *me* sign now. Both ASL and Indian sign (I'm not very good at either).

Crow Dog does not believe this. We have waged wars about it. Crow Dog has hanged himself from trees because of this. He wanted to die, and he meant it. Crow Dog does not do things he does not mean. Crow Dog does not say things he does not mean.

The students he teaches art to in Head Start are beginning to find that out. It's good for them to know a male who means what he says. Period.

But Crow rejects the notion that I *love* his voice. I find it musical. Like a deep flute lost somewhere in a canyon.

Awee loved it, too.

"You guys are ganging up on me," Crow would say.

"No," Awee would sign. (He had enough sign by now to be able to sign it, sign being another trick in Awee's magic bag of secrets; he studied it on the Internet when Crow got tired of him.) "You have a nice voice, Crow Dog."

"I h-h-h-h-haaate it."

Crow cannot hear the beauty in his voice.

But I want him to trust me that it's true.

Over the course of Crow Dog's life, I have popped surprises at him.

I know that smile. I live for it.

I know he *loves* surprises.

Yes. You do.

I want to be the one in charge of the surprises. I want to be the one who decides what to cushion and what not to cushion.

There had been a hole in my head and my life (and yes, my penis) that I did not understand how to fill.

I had left my son.

To fend for himself.

Crow Dog! I need you to forgive me.

Crow Dog needed to be with us.

Beside me. Beside Awee.

He surprised me by finding us. It was my turn to be surprised.

I surprised him when he was a little boy, and I would go over to the trailer where he was living (that dump), and Crow Dog would be hiding under the bed during electric storms.

Alone. He was always left alone.

It made me angry.

Still, I would go over there, and drag him out from beneath the bed. He would crawl into my arms.

It was not the sound. It was the sight.

Of black clouds, and lightning flashes.

I surprised him once when I showed up at his trailer (Crow had been left alone again) to find him in his living room nude, tied with rope to a chair, cigarette burns (I know these burns because I have a few but not as many as Crow) all over him like huge bug bites, a rag in his mouth for a gag.

He was a little glad to see me.

Crow and I are a soldiership. We do not speak of this. I untied him and he melted. It still makes him cry to remember it.

I surprised him when I would show up at his school and speak with his teachers about his progress. He wanted to hide back then.

His scrawls on paper had passed for writing. I wanted higher standards imposed on him.

I surprised him when I showed up at a hearing once. Where Crow had been dragged before a judge.

For burning his mother's trailer to the ground.

I surprised him when I said I would take him in.

I surprised him when I cut him down from that stupid tree, and refused to let him die, not really caring what he wanted.

I surprised him when I had him transferred to my sixth-grade classroom. I surprised him with the red bike even if it did have a basket.

I surprised him when I walked into a high school bathroom and caught him red-handed smoking dope with the dope brigade (yes, I *am* a hypocrite, a big one, and an asshole, too). But this problem ended. He only needed help.

I surprised him when I got him the job herding cows.

I surprised him with a fishing trip to Canada.

I surprised him with speech therapy and hearing aids.

I surprised him with Awee.

He surprised me with his expertise (it comes naturally to him) teaching four-year-olds art.

He surprised me with ASL and Indian sign. Yes. He should learn these things. They are only other languages.

Like Navajo.

I had a surprise for him in that small apartment, that room we lived in with Awee.

I did not know how to tell him. I kept it to myself.

I have another surprise for him.

I am going to spring it on him when he reads this.

I will send him on this journey to search for typos.

My helper.

I am not a typist. I make lots and lots of typos. His mission is to spot them and scrunch them out like bugs.

Crow, this summer I want to send you to South America. My daughter, Kree, wants to take you to Brazil and Machu Picchu.

The Andes of Peru.

You are not to worry about the money. Kree and I are taking care of it.

Hey, Crow Dog, look in my cookie jar where the money from my newspaper articles goes.

Kree wants to know you, Crow.

A sister.

Crow Dog adores my Kree. She teaches Indian children (kindergarten) in Paraguay.

Surprise.

Daddy, you still loves him.

Yaaaaa, Awee. I do.

He will see the whole wide world!

I hope so. It's a pretty big place.

He's gonna be a little scared.

Probably.

He learns fast and figures out how to get around. He figured out the city. He'll be okay.

He still gets lost.

I will be there with my maps.

He used to hold your hand.

Yeah, in crowds. He was afraid someone might snatch me.

Remember the Hispanic festival?

He would not let go of my hand!

Well, you were a little shaky on your feet, you know.

He carried me to the barbershop.

You weren't walking then.

He wanted me to be handsome.

Yaaaaa. No matter what.

Crow is always nagging me to let my hair grow out. I ignore him. Then he accuses me of being mean to Awee.

"What do you mean—*mean*?"

"I mean he needs a haircut. You're the dad. It's on you. And I don't mean one of your buzz cuts or a mohawk."

"I want a mohawk," Awee said.

"I want him to be handsome, Dad. He *is* handsome. But he needs a haircut."

This is why I love Crow.

There was a barbershop across the street.

The barber was an elderly African-American gentleman who wore shiny shoes and a hat. It was just a matter of getting there.

It may as well have been Mars.

I was always having to decide (it wasn't easy) how much activity Awee could handle on any given day. Days when I wore him out (like the Hispanic festival) were days that could lead to real setbacks.

A week in bed for the twelve-year-old. By the end of the week, they hate you.

I look outside across the street from our fleabag apartment at the barbershop. Okay, cookie, how much will we bite off today?

Some days you just don't move too fast. Awee was slow and far away today. He seemed to go about as far as the window.

He looked out at the world like he was about to fall over at any moment, and one of us was going to have to catch him.

He watered his Wal-Mart plant. Then he had to sit down to catch his breath.

"What's wrong, Awee?" Crow asked him.

Awee just looked at him. Awee was in his pajamas.

His hair a mess.

"Go give him a bath, and sit in the tub with him," I suggested.

Crow looked at me in horror.

It was one thing to comb his hair (three hundred times).

It was another thing to be nude with him. Awee was twelve and sexual. He was not a one-year-old.

Yaaaaa. So what. He was a boy who could barely move.

"Yeah, okay, okay," Crow said. "He should be clean."

I got called into the bathroom.

Crow is holding Awee up between his legs.

Sometimes the only way to know a thing is to get that close. It just is.

"Daddy, what is this?"

Awee is in that warm tub place, lost between the morbid and the mystical, the musical and the misbehaved. His eyes half lids.

Crow shows me under Awee's testicle. A purple spot.

I sigh. I know Karposi's sarcoma when I see it now. The purple is so vivid it feels dangerous. It is dangerous. It is cancer.

There is another one on his neck.

"Boys get bruises," Crow said. "It is a bad thing, I think."

If I had hair, I would pull it out anyway.

Awee is in bed.

Crow and I feel so alone.

There are things I want to say to him. Now. They cannot wait.

"Crow, I want you to forgive me. I blocked you out. I can't do this alone, Crow Dog. I need you. I need you now more than I ever needed you."

"No shit."

"I fucked up. I'm sorry."

"Stop being sorry. I'm here. Awee needs us. He doesn't have time for you to be sorry, Dad. When are you going to start letting me be your son, too, as much as Tommy ever was, and as much as Awee is right now? I want to know. When can *I* be your son? What do I have to do?"

"Nothing. Just forgive me."

"There is nothing to forgive. You and Awee are the only peoples I want to be with now. But don't shut me out ever again, okay. Go ahead and kick my ass when you think it needs kicking, but don't shut me out cuz it is the one thing I can't handle or live with."

"You've had a lot to handle for one life, Crow."

"There's always more. Isn't that why we're here, sitting at this table, with my baby brother over there with cancer in his balls, there's always more and more."

"I got an e-mail from Aunt Verna."

"Aunt Verna can't send no e-mail."

"She went into town. They sent it for her at the insurance office. She has a friend who works there. The one over by the BIA."

Crow looks up at the cracks.

"Okay. Just hold my hand. Just hold it and tell me."

I held it. It had just bathed my other one. So it was warm, and slightly wet. I held it for a good twenty minutes.

No words.

"It's my mom."

Just hold his hand.

Crow Dog looks at me right in the eye. It is not something we do. It is left for those moments in life that stand out from the other ones.

"You have some sign," he said. "Please tell me this in sign, okay."

He took his hearing aids off and put them on the table.

In order to express the concept of death in Indian Sign Language, you first make the sign for die, and then you make the sign for sleep.

There is always a beauty to something that cleanly simple.

Die. Sleep.

I was going to tell him (using speech) that there had been an accident.

But it was a lie. There had been no accident.

I did not have all the facts. Crow's mom had just reached the end of a very hard road to walk. Drunk and frozen in the snow. It happens. It happens a lot. It was a surprise it had not happened a long, long time ago.

I h-h-h-h-h-hated her. My *own* stumbling admission of the truth. I hated what she had done.

To someone who had once been perfect.

He had been perfection.

Crow took off his shirt and sat at that table with me by that window and touched his old cigarette burns. The ones on his arms. The one that had burned his breast.

There were no tears.

He was perfection. To me.

He was perfection to the boy across the room. The one asleep.

"I don't want to go, okay. Dad, help me. Don't make me go to some funeral, please. I want to be here with you, and Awee. This is where I am needed."

I put the laptop in front of him, and he sent Aunt Verna a long e-mail.

Then, so did I.

He was where he needed to be. Aunt Verna and Jimmy Dog would tend to this.

They would still love us. I trusted them.

They would bury her quietly and finally and forever.

At night the barbershop across the street did not light up. Everything else seemed to glow in neon. Crow Dog went to hold and rub his brother's back.

I do not sleep. I sit by windows.

Late and late in the land of pills.

I am losing the little one to hornets. The big one I must keep.

The little one will teach both of us things we did not want to know.

The watchman lights his lamps.

Deliver us.

From this childhood of violence and abuse. You only *think* you are tired of hearing about such stories. *We* have not begun to tell them. But *we will*. We will do it from every angle. Even from the perspective of the abuser. We must even hear from him. We *must*. We must take this fantasy that we have made of childhood, and look the thing clearly in the face, and we must begin to articulate in all our languages what the animal is really like. I was horribly abused. I was raped once by a man who should have loved me. My rage and my revenge is to take these things that are our private places, and to write them here. To put them in the face of the culture that has abandoned us. Us. I call them honey. They are my boys. He came to me by that window by the fire escape. And I held his seventeen-year-old head on my lap. And I held him, too, because it's what I do when the barbershop is closed, and the dead dance not softly, but with the other creatures on the street, and in the Dumpsters where the other children live.

Awee stirs. Takes no prisoners.

He has wet the bed.

Crow picks him up. I will change these sheets. I will make the bed again. It will survive. This. Us. Our secrets.

We have none.

Pills. The cup from Wal-Mart. Drink water, honey. His eyes are black. He lets me look into them.

Says . . .

"Daddy."

Gulps.

His arms like matchsticks. I towel the sweat from him. In rivulets.

Now we just hold him until the sun comes up.

We rode together on our clunky bikes to school in the high-desert morning past the fancy inn where the white people came to ski, buy art, trinkets, and to hobnob with Indians. Riding past the courthouse on Paseo del Norte where his custody had been adjudicated, and where his mother had stood, red eyes, heavy in her whiskey bloat, facing a tribal judge who had given him to me to see if there was any hope that could be squeezed from this rock of revelation and atonement.

Riding to school on our bikes where I would teach a classroom of them—these boys from hell—and he would lock his bike up, go into the office, his job, to fly the flag, to hook it up to the ropes on the flagpole, and to not forget that all of us have a function here. His was to fly the flag because the janitor was busy, and from the corner of my eye I would see him, alone and apart from the chaos of the other boys, tending to his responsibility just before the bell.

Crow Dog carried Awee across the street. Awee still dressed in his blue pajamas. The door had a bell that rang when we went in. The barber was kind and gentle with my baby. He went around the lesion on Awee's neck softly with his razor blade.

Crow Dog reading *Penthouse*.

I tried to pay this man, the barber, but he steadfastly refused to take my money.

"Look," he said. "Don't insult me, sir. I don't often get a chance to do something meaningful for someone. I need to be needed, too. Don't you?"

Yaaaaa. I do.

My boys are the strength of winter's thirsty trees. Their leaves a flowing in the blowing of the breeze. Awee was perfect now. He has put himself in arms, the adverse winds, you stain your swords and words in blood, and dragons with their sins. Sleeps with brothers deep in dreams even as it dims. What handsome warrior heads are these. The holding onto limbs.

23. Runs with Wolves

I had abandoned a woman I loved to do this with Awee. I would call Tina on the pay phone, and pump that hungry thing with quarters. Tina. T. Tee. Sometimes I called her Tenacious. Anyone who wants to know me is that.

I am seeing Awee through from one abandoned place to some other abstract landscape I can only hope (I do not know) is more about embrace than abandonment. I want my son embraced. I want him held. I want his shit licked clean by some mother wolf inside the den with all her titty pups.

Wolves do not abandon their infant offspring.

Ever.

In fact, parenting itself is a complex, many-layered set of pack behaviors not at all limited to the biological mother and father of *Canis lupus*. All wolves in the pack participate. Everyone has their turn.

This is where the wolves learn to play. To hunt. To cooperate to bring down much bigger prey. Wolves are instinctually opposed to abandonment. It simply never happens.

I knew Awee's biological father. Awee's mother was more of an enigma. She seemed to be a shadow who stood behind the more dominating male. Awee did not refer to her very often, as if she simply hadn't been there. When he did refer to her, it was always in the context of her illness.

Then he would get this numb expression. He would look away. "I don't think she wanted me," he once said. "I don't think she liked me."

We see motherhood itself as almost inviolate. Always nurturing, the mother cares for her young when they are sick. Our mothers kiss us, and tuck us in, and make sure we are well.

That Awee's mother had dissolved into a shadow was something the woman I loved had a hard time accepting.

"Where was she?" Tina asked. I could just see her shaking her beautiful head. That a mother would not *be there* for her kid was something Tee has always categorically rejected. As a teacher in Special Education, she had certainly seen it enough times. That doesn't mean you are able to accept it.

I have never seen motherhood as inviolate.

My mother left my brother and me, before I could speak English, with the most vicious, violent wolf who had ever drawn breath.

That women would walk out is my experience. I have seen it a hundred thousand times.

I am glad for those people who have not seen it, who deny that mothers would ever leave their children.

Ignorance must be amazing bliss.

Some children would be lucky to live with wolves.

Many of the things I do with Awee are things most people would not necessarily approve of.

I am not very nice to doctors and nurses.

I take Awee on motorcycle trips.

We camp in the desert where there are no hospitals.

I let him drive the jeep down old dirt roads.

I let him join a baseball team.

He kisses the dog.

I am not worried about how well he does in school.

He is not in school.

Although Awee reads more than most adults (when I started writing this he was reading a book about the human genome).

We live in a dump of a hotel with whores and junkies so we have access to pain medication.

We sleep in the same bed.

We come and go as we please.

We answer to no one.

"What do you mean, you're taking him to the wolf ranch?"

She is impatient with me. "It's not too far."

"I didn't ask how far it was. I said: What do you MEAN, you are taking him to the wolf ranch."

"Wolf Rescue Ranch."

"Whatever."

"It will be good for him."

"WHAT! To see a bunch of mangy wolves?"

"Yaaaaa. To touch wolves. It's dangerous. It can be healing."

"And what cosmic crystal ball tells you this? Since when did wolves become healing? He sounds pretty sick to me. You better GET him to a hospital."

"Oh—that's healing?

"It CAN be."

"We've been to hospitals. Where they give him drugs that end up dissolving his bones or the bones just die. Where . . ."

"Speaking of bones . . ."

"I'm fine. Could not be stronger. Might just join the rodeo. I am going to need the money."

"How are wild animals going to help Awee, Nasdijj?"

"They will remind him he is alive and among them."

"It's a lot to expect from a sick child. I don't understand why he isn't asking for his mother."

"He's afraid of his biological dad. He calls me daddy now."

"I'll bet that makes you feel good."

"Is there a law against my feeling good?"

"I just think he needs a mom."

"He has Crow. He has me."

It would have to be enough.

Awee would have running with the wolves.

Awee was becoming severely depressed. There is something that grates, here, a flaying of the flesh, it's like holding barbed wire and squeezing it when a child is this depressed. Children are not supposed to die.

I just want to pick him up, hold him, rock him, and tell him it's going to be okay, but Awee is too smart for lies.

It's the razor blades again.

The ice picks in his legs and feet.

The neuropathy.

Some of the medications worked a little bit. For a while. Now they don't work so well anymore. No one knows why. No one has more than five minutes to deal with him. No one listens to him.

He is in pain.

He tolerates some pain. More pain than most people would consider tolerating. But then he reaches the point of no return and the pain is so intense, he disappears into the vortex.

The doctor who had been living upstairs in the Whore Hotel up and disappeared.

Poof. I had seen it coming. Too many hookers up and down the hall had warned me to expect it.

The Wolf Rescue Ranch is in a very remote place ironically connected to the Navajo, who traditionally herd sheep. And yet many Navajo understand the mystical connection they have with a species that was almost wiped off the face of the earth.

Abandoned.

I was going to tell you where the ranch was.

I typed the location in and then was horrified to read it.

I do not want you to go there.

I will not tell you how to find the wolves.

We sat Awee on the ground. In his blanket. And we left him there.

We were not far away.

But Awee did not know that.

Sick or well, he was there to face the world. To be *in* the thing.

The wolves were cautious. Yet they approached. I suspect they knew Crow Dog and I were there. Wolves smell everything. I don't know that you can hide anything from them. We did not really try.

They could have eaten him. He might have welcomed it. But he was there to face his life on his own. Perhaps his death. No one knew.

They circled him. They smelled him. They licked him. And they howled.

And then they ran. To play.

To be licked clean by wolves. He was breathless.

He would have enough to talk about nonstop for at least a week. He had been very brave. To face the wolves.

Who had rescued who?

We scooped him up. The wolves were gone away. Who from his own invisibility has come to abandon death today.

24. He Doesn't Stutter When He Sings

Awee owned a few used CDs: *Peyote Songs of the Native American Church* by Verdell Primeaux and Johnny Mike. *Land* by Robert Mirabal. And *Living in the Ground* by Ben Weaver.

Awee owned a blue wallet. Held together with Velcro and duct tape.

There was no money in the wallet. I don't think the wallet had ever seen a dollar bill. But there was a picture in the wallet.

Of Awee.

The child was obviously Awee. Awee as a baby.

A baby picture. Torn. Ready to fall apart.

The kind of baby picture a mother might take.

Awee in his diaper and ready to eat his toes.

Happy Awee.

You could kiss his tummy and smell the baby powder.

As children, we never had a camera.

Both my mother and my father were threatened by the notion of a camera.

There was a *sea* of superstition both in the migrant world (of my father) and the Navajo world (of my mom).

Photography has always been an enigma to me. One that has both released me and hemmed me in.

As I write this, I have not seen the photograph Awee kept in his wallet in quite some time.

I had to throw the wallet out (it was disintegrating) so the photo has been sitting in the bottom drawer of my desk.

I am opening the bottom drawer.

I am taking out the envelope the photograph is in.

I am holding the envelope. I am not sure.

That I want to do this.

There is a power in this envelope. I can feel it.

Awee, talk to me.

Daddy, it's only a photograph. Of me! Your Awee.

But I didn't know you then.

Silly Daddy. You would have built me a cradleboard.

Yaaaaa. I would have liked to have carried you around. You would be all wet against me. I would have loved you then. I would have whole picture books filled and overflowing and falling on the floor with you everywhere.

One will be enough. It is all there is.

The photograph is too dark. I think your mom took it. Darkness everywhere. I can barely see you through the darkness. I can barely make out your diaper. Your kicking legs and feet.

It was me a long time ago.

You don't remember the photograph being taken.

No. We did not take photographs. I don't know who took this one. But it might have been my mom. It probably was because he was more traditional. He would not have wanted a camera in his house. She always did what he told her.

Maybe the photograph was a secret.

Maybe. We had a lot of those. Like AIDS.

Photographs tell the secrets. This one is so dark. There is an awful lot of descending darkness in this house, and yet there is a baby in the middle of the shadows who is attempting to know his toes.

I found the photograph in her purse. She was hiding it. She was hiding many things.

You were looking in her purse.

For money to buy food.

Did you buy the food?

Those little cans the sausages come in. I was hungry. It was a hungry house.

Awee, I am going to put the photograph of my baby in my wallet. That way it will be close to me.

Crow liked it.

Yaaaaa. You guys were looking at it in the bed.

Sometimes I was a baby then and he was not mad at me about it. He was gentle. I needed him to be.

He changed your diapers. You had lost a lot of body mass, and did not have much strength.

I did not want the diaper. It made me cry to wear it.

But Crow was kind to you.

He changed me. Then he rocked me in the rocker. I remember him holding me, and sometimes he had a bottle.

You were dehydrating. Vomiting. Diarrhea.

Daddy, he sang Navajo songs, and he didn't stutter.

No, he doesn't stutter when he sings.

Crow Dog will not look at the photograph. He will cry, he says. He doesn't want to see it, or be in one, or take them right now (maybe someday). It is too much. I put the photo back in my desk. I will slip it into my wallet later. For now, Crow walks around my desk as if there might be an animal I keep inside, and if he is not careful, it will snap and bite him.

It's only a desk, I say.

"Sure, and a photograph is just a piece of paper. How can you sit there and talk to him?"

"It keeps me sane. Sort of."

"Where is he, please?"

There are no words. All I can do is show Crow Dog my brown Navajo eyes. They are the only thing I have that are distinctly Navajo. Except for my dick. The rest of me is white. But my eyes are as Athabaskan as the desert on a night so liquid dark even the moon seems cold when you touch your tongue to the steel of her winter wetness. You will freeze to know me then. Crow Dog did.

"You know."

"Yaaaaa."

"Where do you see him?"

"Everywhere. I don't need photographs, really. They are supposed to take your soul away. Stealing moments from the light." I frown. I shrug. I know nothing of moments or of light. What I know is in my leather *jish*. My place of secrets. Corn pollen. A shell. A lock of Tommy's hair. A small piece of moccasin. A small red cotton heart from a T-shirt that once said: *I Love New York*. All I need is the heart so I cut it out with scissors.

"I will show you my *jish*," Crow said.

"You don't have to do that."

"I want to."

For a Navajo man to show another Navajo man his *jish* is to go into that place the photograph is supposed to steal.

His place of secrets.

Corn pollen. A ribbon from a prayer bundle. A stone from a volcano. A hundred-dollar bill from a bank his mother robbed. Sunflower seeds from an August sunflower he had picked with Awee from a ditch. A pebble from the grave of Geronimo. A small white cotton corner cut from what had been a diaper.

Just big enough to smell.

"I smell him, Daddy."

Crow eyes soft as a mushroom in the woods.

"You changed him when he hated the diaper. You were so gentle with him, Crow, he didn't mind it so very much."

"I thought the diaper would make me sick. Now, I only miss it. I miss all his smells. All of them. I still see him in that bed. But I know he would not stay in no bed long."

I laughed. No. He would not stay in no bed for very long.

"I see Awee on some ferocious ship that sails silently among the mystics and the marvelers to wizardries in wind that breaks like regret scolds and exposes everything in the passion of the shadows and omnipotence of light. Like you said back then. It's like giving birth—you, holding him in the rocker that I sit on as I bring him back every time I sit here so I might write. The music of this rocking. The creak creak from this rocking chair. I see his chin resting on your shoulder. One boy is giving the other boy the courage to face the history of his existence. He gave so much to me. Sometimes I forget how much he gave to you."

My boys cry from time to time. We often laugh as well. We do not need photographs to do either one. We are the photograph, the father, and the son. One boy is the other. Each has given birth to the other. Each one dies every day in the other's arms a little bit. All of this in one small room where nothing happens by that enfolding small river that wanders wet through our dreams. The image in the wallet will dissolve to stars and dust. The stories that we rock will be the stuff of us. Death is like the gentle bird that arrives upon its wings. Yes, he stutters when he talks—but never when he sings.

25. The Roof

We took Awee up to the roof of the Whore Hotel.

Another world. You seemed to float on the breeze up there.

I should say Crow Dog took Awee up to the roof.

In his big warrior arms.

Crow Dog and I were doing more and more carrying now.

Awee's pain was electric. It would shoot through him, take his breath away, and crackle.

Through him. Through me.

The pain was so pervasive *he could not breathe*.

I have attempted to engage well over a hundred medical researchers in this discussion.

But they will not be engaged. Not by the likes of me.

They look at the floor.

They grind their teeth.

The intuitive part of them understands that I am speaking the truth, but the truth is an elusive animal.

They want to hold it.

Unless you can weigh it, see it move under a microscope, watch it reproduce, you can scientifically deny its existence.

What is pain? Why has it always been the province of the

metaphor? The tool of the writer. Does pain *not exist*, or has it been such an inherent part of the thing we refer to as a person for so long that we only see what we want to see, what we want to touch?

It is impossible for medicine to conclude that HIV itself is the cause of pain.

We are suspicious. The people who are infected with HIV complain of pain. Yet we know who they are.

For one thing, we do not know what pain is.

Every medical researcher I have talked to about the fact that HIV itself is the cause of pain shakes his head that, yes, that might be true, but so what.

What do you expect me to do about that?

They ask.

Nothing.

I expect nothing from you anymore.

Go ahead. Look at your floor. Study your shoes.

I will find my own universe of answers.

The pain I speak about does not exist. Stars are constant, and their orbit never wobbles.

Awee experienced several kinds of pain. One pain had to do with his dying bones getting a sufficient blood supply. The twelve-year-old had been attempting to explain this pain for a year, and then it was substantiated on an MRI. Goodness, it was real. Imagine that. Awee had been doing battle with this pain since the age of ten.

No one had believed him.

I found it incomprehensible that a ten-year-old would have to suffer through what is essentially bone pain. Deep and fundamental. Like a stone that shatters. Awee's other pain was the neuropathy. This was thought to have been the result of an allergic response to one of the HIV "miracle" drugs. Basically, Awee's nervous system was like a rocket ship that had burned up its electronics, had emptied its fuel tank, and was now riding through the universe on piano wire.

On the bad days, Awee had no balance. He wobbled like a star or a boat far out at sea. Bearing his weight on his feet was so traumatic, he would scream.

Bloody fucking murder. It was the kind of scream that sent onion worms biting through your veins.

He just couldn't. He would weep: *the razor blades*.

To this day, well-meaning but misinformed people will look me right in the face and suggest (like they know what they're talking about) *pain management*. It sounds so clean. So professional. So scientific. There were some pain management clinics that refused to accept us, never said why, never responded, never returned phone calls, as if they could tell from our names that we simply were not white.

We did not exist to them.

I would have been better off buying him heroin on the street. Don't think for a minute I did not consider it.

I did.

But if I had been arrested, then who was going to be there for Awee financially?

Still . . .

Awee would sign to Crow with his hands (so I didn't have to hear it, but I saw them anyway) to please just let him die. Awee begged.

Let me gooooooooooo.

Please, Crow, please.

But Crow would hold Awee's smaller hands.

Still.

Just still. Don't say that. When Crow cries it's enough to soak everything.

Awee would melt back into the bed.

He was in pain again. He wanted to die again. No one would help us again. I did not know what to do. I was insane with rage. At the people I saw as refusing to help us. We seemed to be at the end of some old dirt road.

Crow would lift Awee up and hold him in the rocking chair by the window. So Awee could see out. Escape.

There was life outside walking around on its own two legs.

Look, honey. It was more interesting to look at than the wall. Crow would tickle him and try to make him laugh and hold him up and up . . .

Awee wasn't heavy anymore.

Crow made a picnic out of it. We had blankets, chips, that red Safeway gunkpunch Awee liked, potato salad from the Safeway deli, and all the things that made it a party for Awee. Who had lost his voice. Another lung infection. Just another thing to try and get through.

Big horse pills for anitibiotics.

Crow and Awee were having a great time with sign language (when Awee's fevers would go down). Awee would tease Crow by pretending not to be able to sign correctly. Crow would go *no-no-no.* He would take Awee's hands (which is what that little squirt wanted) and show him how to do it right.

Touching.

There was nothing Awee liked more than being touched. Nothing.

Awee was seductive. He knew it. He would look at me shyly from the corner of his eye. Because he knew I knew it, too. He would have seduced Crow in a minute if left to his own devices. He was not.

He knew I was on to him.

There was not much he could do about it, really. I would sometimes tell him he could just ask Crow for what he wanted (it would have been more honest), and Awee's ears would turn a little pink. But they did have fun together even if we were scrunched into that prison of a room.

Sometimes we had to leave it or go mad.

I had been writing a book on the little table in that room. A childhood memoir called *Geronimo's Bones*. It is an angry book.

I wanted it to be a follow-up to *The Blood Runs Like a River Through My Dreams*.

It is a detailed account of my migrant years, and living with the raging monster who had been my migrant dad.

Just writing about the violence of those years—looking back—in that little room with that sick boy with AIDS in that bed was everything I could do.

The past, the future, and the present had finally collided.

The nuclear fission was internal.

Money worries had returned to me. I would go into the bathroom, close the door, and literally vomit, hoping I was not making too much noise because my boys had other worries. But I knew *one horrible thing*, and it scared the food from my bowels: If I had failed as a writer to support us (and I had), the life that waited for us out there was the migrant life. Shithole or no shithole, I understood it intimately enough to know it would pay me in cash at the end of the working day.

Crow Dog had swept up all the broken glass on the roof. The liquor bottles were gone. It was nice.

It took me longer to get up there. The bones in my hip kept popping out.

Navajo stayed with me. My girl.

Stairs are hard. I used to think that if your muscles were in good enough shape, they could hold you up. I do not know what caused me to think this. My muscles are in great shape. In fact, they're in extraordinary shape. But you need bones to make it up the stairs.

"There's something I want you to see," Crow told his little feather.

Awee was his little feather. Awee would always grin.

Crow handed Awee a small boxlike thing that at first appeared to look like a radio with a lot of buttons. It was actually a small computer about the size of a dictionary. "It's my voice," Crow said.

I was surprised to see it. I knew what it was. I had lived with it long enough.

When Crow was in the sixth grade, he stopped speaking entirely for a good, long while.

Just brooding silence.

Crow as a twelve-year-old was tired of it. The battle with language.

He had a terrible stutter. He would not wrestle with it any longer. Enough was enough.

I drove him to the University of New Mexico, and we met with some speech pathologists, and some communication software specialists. Crow Dog was silent during that whole long, grueling trip.

Arms locked in protest across his chest. We left with the machine Awee was holding now. Crow had not used it in a long time. He had not needed to. It was called a touch talker.

The touch talker was Crow Dog's voice, and that was what we called it.

He would put *his voice* in the basket of his red bike before we rode to school in the morning.

"Don't forget your voice," I'd say.

"Do you have your voice?" the other teachers would ask him.

Quite simply, you just pressed the keys, and it talked for you. It helped to press the right keys.

The other sixth-grade boys thought it was the most intriguing thing they had ever seen. Everyone wanted to play with it, but I would not allow this. Your voice is not a toy.

We did play a game of Simon Says. The look on Crow Dog's amazed twelve-year-old face when thirty other boys are doing what your voice is telling them to do was *out* of this world. Simon Says sit down. And they did.

No one listens to children with problematic speech. No one does what these children tell them to do. Certainly not their peers. When Crow *saw* other children *doing* what his voice told them to do, I thought he might wet himself.

The only problem with a touch talker is that you have to lug the thing around. But if Crow was not going to talk, there was going to have to be a trade-off somewhere, and this was it.

Everyone trades off something once.

I wanted this picnic up here on the roof to be one that was pain-free for my twelve-year-old. Awee was coming to us with his history, and we were coming to him with ours. Awee was fascinated with the old touch talker.

I had something for Awee, too.

Crow was a little shocked.

I knew he would be.

"Daddy, what are you doing?"

"I'm washing Awee's arm with alcohol."

"Why?"

"Because I'm going to take away his pain, honey. No one will help us, Crow. We have to help ourselves. We won't be the first people to use heroin up here."

Crow had to look away. Awee was still. Almost lifeless.

He had always tried to cooperate when he had to have blood

drawn. There had been a few times when he had lost it, and I had had to hold him while he screamed.

But he had gone through it so many times by this point that there was nothing unusual to him about turning his veins over to someone else.

The rubber hose.

The sterile needle was disposable.

"Crow, I need you to help me hold him so he's comfortable."

"Okay."

Crow was so sad. But this was his brother. And his brother was being destroyed by pain. Horrible pain. His brother wanted to die. Awee begged and begged us to let him go.

There had to be something better than that.

Awee's veins were always black and blue anyway from the bloodletting that was his life.

To squeeze the pain of juice for just a while.

Oh, Daddy.

Awee sighed.

Relief.

From the razor blades and the ice picks and the bad things that ate at him and took all of his energy away.

From us.

I was scared to death to do it. I had tried everything. But this. Let them put me in jail.

I am *not* going to sit there and see my child sick and screaming with pain while everyone did absolutely nothing.

Live with it.

He could not live with it.

Neither could I.

"This is why you went out for a while last night," Crow Dog said.

Yaaaaa.

.   .   .

Awee grew still.

Good good boy. It is over before you know it. Shooting heroin is not rocket science.

The unruined rivers running hot inside the chambers of your skull give rise to carnivals and flares. The latitudes of night swim like bitches sing the blues, wild and with you, tormented, the strings of violins popping inside your eyes, finds me austere, catapulted, vast hordes of suns making contact with the center of the earth, a heat rising from your belly to expand like molten lead has burned the hearing from your ears.

Awee floated and smiled with me just a little.

Sounds like a humming came from him.

His eyes were half-lids but he was with us. Really with us. He looked at me with the biggest look of surprise on his face.

Where did all the pain go?

I had some of him back with us. That is all I wanted.

That slow and languid day we had up on the roof with Crow Dog's voice—and the heroin—was one of the *best* days I have ever had. Anywhere. With anyone. Ever.

The first time I attempted to write the story of this day, I left out the part about the heroin.

"I think you should tell what really happened," Crow Dog said.

I was afraid.

That *they* might lock me up.

I am always afraid *people* are not ready to hear the stories in our bones.

All my boys have come with courage. My daughter has it, too.

It takes courage to find your voice when you have lost it to the wolves.

Awee could not speak up on the roof that day. But he reached out and playfully touched his bigger brother's lips. Crow Dog kissed his fingers.

There's an old programmed Crow Dog voice on the touch talker. It startled me to hear it.

Like something from the past was laughing at the bottom of the hill.

Hi! I am Crow Dog. Born to the Water Flowing People Clan for Salt. I am twelve!

It just hit me as being so funny I rolled around on the roof up there like a hysterical idiot.

Sing, goddess, the anger of Peleus's son Achilles and its devastation, which pains thousandfold upon the exiled of us hurled in multitudes to the House of Hades strong souls of heroes, but gave their bodies to be the delicate feasting of dogs, of all birds, and the will of Zeus was accomplished since that time when first there stood in diversion of conflict all the sons and lords of men and brilliant Achilles with his blood-soaked fields of supplicated backs and beating hearts.

You are your mythologies.

Crow took his hands, and gently guided Awee's fingers to buttons on the touch talker, which has had hundreds and hundreds of stories told to it by a boy who has had to tell them.

He has not changed the programming of his voice in six years.

Crow will be eighty, but the voice in his machine will still be twelve.

We had stayed up late back there in the sixth grade. Night after night. Programming Crow Dog's voice. Fingers touching fingers. Attempting to communicate with someone who has had his language taken from him like his tongue cut out. Crow had taken my fingers, and, touching them, had moved them to his arms, his chest, places where he had been burned. They had hurt him like they might an animal. I knew what those places were.

If you pressed certain combinations of buttons (what you can do with a touch talker is practically infinite), the touch talker would articulate Navajo. *Da'ahijoogaa'*: there was war. Many of Crow's stories began with this. Listening to the touch talker up there on the roof was not unlike being inside Crow Dog's twelve-year-old mind. Now he was a man. Responsible for someone who was the age he had been when he had finally arrived in fits and sputtering to live with me. Rope burns fresh and black around his neck. Stuttering. Stumbling. Refusing to speak. Six years later is an eternity of sorts.

I sat on the blanket with Awee's head in my lap while Crow Dog went and painted the city all around us. The city with its terrible eyes shining.

I just kept combing my fingers through Awee's hair.

I knew the antibiotics would work, and his voice would return. Awee was deeply invested in communication.

I also knew that I was going to have to do something about keeping Awee out of pain.

I keep trying to make the abstract connection between how we communicate and how we deal with pain.

I keep arriving at Awee.

When the infant screams, he's either wet or he's hungry.

He understands that his screaming brings you to him.

You pick him up. He likes it. The brain releases chemicals that the infant experiences as pleasure.

Studies with neonates show that within a day or two of birth, an infant is moving his arms and legs in rhythmic synchrony with the pulse of the mother's words. The newborn is literally dancing to the sound of language. If language is an expression of certain innate structures, then it is the structure that is important, like the roof, and not the pieces.

My sons were works of art themselves.

If we try to do without poetry and esoteric mythology—those places that take us out of ourselves, and are, ironically, places in the brain not disconnected from the pleasure center, the neurological mechanism that allows you to experience such chemicals as heroin—to describe precisely and scientifically how language evolved, we find no casual explanation.

For what is all around us.

"Will you let me go, Daddy," Awee signed.

He meant to die.

He was not in pain. But he could say it. Perhaps he needed to.

"Do you need me to?" I asked.

"Not today," the fingers told me. Maybe someday. But not today.

He made the sign for find. Then pointed to his throat. He would find his voice again.

Awee would heal as was his way. Again and again. Like a skin sheds its second self repeatedly.

"Why won't Crow let me die?" Awee would ask me when we were alone one day in the jeep. Crow Dog in Wal-Mart buying something.

"Crow does not want you to leave him to the loneliness of his life. I think you can understand that."

Awee said he could.

It was as good a time as any to relieve Awee of his pain again.

We had our own pain management program.

We were very careful not to get caught. We parked away from everything. It was dangerous. But so is living.

Crow would grow very, very sad when we did this. I knew he hated it. It went against everything he had been taught.

So we tried our best to do it when he was not around. That was not always possible. Shooting Awee's veins with heroin. The

alcohol. The rubber tube. The disposable syringes. The para-
phernalia of relief.

Crow gets back in the jeep. He says nothing. He knows. You
can smell the alcohol. Awee quiet. Those vast hordes of suns
making contact with the center of his worlds.

There is nothing *peripheral* about a life locked tightly into the
agony of undiminished pain. What merciless slavery is this loneliness whose burned beginnings cut through instruments of
truth and veins. That bleed up on the rooftops of the whores in
rain. My sons stand mute to the everyday amazements where the
sky is black with glass. And loneliness is more than pimps who
peddle ass. My sons stand mute to the testaments of hope. Where
one was touched by the devil that is dope. Two children not connected to the simplicity of lovers. More complex than sanity,
they were the music of two brothers.

26. Rocker to the Woods

We hauled the rocker to the woods.

I say we. But it was Crow Dog who hauled the rocker to the woods. It was my idea. Crow thought it was a good one.

I feel things from objects. It's hard to explain.

To white people.

A lot of my Native American friends say: *Oh, there he goes again with all that Indian shit.*

Yaaaaa.

White people think I am insane.

I keep my mouth shut when I am around them. They do not think that things have lives or speak.

Things have lives, and they speak. Stones speak of joy and they know they will be here. Stones are the happiest.

Things often speak in agony. Especially trees.

I pass them and I have to say: *I know I know I know I know. Stop hounding me, please. I know.*

There was a woods behind the Whore Hotel. Most urban places on the planet only look like they are forever. There are statues in Rome that feel that way, too. *I* am here forever.

I want to say: *Honey, your arms got cut off in 300 B.C., and your nose cracked during an earthquake, and your tits have pits in them.*

Statues are arrogant.

Forever is always an illusion. The jungle waits quietly to reclaim itself. Concrete breaks. Suburbs die. What was once the woods becomes the woods again. The worms just work at it. Even the Whore Hotel with its retinue of sex misfits and addictions will be replaced. It will probably go condo. There is really only one artifact that lasts, and it lasts because it adapts, and that is language.

From the roof of the Whore Hotel you could see the woods in the distance. As if the woods itself was in yet another kingdom. The kingdom of leaves and shadows and logs to sit on and creeks and spiders and their webs.

First, you had to walk through a field. Sad thing of rag weeds. Littered with the carcasses of rusted cars. Old tires. Then you came to the woods.

Crow did not take the chair all the way to the milkweed pods. They were too far away.

There is always magic in such a woods.

The kind of woods where children played.

We could hear them.

That laughing in the distance.

We could see evidence of children. Ropes on trees. The residue of forts. *One* roller skate. Or rather Roller*blade*. Today's junk is modern.

It was a nice woods. There was nothing dangerous there. It sort of quietly welcomed you to come be inside the woods. It was odd to haul a rocking chair out to the woods to rock some sick child and his dragons—the smoking pain and flames of fire that seemed to fly soundlessly just above him—but the woods did not care. About dragons. Dragons came. Dragons went. This woods did not fear silly dragons. This is where you left your pain behind. This was the woods of *nice* children. Children who had no parents (mean people who could tell them when to go to bed). Children who lived in elaborate tree houses, who performed good deeds, and ate cookies whenever they wanted. To such a place with such wizardry fire-breathing dragons were ordinary.

Pain meant nothing here. *Be gone.*

The princes of the kingdom would banish it, but the dragon that is pain usually came crawling back.

Breathing revenge.

Looking as black as thunder.

The dragons of the woods are not unlike the poison ivy there. We ignore it. We pretend it does not exist. We do not touch it. We love the woods.

Crow had picked a great place for the rocking chair. He set it in the middle of a path.

Dragons could dance around. Being stupid. Be gone with you.

The woods seemed to sing to me. *Bring him to me. Let me soothe him with my soft wind and leaves.* So Crow hauled the rocker to the trees (he did not see any witches there) so we might rock Awee as the wind and leaves played piddle all around us.

When Crow returned from the woods, Awee was (as usual) in bed. He almost seemed to be sleeping.

The dog was at the foot of the bed.

I thought now was as good a time as any.

"What do you see?" I asked Crow Dog.

Crow looked at the floor. "Awee's sleeping."

"You're not looking at him."

"Why are you making me do this? The rocker is in the woods. I'll carry him. Let's go."

"No. I want you to look at him."

"I can't."

"Yes, you can."

"No, *I can't!*"

I went over to the bed. The dog moved. I threw the blanket off. I threw the sheet off. Awee was naked, and curled up in a fetal position.

Just barely shaking. Thumb in mouth. He was not asleep. He was wide awake. And yet he *appeared* to be asleep. But not quite.

He began to crawl.

It was slow. It only looked like crawling. It had the movements of a child crawling. The arms moved like claws. The legs moved like claws. Crawling, clawing at the bed.

I tried keeping his fingernails cut short. Hold still.

This is often what we (fitfully) slept with, too.

This *thing*.

With the black eyes. With its diarrhea thinness. With its matchsticks for bones.

Shaking. Crawling. Clawing at his bed.

"What do you see now? Do you see Awee asleep in bed? Crow, honey, you are seeing what you want to see. You want to see Awee sleeping nicely in his bed like a nice boy. Look at it."

"I can't."

"Tell me what you *see*."

"I see Awee in pain. Awee is clawing at himself in pain. It is eating him alive and I don't know *what to DO!*"

"Well, I do."

It wasn't pretty. But it hadn't been particularly pretty in quite a while.

"Hi, Daddy."

"Hi, honey."

"Are you my arm?"

"No, Daddy's not your arm. Daddy is giving you a shot so you can feel better for a while."

"Oh, Daddy, the razor blades are hurting me again."

"I know, honey. I'm sorry."

"Daddy, the ice picks were stabbing me."

"I know. You'll feel better now. You already do!"

"Hi, Crow."

"Hi, Awee. Are you with us now?"

"I don't got no clothes on, Crow. I'm bare-naked, please."

Awee covers his penis with his hand.

"I will dress you, Awee."

"Do we have to do the diaper? I don't like the diaper one."

"I'll pick you up, and you pee in the toilet. And then maybe we won't do the diaper one, okay."

"Okay."

Awee lifts his arms up. His brother carefully carries him into the bathroom.

I feed him pills. One pill at a time. There are over twenty pills. He wants *his* Wal-Mart cup (we are not to use it as it does not belong to us). Awee gulps the pills down with water. The water falls down his chin, drips on his penis. He looks down.

Crow dresses him. Tickles his feet (Awee smiles but his feet are impervious to anything). Unders. Socks. Shoes.

Quick. The toilet again.

His guts explode.

Everything in him drains.

The ritual of the cleaning.

Awee plays in the tub with plastic lemons that lemon juice comes in. The kind that are almost squirt guns if you fill them with water.

Crow is patient.

Even when squirted.

Awee laughs.

Crow attempts to tie the shoes. Getting anywhere takes awhile.

If you can't accept that then you may as well forget, forgive, and flush yourself away.

Everything takes time. Awee's feet slowly seem to realize they are being encased in shoes.

Awee screams.

The icebergs crack again.

The ice picks and the razor blades.

Something inside the boy is mad with sullen venom.

"Daddy, I'm gonna throw up."

But he does not throw up.

The medicine inside of him sings numbing songs to the furies. Hyenas jump from inside his eyes. Deliver us. There is a war going on inside every cell of this small body. We leave the shoes behind. We are going to the woods where the forest children and the dragons do not wear shoes.

"What do the woods children wear for shoes? What do dragons wear for shoes?" I am asked. He is sucking his thumb again. He is trying almost desperately to be playful. There is a powerful healing element to play. It restores in the same unconscious way as sleep.

For such an arrogant species who pretends to understand everything in the universe, we do not even begin to fathom something as mysterious as the disarray of sleep.

"Rollerblades, honey. The forest children all wear Rollerblades. Everyone knows that. The dragons wear booties." Awee laughs now. He is carried to the woods.

Go down this path. With me.

We will listen intently to the happiness of rocks.

Awee was a complex child. His escape into a temporary infantilism was, in fact, the high vengeance of a noble scorn. To walk carefully away from the savageness of the virulent persecutions that burned at him. This was not a simple thing. It was taking the abstraction of the internal and rendering those symbols he found there—the mania of what is essentially nightmare—into externalized destinations, the Ides of March, and sweeping up, instead of being swept, the spellbound child subverts the instability he finds beyond the grave, unleashing a coup d'état, defeating death. He goes back all the way to babyhood, a mutiny of beginnings over endings, cutting the cord that has tethered him to torment, he flies off on wings to elysian fields that lie beyond the purchase of humanity. It was an intricate letting go. It came with depth, and layers, and Awee's inherent ability to examine who he was. Why he was here. How he was here. And with whom.

What men can say they have done this thing?

Crow rocked him first. Crow had a baby bottle of the nutrients we fed Awee. Soy protein. Vitamins. Awee liked it. His eyes and Crow's eyes would make allowances while Awee sucked.

I sat under a tree. On a very nice sitting log that seemed to have been put there just for us.

And one bug.

Me in my brown leather cowboy hat.

Listening to the whispering and the singing of the woods. Petting the dog beside me.

I was sitting far enough away so as not to hear them. I wanted whatever they had to say as brothers to be private.

But I knew what was being said. I knew it word for word.

Because I knew these children like I know my scars and wounds as I have licked them at least a hundred thousand times.

The big one was the one in pain. But he had to deal with this. The little one was telling him to not be sad when he died. The big one was saying that he really had no choice in it, the sadness only was. There was nothing he could do to make it go away.

And please don't die. And please don't die.

The big one is biting his lower lip so something else will hurt, and he doesn't have to cry. Now. Here. In this woods with these dragons who lived for it. Who refused to be left at home.

The three of us were learning not to be afraid to cry. We were doing it now almost every day. One of us always on the verge of it. The other two always ready to catch somebody before they fell off the precipice.

Down into the blackness of the hole where the dragons lived.

I sat down in the rocker, and Crow handed me the child who felt as if he weighed about as much as a cowboy boot.

Crow sat on the grass.

"Do the Navajo believe in monsters?"

"Yes." He knew they did.

"Do the Navajo believe in monsters in the woods?"

"The Navajo believe that Coyote lives in the woods from time to time. But then Coyote lives wherever he wants to."

"Will he trick me?"

"Oh, yes. He tricks boys every day. He's probably tricked a hundred boys today."

"Did he ever trick you?"

"Me? Oh, yes. Coyote tricked me yesterday."

This was most amusing. That I would be tricked.

"How did he trick you, Daddy? Do you have ears?"

"Do you want to touch them?"

"Yes, please."

I let him touch my ears.

"Do you have a penis?"

"You're sitting on it."

"I will touch it."

"No. That would make me sad. I don't want you to."

"But you touch me, Daddy."

"When I am cleaning you. Bathing you, honey. Touching my penis is not a game, okay?"

"Okay. Do you have hair?"

"Do you want to wear my cowboy hat today?"

"Yes, please."

"You look very silly," I said.

"I'm a cowboy."

"Definitely."

"I don't got no shoes though."

"You are a cowboy who doesn't need shoes. Remember when I used to bite your toes?"

"Only it would hurt me now."

"Yes, probably."

"Cuz that is where the razor blades are, in my toes. Cuz the razor blades."

"They hurt you."

"It hurts terrible when they come. And the ice picks."

"Tell me about the razor blades and the ice picks, please."

"Do you want to know?"

"Oh, yes."

"Well, they come, and then they stab you like in the toes, and then in the feets, and then in your legs, and then inside your bones, and then . . ."

He sighed deeply.

"And then sometimes where you go to the bathroom, you know, pottie."

"It upsets you when they come and stab you. There is a nerve by your testicles. Remember . . ."

"It makes me have accidents."

"Yes. That is why Crow puts a diaper on you sometimes. That nerve is damaged. I am told that it is terribly painful. It amazes me you do as well as you do. I know for a fact that you do better than many, many grown men would."

"I do?"

"Oh, yes."

"I like the woods. I am glad you can bring me here."

"I like to rock you. It makes me feel very nice. This is the woods where you found the milkweed pods."

"What are milkweed pods, please."

He did not remember.

When you are not in pain, after you have been trapped in the kind of pain he has been trapped in, what you remember is pain, and what you fear is the return of the dragon.

"It's very important," I explained, "that you do not go *anymore* into the kind of pain you have been in. It's going to be much easier to control if we don't let it get that far. So far into you that we can't bring you back. Do you understand?"

He shook his head that he did, but he did not. I *know* every molecular nuance to his liquid black eyes. He did not understand.

Try another way, Nasdijj.

"You will need more of the medicine that has been helping you be with us and not be in all that clawing pain. I am really, really sorry I let you be in so much pain today, but I wanted Crow to see it."

"See what, Daddy?"

"Little one, he saw all he had to see. Sometimes we only see what we wish were true, or what we wished were there, and sometimes it's difficult to see what is really there, but Crow saw what is really there today. And we are not going to let you be in that kind of pain *ever again*. You have different places on your beautiful, beautiful body we can give you the shots, and then there's a game I will teach you."

"What is the game, please."

"It's called chasing the dragon."

"Will I chase a dragon?"

"Oh, yes."

"When I die will you miss me?"

"I will be *insane*. I love you. I do not know that I can live without you. I cannot imagine it."

"I do not want you to hurt yourself. I do not want Crow to hurt himself."

"If that is what you want."

"I do. That is what I want."

"Are you sure?"

He thought about it. The wind.

"Can you say that if we were all dead we would be together? If you can, then say it, and I will say I want us to be together. But if you can't say it, then you don't know about being dead. If you don't know about being dead, then I want you to *not* hurt yourself when I die, and I want Crow to *not* hurt himself. Do *you* understand?"

Do I understand the Ides of March? I think I do.

"I do not know about being dead, Awee. Many people have what they call faith. That is fine. For them. What I know has to do with about being now. Dead is a mystery to me."

"Then we have to be together now, and that will be enough."

"It will have to be."

"Do you have a throat?"

"Oh, yes. Do you want to touch it?"

"Yes, please."

He touched my throat.

I was looking up.

"Will I go to heaven?"

"I don't know."

"When you die, can you be naked?"

"If you want."

"When I am dead will you make love to Crow?"

"No. Do I make love to Crow now? You sleep with us."

"No. But you love him."

"Like I love you."

"If I was a girl would you make love to me?"

"If you were a girl you would be my daughter instead of my son, and I would take care of you just like I am taking care of you now."

"Okay. I'm tired now."

The sun was going down.

"Do you want to sleep?"

"Yes, please . . . Daddy?"

"What, honey?"

"Will you write about it?"

"Write about what?"

"Us. This. The woods. Rocking me."

"I suppose. I'm trying. Do you want me to?"

"Oh, yes," he said. And then he drifted.

Way out far, and on that fatal sea, and star to star, he drifts through all antiquity. The woods sang songs. The dragons in the leaves. The children of the forest. Stealing time. We were like thieves. The rocking chair a throne. It makes a creaking sound. In nakedness a son is born. A father can be found.

27. Charity

I was sitting on a park bench in a city park.

I looked like any other dad with his dog and kids out for a walk.

Life was good and the sun would break from behind the opalescent clouds, warming my face.

It was like a billion other city park benches. Green peeling paint. The park itself was ordinary. Crow and Awee were not too far away. They were playing in the sand.

Most of the other children in that city park were playing on swings and monkey bars.

Awee no longer played on swings and monkey bars. Crow chasing him.

Now they played sitting in the sand. We used to call the things they were building with their hands sand castles, but these were more like mud castles as it had been pouring cats and dogs for days, and it was chilly enough even now for the three of us to wear jackets. We had been cooped up. We needed to get out. Stretch. Feel the earth. A little mud never hurt anyone.

Mudpies.

Want some, Dad. No thanks.

Puddles. Dog poop. Syringes. Trash. Crack vials. Grass on the verge of deadness doing what it can to hang on.

Toddlers in their Buster Brown boots running from their moms (because they can) with thick goo dripping from their snorting noses like green snot machines.

Yuppies wearing helmets and dressed in spandex on bikes flying through. Sliding by the crazies, and weaving past the tottering drunks as if the drunks themselves were yet obstacles like stone, the accent on health, the asexual affluence reminding everyone that it had left us all behind.

Fourteen-year-old boys in baggy gym shorts and not much else chilled to the titties and pretending not to care with skateboards rumbling by you on some internal dare.

Girls in clean socks with their sisters' stare.

Picnic tables carved with the names of gangs. The Bloods and South Side Rulz.

The graffiti of harangues.

A baseball field now almost a lake.

A toilet where gentlemen came and left. Came and left.

We always had to know where the toilet was. But Crow would not take Awee in there.

I did not exactly blame him.

Awee was wet. He had peed his pants. His brain could no longer differentiate wet from dry. No one cared.

Crow just played with him. Gave him attention. Awee was delighted to be here.

Awee's world was now that thing like light that danced caught glittering between the miniature and the minimal, the modulated and the misinformed, the morphological, and the monsoons of mistakes that blew in from some oceanic heaviness wet with rain and the smell of sea.

"Is that him?" the young man beside me on the bench asked.

Yaaaaa. My boy and my other boy. I nod.

He nods. Removes his tough-guy sunglasses. Squints.

There has been no sun for days.

"Fuck you, man. Just fuck you."

"Yeah, fuck me. But it won't help *him*. I just wanted you to see him."

"Yeah, motherfucker, I see him. What makes you think you're so fucking different?"

They were wrestling now.

"They both do," I said.

He could see that. He was a great judge of character. He has staked his life on it.

He was well-dressed. Nice expensive stuff.

He had everything. Nothing harsh.

Appearances.

"I can only do this once, you know."

"I appreciate it."

"Yeah, you fuck. I'm sure you do. How did you find out about me? Had to be a ho, had to be."

Tough-guy bravado. He who demands loyalty from all languages and tongues that he might conquer loneliness like a woman licks the sun. His ancestors had once lived in what is now called Kenya. He at one time was determined to go there, curious, but since that time had changed his mind, and now he was more prone to stay at the Holiday Inn in Samoa. He did not like to think too hard on his ancestors. He was not like them. He was in charge of his destiny, no one else. Tough guy thrills and chills. Deals and steals. He drove a red Camero. It was parked around the corner. He was even early, as was I.

Tough guy with his wings gone mad. Never sample the merchandise. You lived by rules, and you died by them. Well, of course, he had. Sampled. Dipped into it. Only recently. He knew this: *It was over now. Done. He would be a confirmed junkie now in a matter of days, hours, really. Hours were all he had.* He had sailed too near the wind, and even his plans to kill himself in a room at the Holiday Inn in Samoa drained him of his street-smart postures, the arrogance of his caricatures, his posing, when he thought about it, which wasn't often. There was nothing to think about.

It had been decided.

The ticket to Samoa was in his suitcase, which was packed but not with much. He had acquaintances in Samoa—all the friends listed in his pocket PC were acquaintances—even the one who would deliver the gun he had already purchased. It was a planet of acquaintances.

I had sat on his couch and we had discussed all of this for some hours as he drained himself of words. Dope will make you talk like that. On and on to deadened strangers who have arrived at a particular time as if they were themselves the hidden souls of angels. The image of the gun in his motherfucker mouth was like some phallic gesture to the horror of the sky.

"One hooker leads to another hooker. You just follow the scent. It led me to you. You know that."

"What you need is charity, man."

I almost laughed. For the past two days I had been exchanging e-mails with people in the Public Relations Department of the Robert Wood Johnson Foundation.

They fund things like public television documentaries on pain management and death.

I needed money. I needed money to buy drugs.

They do not fund individuals seeking funding to buy drugs.

The e-mails ended. They were not helpful.

The whores started coming to me. I had been buying dope

for Awee but my ability to keep doing that was about to end. If there is anyone who could understand my situation, it was going to be a whore.

I loved them.

Warts and all.

Many of them had HIV.

His name was Noah.

He sold heroin to whores.

He had been infected.

Most of the girls in his circle knew it.

"Look, you can't tell him I was the one who told you about him, okay," she had explained.

I had been buying her drinks. She needed drinks.

Her name was Tammy.

She said. Who the fuck believes anything a hooker says.

I do.

I had been buying her cigarettes. She needed cigarettes.

I do not know her real name. I do not know that she had one. I had been buying her time. She needed time.

"You wanna fuck me?"

"Not really. Tell me more about Noah."

Twenty dollars helped.

She crosses her legs on the bar stool like a professional. She is a professional.

"He's a really nice guy. A little intense, you know. *Never* fuck around with him. If he figures out who the girl is, she's as good as dead, you know what I mean? It sure as shit wasn't me."

I knew what she meant.

"Some guys just don't want to go through it. They like being who they are. Strong. In charge. You know, tough guys. They see it all. The pills. The doctors. The slow, you know, grinding down, and you can't even fucking drink on those pills, you know,

but everybody does, and coke, you got any coke? There goes
Debby, she always has coke."

Another fifty dollars bought some blow.

Debby was the cocktail waitress.

Blow, as every pimp knows, makes a ho's tongue go looser
than her booty.

"Noah's gonna have a party. A big motherfucker bash at some
swank hotel. The Jack Tar. This weekend, *try* and keep me away,
free drugs for everyone. Free drinks. And not that cheap shit
they sell in this swill. *Nice* booze like that Johnny Walker Black I
can never afford to buy . . ."

She exhaled.

The way only a whore knows how to exhale. The smoke from
her lipstick lips like surrender circumnavigates the air, and what
do men know anyway about the sadness of women.

The contour lines, and the stretched landmarks of her life
were like features on a moon of broken glass. She flirts with the
neutral eyes of an alcoholic broad who moves in slow reflection
like the smoke that drifts from the cigarette she holds as if it
were a weapon welded to her hand. Her fingernails are fake, and
even her death flows serene beyond the superficial reach of
splendor. The bar we were in featured a South Sea Island motif.

"Noah drinks here," she said.

Another state secret.

There were so many.

She was from Miami.

I bought her a bottle.

I do not remember of what.

Tammy from Miami. Even her apartment had a plastic potted
plant.

She lived two floors up from me and down the hall. When

the women in that corner of the building were angry, all their wailing places would descend within these walls, and break with equal fury all the shot glasses within a six-block radius. She was in love with a Colombian we called the Boneman.

There were rumors he might slit her throat. We figured most of them had been started by Tammy herself.

"Do you miss Miami?" I asked.

"What's to miss? My old man down there used to take me to the Opa-Locka ABC. Wow. I could get double gin martinis if I wore my fuck-me shorts when I was thirteen. Hey, you know, only a year older than that boy you have, the little one. I was a waitress at the International House of Pancakes by the Hialeah dog track. The tips were good." She shrugged. "I suppose I could hook you up with Noah before he blows his brains out."

"Blows his brains out?"

"Look, you know and I know that the medication does not work for everyone. Noah sees girls that used to work for him— when he was a pimp, but he's not pimping girls anymore—down in the gutter on the street selling pussy for a subway token home. Only they ain't got no home. Noah has seen it all. Done it all. Now all he wants is to check out. Can't say I blame him, but, hey, the drugs work for me, so I think I'll stay around. But I know Noah. And the party is Friday night if you wanna be my date?"

I did not want a date.

But two bottles of Johnny Walker Black and a carton of cigarettes bought me Noah's number.

I called. We connected.

He didn't look sick.

Sometimes you just want to talk.

It happens to everyone.

You want to talk. It does not matter to who. You want someone to know that you are here. You are still here. And this is
where I hurt. And here. And here. And here.

"I got a kid, too, you know," Noah said as we sat on the
bench in the park.

I had seen a few things in his apartment.

I had seen a new catcher's mitt on the dining room table. So
new you could smell the leather.

He had a picture of his son in his wallet. He showed me
DeShawn, who lived with his mother.

I had seen a picture of DeShawn, too, by the television. The
picture in the wallet was the same picture as the one by the big-
screen TV. It appeared to be a middle school photograph.

They are so vulnerable at that age.

Caught. Between. The stars.

Noah studied both my boys. Playing in the sand.

"My boy don't need no sick dad in his life."

He almost whispered it.

This is where I am supposed to say: *Don't do this. Your kid
needs you. You will be okay. The medication really does work. What a
waste.*

This was not a man you argued with.

I wanted charity.

I wanted heroin for my kid.

So Awee would not be in pain.

I was at the end of this rope with Noah in a city park where it
had rained solid. Everyone was out. The air smelled clean.

"Don't do this. Your kid needs you. You will be okay. The
medication really does work. What a waste, man."

"It's not your business. I have a ticket to Samoa. Did you cut
this stuff like I told you to?"

Yaaaaa.

"Did you bring it down like I told you to—shit, that kid can't weigh but fifty pounds. Keep it low. He will still get hooked, and you'll have to jack the dose up, but keep it low like I showed you. Be careful, motherfucker, this junk is lethal, it has not been cut with no baby laxative or any other crank shit, you got that. It's *pure* horse, man. This, motherfucker, is *charity*."

"Thank you."

"Don't thank me for shit. And it's not for you. It's for him. *Not* you. *Him*. Cuz if I hear you been high even one time, I'm coming over here, I'm taking you with me when I go, and you *do not* want to make me angry."

No fucking way.

"How do you want me to pick it up?"

"It's already in the pocket of your jacket. It's a *lot* of dope, man. Do not tell anyone you have it. There goes my party. It will be BYODYH. Bring Your Own Dope You Hos."

He slapped his knee and laughed, flashing his gold front tooth. Now I could feel the package in my pocket.

"You're okay, Tonto."

"Hey, I . . ."

"You begged. Not many do. People don't beg. They too stupid to beg. You got right down on the floor, baby, and you begged in my apartment. I know. I sell dope. Mostly to junkies, you know, got their shit together. People think junkies don't have no shit to put together. That is fucked thinking, my brother. Fucked thinking. I know some skag queens who have lived eighty years, and they still hitting on that goddamn needle. She don't beg for shit. See, we don't hear about the ones who live like an old leather shoe forever. Why would we? They do it quiet. They want it quiet. They live in one room and all they want is to be left alone. But they don't beg cuz they don't have to, man. You begged. Really begged. My junkies don't beg. Fuck no. You said your boys were beautiful. You were right. I see that. I might be some lowlife. Sampled his own shit now. That is death to a dealer. I am lowlife. I know that. But I am not so low I can't recognize beauty. Do me a favor, motherfucker."

"What?"

"Don't beg. Don't ever do it again. Not for dope. Not for anything. Do that for me, okay?"

"Sure."

He left me sitting there. They say charity is dead. I do believe it.

Two kids playing, making mud and castles in the sand.

One had wet his silly pants. The other held his hand.

28. Geronimo's Grave

There was work in Oklahoma. There is always work in Oklahoma. In Oklahoma, the sun burns on your neck, pushing you down until your face can feel the dirt, and you can definitely smell it. It is not the kind of work most Americans want to do. Picking food, loading it onto trucks will break your back, and it will break you, too, and there will not be scars in the broken places, you will not be stronger there, you will only be broken.

I had failed as a writer.

I had failed as a father, too.

I had failed to provide for my boys.

I would rather return to the migrant camps than have to go on welfare because welfare demeans me. It puts the orange jumpsuit on you, and you end up picking candy wrappers off the lawn at the county courthouse. For this you get food stamps. At least harvesting food means something.

At least it's real.

The problem with the migrant bosses who will pay you at the end of the day (they don't really care to see your papers or know your name) is that these guys do not run the best migrant camps, if there is such a thing. Such a distinction.

The best migrant camps.

The ones with real toilets.

The ones with water.

The migrant camps where you are paid at the end of the day are the worst migrant camps. They are glad to see you go. People who stay too long can be a problem. People who stay too long begin to complain. People who move on are not there to complain.

One of the biggest problems among female migrant workers is kidney disease. There are no places to go to the bathroom. You attempt to limit your intake of liquids so you don't have to pee, and you end up passing out in the fields from dehydration.

Crow had never worked the fields before. "When you gotta pee," I explained to him, "you just go pee. Do not be embarrassed. Don't hold it in. And drink. Drink a lot."

Sometimes they bring water to the fields (in the good camps). But I made Crow carry Gatorade. I was his mother hen.

It felt like all of my effort on *Geronimo's Bones* had been wasted. The dirt in the Oklahoma fields would shimmer in the distant heat, blowing around the topsoil, and I could see Geronimo among the migrant workers. His bronze skin burned like mahogany. I was distraught. It had taken so much sweat to write that book. Years wasted. All down the drain like some Oklahoma migrant toilet dug in the ground and overflowing with human shit. I didn't have many more years to waste. I didn't know if I could pick myself up off the floor by my bootstraps again. My bootstraps had worn thin. The boots had holes. They were not the kind of boots that were going to make it through a winter.

I am not afraid of work. I knew how to find it. My problem was my bones. Sometimes I was using crutches now. Or I would just limp along the rows and rows.

Awee was in a wheelchair. The ice picks and the razor blades made walking a complete torture for him. He would weep and scream. The wheelchair helped a lot. Except for the pudendal nerve entrapment that made him squirm like he had been wounded.

Awee did not want to be in a wheelchair. But Crow and I made a big deal out of how cool it was.

It *was* a cool wheelchair.

If we put a nice pillow on it, it helped with the pudendal nerve.

Awee would hold himself, bent over in agony, when the nerve itself seemed to scream some silent, wrathful hornet's nest of burning teeth. I wasn't going to write about the wheelchair. Because Awee never really saw himself as *handicapped*. I was going to ignore the wheelchair because it would not be the way in which he would have wanted to be portrayed. I wasn't going to write about the heroin either. I felt bad about a lot of things. Just limp along the rows and rows. Wondering how Awee was back in the migrant shack. Both Crow and I would stop and briefly look off in that direction like we had lost something. Then back to work. I could weed the crops with a hoe versus hefting heavy things like melons, although sometimes hefting things like melons could not be avoided. The pain was far worse than holding up the bike. I had finally sold it to pay medical expenses.

I had seen handicapped athletes use these wheelchairs at the Para-Olympics in Barcelona. The chairs are quite light. Awee's wheelchair was sky blue.

It was the last of the book money. It was the last of *The Blood Runs Like a River Through My Dreams*.

It was time to find a migrant camp. It was a going back in time.

Migrant camps exist frozen in a time warp.

They are a dime a dozen in Oklahoma. You can get paid in dollar bills (they count them one at a time) at the end of the day.

I liked that. Even if they did charge you "rent" for those vermin-infested shacks they put you in. The three of us would rather sleep outside on the ground. At least here there were fewer rats.

During the day Awee would go outside in his wheelchair (against my orders) and sit there waiting for us to return rather than be inside the shack with the rats. Crow and I could be as far as twenty miles away.

We had all been buried by the dirt and the Oklahoma sun.

Geronimo is laid to rest just outside of Lawton, Oklahoma, on a military reservation, Fort Sill. The cemetery is near the back end of the reservation. On an old dirt road. It is a fenced-off and quiet place surrounded by huge trees whose sweeping branches seem to reach out to protect the Chiricahua sleeping here. The babies and the elders. Awee had heard all about Geronimo from me.

I spoke about Geronimo as if he were a hero. He was to me. Geronimo had single-handedly kept the entire United States military machine from finding his people. Surrender came with imprisonment.

Geronimo had been forced to be a farm worker.

The cemetery he is buried in almost whispers Chiricahua lullabyes.

Awee wanted to see it. He had just endured his first migrant camp. Crow Dog had had to heft more melons than his share. He had had to heft a lot of my share. After a day of hefting melons, it begins to feel like you are hefting rock. Geronimo did not care much for it. Neither did I. Neither did Crow Dog, who never said a word.

Awee waited inside his little shell all day for us to come home.

In from the fields drenched in the fatigue of sweat. "But I want to help."

"If I see you anywhere near these fields, I will heft you *and* your wheelchair into a huge, loud, regurgitating, electric spanking machine that will turn your—"

"It's already red," he said. We had all shared the same mold-crawling concrete showers. Awee's butt was the color of the inside of a ripe watermelon. His skin was a mess of fungal infections. He could barely sit in his new wheelchair.

I tried getting doctors to prescribe Diflucan. It was useless.

The other children in the migrant camp thought it fun to push Awee around. They were "helping." No one said AIDS. We just told them Awee could not walk. People would nod nicely, cross themselves, and say something soft about God's will.

They were nice people. They worked hard. They moved on. You never saw them again. Sometimes you had to sleep with them in a big barn of a migrant shack. *Shack* is perhaps the wrong word (some of them were Quonset huts built around 1940), but I do not know how else to describe these places. One old stove. Maybe water. Migrant cots wall to wall. All-night coughing. Men playing cards. The all-night music from a radio playing salsa or something that reminded someone of home.

Children everywhere.

Awee did not believe there was a spanking machine. Crow and I assured him there was one. There was one just for Mexican children. There was another one for Native American children. There was a big mean one for bad white children. There was one for African-American children. But the biggest, meanest spanking machine was for the Navajo. It was red, too.

There were a lot of loud machines in migrant camps.

You never knew.

Awee claimed that if there was such a thing as a mean spanking machine, there would definitely be one for writers.

I knew an editor who would have agreed with him.

I had spent years attempting to capture (in something as blunt as English) the spirit of Geronimo the warrior.

The spirit of Geronimo dominates everything in the isolated cemetery place he is buried in. Yet finally the spirit of Geronimo is one of surrender.

Coming here, pushing Awee through all these graves, causes me to realize that if my book *Geronimo's Bones* was in the final analysis correct, if I were actually bringing you something about who the old man had been, the book itself had to be about surrender, and, now, it was.

As was Awee. Surrendered in his wheelchair. We were among the Chiricahua. Who were not to blame. Dead children buried everywhere. Lost to starvation. Lost to tuberculosis. Lost to smallpox. Lost to alcohol poisoning. Just lost.

Geronimo's children are buried all around him. He never returned to the Gila Mountains he loved.

"There are two things that kill people," Awee claimed. "Sadness and loneliness. Our house has neither one. Even if our house is really just a jeep."

We were becoming better at climbing over the barbed-wire fences of sadness. None of us was lonely. Ever.

We had one another. Our little lost tribe.

Loneliness was not an option. Especially not in the fields where people were generous and hefted melons for you if you were someone whose bones had turned to dog shit.

Awee had spent many hours with me as I had torn my hair out by the roots over *Geronimo's Bones*. He knew a lot about Geronimo.

Who could see things.

Geronimo had visions. His visions were what had led his people.

Geronimo and his people had evaded capture for many years.

Because Geronimo could *see* beyond the Apache shadows of the desert night.

Awee grew very solemn.

I knew him well enough now to respect him when he did this. He always did it for a reason.

Crow was putting a medicine bundle in the tree that towers over Geronimo.

"Daddy," Awee said.

"What, honey?"

He sighed. His tone was loving, quiet.

"I'm going blind."

Big old blobs of blobby tears ran like rivers from the liquid blackness of his Athabaskan eyes. Most of what we are is liquid.

I knew enough to know it was the optic nerve. All of Awee's nerves seemed to be dissolving, and Awee with them.

We found a Motel Six. They take dogs. The room was nice. There were two huge beds. But the three of us slept together. All around Awee. Holding him. He had been slowly losing what he had of sight. No one to blame. Nothing to do. No way to make it right.

29. All the Way to China

The migrant trucks arrived early in the blackness of the morning. You could see your breath like frost. Awee in his wheelchair saying good-bye to the working men.

"Are you gonna be okay today?" I fussed.

Yaaaaa. My line. "Don't worry, Dad."

Right.

I hated this. I had always hated this. I was always the last caballero in the pickup. Crow would be with the other men waiting for me. It took me time to fuss and cluck around Awee. Making sure his shirt buttons were buttoned.

I'm coming! I'm coming!

Our truck was always late.

Sometimes in the evening, if we had not worked all the way to dark, the migrant men (who liked Awee and were very kind to him) would give Awee rides in trucks. They were always very tender lifting him from his wheelchair and setting him on blankets in the back of pickups. Awee leaned on the inevitable spare tire.

Not going anywhere really. Maybe to the store for beer.

It was okay. Crow and I would ride with him. Sometimes we

would lie down in the back of the pickup. Looking up at the sunset shadows of the clouds that would pass by. So far away and
way up high. Star to star and light fantastic, swimming in the migrant sky.

Awee was the only child I knew who could see all the way to
China even from the desert, which is where we were once again.
"I can see China," he would say as I held him. For someone go-
ing blind, this was our small, somewhat private joke.

Yaaaaa.

"No, I really can."

"Okay, where is China?"

Awee would point at some faraway set of shadow mountains.
"You have to close your eyes," he said. "You will see across the
ocean. I do." Then he would close his eyes. To see everything.

He would gently take his fingers, and close my eyes so I could
see everything he saw. All the way to China. It was far, far away.
But so was Awee by then. As he was touching my eyes, I could
smell his hands. Ships. I could feel him slipping. I did not have
to close my eyes to know it.

Awee went from touching my eyes to pinching my lips
together.

Hard.

Owww. It hurt.

Awee was *always* pinching my lips. To see if I was real.

I did not want him to go. To China. Or anywhere. In ships.
Awee, standing alone on the deck. His face yet into the wind.
His hair blown back. *Awee, don't leave me here.*

Kites.

We found them in the most unlikely place. A kite shop in a
nowhere town. Almost a ghost town. Like any of the other
towns in dust we had spent the night in. But this one had a kite
shop. The kites were in the window of what had once been a

general store. All the kites were brilliant colors. Oh, we wanted one. I bought three.

Awee's kite had the image of a bird. It was a bird kite.

Knock knock.

Who's there?

Awee.

Awee who?

Awee gonna be birds when we fly the kite? Ha! Ha!

Birds. Yaaaaa.

The mesa is a place of wind. The kites were our private sailing ships. Sails unfurled. Crow Dog would run fast—Navajo chasing, barking—to make the kite fly high. Then he would hand the kite to Awee who would hold the kite for a bit from his wheelchair. Awee out here sitting in his mobile cage. With the gopher snakes, lizards, piñon jays, coyotes, ravens, saltbrush, Grama grass, bobcats, wild horses, and the prairie dogs. In the end, we are only animals among the animals and glad for it.

A small family of sparrows flies away. There are times in life when you are compelled to put your anxieties away. Your work. Your worries. It all ends here. Birth and death are two of those times. We had shared our scars. Milkweed pods. The men he kept in boxes. Jesus was a statue. Reading to Head Start children. Two boys dancing in pajamas. Dancing with shy girls at powwows. Building houses. Trembling. Fixing motorcycles. We had worn the masks of gods. Played baseball. Had our hair cut in barbershops. Run with wolves. Seen the stars from rooftops. Touched Geronimo. Gone for rides in migrant trucks. Flown kites.

Poetry is the only real language that I know. It carries you down like the arms of Sa. It is the eternal language babbling in my head. A ship. The barquentine. Poetry is a catboat with black sails like a catamaran drifting in the tides and winds of chaos.

.   .   .

"I want to go down to the canyon," Awee said.

We had to carry him there. Toothpicks.

Sa is said to live here but no one knows. No one has seen her since the time of dragons. The canyon is just a place. That is all it is. No one lives there. It is empty.

I look forward to my death. I look forward to this struggle ending. I look forward to being freed from this pain. I know the time. I see the room. I know the window well. In the west, there is the sunset. And that river with my antelope.

The Navajo know where the canyon is. *Let them HAVE their tribal secrets. It is IMPORTANT.* There are many places in Dine-tah that are not even on the reservation. On the reservation. Off the reservation. Boundaries are artificial limits imposed by men.

They used to put the dead bodies of children high up in the trees. Then, no one came here.

The rattle from the desert wind was like the songs from snakes. The rattle from the desert wind was like a thing that takes.

Its time to cum. Its teeth in flesh tasting poison veins that ultimately numb. The rattle of the desert wind twists softly as we run. Like ravaged thirst. A treason to the turbulence of night. Illumination claws to burst. A scaffolding of light. These trails to dreams, and to count the bodies of the warrior dead. Riding naked on our ponies to where Time has cramped and bled.

The desert wind was but the whip, and the sand was but the temple of the swirling earth. The desert wind was but this stinging love for him. The execution of my birth.

The desert wind was a wandering of dim and tangled trails. The center of the dark, I pray for him, a milk of drowning males. An ancient thing, the wind smelled like dried pine, sage, love, sun, salt, sweat, flesh, and doubted it would ever hold the sums of nothing even as it flew into the bleeding wounds of sleep. The desert wind felt hot against the lips like lips are wings against the tongues and what the languages would reap.

In Time, dominion keeps the wind a thing in molten liquid form. The wind is a thing of sand and sing and ultimately storm. The wind was dead and strained to say its noontide perished prayers. Fingers like nerves of steel. Climbs these rocks on stairs. The wind was dead and strained. To eliminate the fever. Trembles at the razor pain. The fingers of the weaver. Cut themselves where probing is the redness of the rose. Cut themselves where probing is the draining of everything that flows.

Through Time. Through wind. Through sand. Through a universe of cold. Through that which makes young thieves grow in symmetry to everything gone old. The sickened sun was shouldered warm like whispers on the rocks. The echo of the empty sky was hard with smoke and shudder mocks the magnificence of eyes. Magnificence a thing of sleep inside my son's black skies.

The silent mute is the magic of the ravens whose song is not in tune. The desert is our bed, our bones upon the ground of doom.

That slaves away heavy in its rages of the clouds. Eternal snakes do rattle blackly in the shedding costume of their shrouds. My son punished kissproof in his songs of morning dust. The desert falls away with secrets. Secrets with their thrust. Like God in bed his eyelids sang the noises of the shells. I draw no sheet over nakedness or demons with their hells. Rumbles deep with secrets. A snake with its silent bowels. Straining to eliminate the snakes beneath the Dog Star of the howls. Erupts with secrets in what must be the strangulation of a lust. Erupts with involuntary crucifixion in the exiles of trust to dust.

He is riding ponies. I see him in my dreams. We talk and dance and laugh and prance. Life is never what it seems.

.   .   .

The elements of surrender, and the canyon stones in canyon walls are torments of revenge, remember.

In the east, toward Chaco, the coming of the sandstorm sings. The stars are broken, the sky will pour with the garroting of ancient kings. The fathomless runs with fury, far, far, and down below. For we shall be our shudders, and everything we know. Whipping the earth to a place bled white. The stinging sweat flows against your eyes of stain and sight. Riding ponies to the tops of mountains dying like our bursts of milky light. The coming and the going from what we know of earth. Dying is but an orgasm and not unlike your birth.

Riding ponies naked. As we ultimately must. Riding ponies naked far above the swirling dust.

The blazing sun has burned our fiery skin like soaring sails. Rippling warriors of the flaming suns. Doom ultimately fails.

I'm standing on some shore, and his ship has disappeared out to sea. Our Sabbath Masses wear the quick away. I am him and he is me.

I held him floating in another land where the sky and Time were low.

Now I had to hold him to me while I let him go.

Three warriors pleasing death outstretched, extended, mere anatomy pulled tight but yet the knot. Distance lends enchantment. Bodies only rot. My wings are done. The sun will run. With wax and tombs of quest. No more rising and the falling of what had been his chest. Incest is the flight of birds and ultimately sin. The desert is an extinct place concealing all that's dim. Our love was just the deepness of the wolves asleep in caves. Folded in our arms and throats. The shadows kiss and rave. Who is he then, this carnage whirling, and the skies will pull on thunder's pour. Our eunuch suns raise up the dead, and speak in tongues of war.

The echoes of our flesh move like blindness in a womb. Riding ponies to our roots. Unhouse the seedless tomb.

The only thunder in this desert is the thunder of the dead. The sun has set. We lay in weeds, and sing of deeds, and make the ground our bed. Him by bags of blood lets out the flies. Lightly as a feather floats away on wind and dies.

We held him one last time.

None of it could touch my grief, and none of it could rhyme. I refused to let them touch me. The woman that I loved. The older boy who needed me. I stupidly would snub. Ponies. Ships. Death is but a path. Launching lifeboats onto a sea of wrath.

The universe does not *hear me*, not my sound, everything I touch is yet unbound. Your son is dead, and stings his eyes upon the vowels found wet upon the tongue. You climb into his grave to be his milk and all the magic you have wrung. From nettles and the wick of words the two of you have known. The stories and beginnings that were told to you by gnomes. When warriors die like dead children unwind the seeds from dust in chords. The three of you are as mad as birds above the warring hordes. That the phoenix would break away in love to find communion in the dark. Runs out the sound in chains, and flies wanton like the lark. Last night in a rape of waves his savage gliding finds you holding what is left of thread. You. Standing in the dark and watching your sleeping son in bed.

Now my other one—the one who cannot hear—holds his hand to me, and makes sure that he is always near. I did not mean to push him so hard or far away. Don't leave me quite just yet. At least just not today.

Awee bathes all our burning in the story that was told. Melting yet the coat of ice we wear, the stars are falling into cold. We are always riding ponies naked to the top of rocky buttes. The other sun in stranger's dust sings myself in flutes. The *yiyol* is an Athabascan sandstorm, and the flames will make you blind. The requiems of whirling, and the bitterness of Time. Flows ponies woundward where the sons stand yet upon the slain, and sandstorm sings of wombs that bring yet naked warriors to the tame.

His ruined body still. It made no forward motion. His eyes could see away and off and far across the ocean.

Eyes to the sky. Hold me, Tina. Please. Hold me. I need you. I want you back.

Death just cums. It takes away the pain. Riding ponies through the mesa. Disappears in rain. Death just comes like the broken pony pulls a plow. I do not know. I do not know. I do not know how.

Sssssssshhhhhhh. Listen. The brother and the dog are running with the kite. Like jumping off of cliffs and wings will give you flight. The memories of boys and dogs are forever worth the keeping. Hush. The boys and dogs are far away. The ships are only seeking. The boys and dogs are done today. The boys and dogs are sleeping.

THE BOY AND THE DOG ARE SLEEPING

A Reader's Guide

NASDIJJ

A CONVERSATION WITH NASDIJJ

JACK NORTON was born in Minneapolis, Minnesota, in 1979. He has lived a life spent on the road: His parents, Pentecostal preachers and part-time bluegrass musicians, kept home in Macon, Georgia; New Orleans; New York; Iowa; and Minnesota. Jack graduated in 1997 from the Arts High School in Minneapolis. For the past decade he has been a full-time singer/songwriter and poet, writing, recording, and performing over two hundred shows a year in North America and Europe. He leads Jack Norton's Wizard Oil Vaudeville Company, a conglomerated touring theatrical troupe of musicians, actors, puppeteers, filmmakers, and carnies. Norton currently lives in Minneapolis. He can be contacted at info@jacknorton.net.

Jack Norton: Explain to me how and why the Navajo refer to themselves as the People Who Walk the Surface of the Earth.

Nasdijj: The Navajo—for good or for bad—essentially see themselves as apart from the rest of humanity. The mythology says that the Navajo are here to endure the hardships of living, and as such they are to offer themselves as examples to other humans. When living is out of balance, as it usually is—and for someone like me, it always is—we are taught to believe that it is our responsibility to facilitate change. White people do not understand that part of who we are. For instance, we do not speak out. Hardly ever. But when we do it is with power. To return the world to balance. White people see us as stationary. But that is an illusion. We are, in fact, a nomadic people. But you have to look at us and our thousands of years of migrating through the lens of centuries, and not with a corporate eyeball where the only thing that matters is how much you made today.

JN: Talk to me about poverty on the reservation.

N: I don't know how to do that. What I do is take one small example like Awee, and I attempt to show you what he had to live in. It is a world of desperation, disease, hunger, and utter personal devastation.

JN: What is this death that comes through uranium mines?

N: All through the Cold War the Navajo reservation was mined to supply America with nuclear material for weapons. Most Navajo miners are dead now. It killed many Navajo, much livestock, and has left the younger generation with enormous health problems.

JN: You write that change is one child at a time. You write that change is changing the madness of culture into the spirituality of the individual one social structure at a time. Do you still believe this?

N: No. I have lost all hope. For society. For culture. For individuals. What I now believe is that it is too late. The corporations win. There is no hope. Not for the Navajo. Not for anyone. I was wrong. The enormity of what the white culture has imposed upon the Native American has rendered anything any of us could do to be totally ephemeral. I have no hope for anything or anyone. All I know is that we all will die and be done with it. That is all I believe there is.

JN: Life with Awee had an immediacy to it that was inescapable. Do you live your own life that way? Was it as intense with Tommy Nothing Fancy? Does your own health cause you to live this intensely?

N: With Tom, life was soft, and I was not yet thirty. I was a warrior and still had hope. My own health has been worn down to the point where my nose is pressed into the grave and it's cold and dark. I rage against it. Dylan Thomas was right. Life is absolutely immediate when what you fight against is being enveloped finally and utterly by what is called the night.

JN: Are there any support systems or health care providers on the reservation that could deal with AIDS?

N: Public health care on the rez is underfunded and overwhelmed. Doctors and nurses cope as best they can. But it's like war there. You would swear from standing in the hallway of just about any Indian hospital that a bomb went off somewhere. It's like Iraq in that respect. But it's here. In America. White people don't see it because they don't want to know, and if they did see it they would be indifferent or they would say, "It's their own fault" because that is what they have always said. No. Health care on the reservation is a nightmare. I have seen people just give up and die and I understand that.

JN: Was it necessary to become as isolated as you did with Awee, living alone in a hotel?

N: I did not think it fair for me to impose AIDS on anyone else. It was my problem to deal with. So we were, indeed, isolated. But I also knew that through that very isolation we would either bond or die. We did both. Awee died, but pieces of me did, too. The

hopeful Nasdijj, the nice Nasdijj, the Nasdijj who believed that
we could solve these problems if we just worked together is dead.
I am numb, poor, devastated, ravaged, and ruined. You cannot
know all of it. I keep it to myself. Every moment I am even here
is almost unbelievable, even to me. By rights, I should have died a
long time ago. My doctors are completely baffled. But sometimes
my rage at the world and at that night Dylan Thomas talks about
infuses me with life. It is why such people as Crazy Horse and
Tanka Yotanka and Sitting Bull survived as long as they did.

JN: What were Awee's dreams?

N: Awee dreamed of better places. Better times. Better ways to
love. He was completely innocent, and unlike most adolescents
who want to be let loose, Awee wanted to be held. I held him and
I rocked him and now I miss him.

JN: Was Awee ever allowed to have contact with the kind of
AIDS support group for boys you run now?

N: I do not run anything. The boys run everything themselves.
Yes, we knew some children with AIDS. I did not write about
everything or include everything in the book. That would not be
possible. Did it help Awee? Actually, Awee was helped when he
was allowed to help. Yes. It kept him going. He was a cog in the
support system. Just like the boys I deal with now. To know you
are a part of something or someone gives you hope that the intimacy you find and the responsibility for another person that you
find is real.

JN: You have said that AIDS is chaos imposed on time. What
do you mean?

N: I meant that even though life is often this hurtful, chaotic
mess that presents itself to you, AIDS makes it incomprehensible. In the face of utter incomprehensibility, time becomes an af-

terthought. It is not like time as people who do not live with AIDS would understand the notion of time. Time in the world of AIDS is again that intense rage against what is blackness. It is as if the speed of light does not pour into your eyes, but pours like milk from them.

JN: You have said that we must make this fantasy we have made of childhood, and look the thing clearly in the face. And we must begin to articulate in all our languages what the animal is really like. Please explain.

N: As a Navajo, I am taught that a child is complete when he comes into the world. As a human being. He is not a blank slate that we are compelled to write upon. In America, we tend to see children through the cutie-pie eyes of Romper Room. This is idiocy. It is disrespect. Just as we disrespect African Americans, or Native Americans, or Hispanic-Americans, or Asian-Americans, we really and truly disrespect children, too. I was a part of the United Nations Assembly during the International Year of the Child when we wrote the basic premise of children's rights. Children have the right to food. Children have the right to shelter. Children have the right not to be physically or sexually or emotionally abused. During that entire fight to get those basic rights approved by the UN, country after country, culture after culture fought it tooth and nail. Including the United States, which was a little unsure around what we meant by shelter. Does that mean that homeless children have the right to shelter? America did not want to go there. Now, we just throw them into a gymnasium and wash our hands of the issue and of them. Today, children in America are disposable, and homeless children may as well be dead. Most of them will go to prison where they will be dead to anything and everything and certainly to hope.

JN: You have said in print that as a child you were raped and abused and abandoned. Is that your aim or goal as a writer—to come to terms with those things?

N: I am homeless now. My entire existence is a coming to terms with those things. They haunt me every moment of every day. Like white on rice. Writing is a way to survive. I am never happy with what I have written. I am never happy about how I get published. I am never happy. I do not fathom—happiness. Or why it seems to be a common goal. I want to exist and get through the day. When I close my eyes I let the writing come to me. It writes itself. I have no idea or notion of having done it. I have spent my life writing. But I do not remember the act of writing for one second of it. I still feel abandoned by white culture. The only warrior weapons left to me are words.

About the Author

PHOTO: TINA GIOVANNI

Nasdijj was born in the American Southwest in 1950. He grew up partly on a reservation—his mother was Navajo—and partly in migrant camps around the country. He has been writing for more than two decades, making ends meet by reporting for small-town papers, teaching, and doing migrant labor. He is the author of the critically acclaimed memoir *The Blood Runs Like a River Through My Dreams*, which was a *New York Times* Notable Book, a finalist for the PEN/Martha Albrand Award, and winner of the Salon Book Award. "Nasdijj" is Athabaskan for "to become again." He lives in Chapel Hill, North Carolina.